Music in New Hampshire, 1623-1800

Music in New Hampshire
1623-1800

LOUIS PICHIERRI

1960

Columbia University Press   New York

The Sonneck Memorial Fund
in the Library of Congress has generously provided funds
toward the cost of publication of this work

Published
in Great Britain, India, and Pakistan by the Oxford University Press
London, Bombay, and Karachi

Library of Congress Catalog Card Number: 60-13940

Printed in the Netherlands

Contents

Foreword

NO ONE interested in the early history of music in our country can be unaware of the frequent complaints that we lack the thorough and careful studies of music and musical life in smaller sections or communities of the British colonies and later of the individual states without which it is impossible to provide a reliable, over-all musical history of the country. Attempts at local histories are not entirely lacking, particularly in recent years; but of the earlier works some are merely reminiscences of the individual authors, often quite valuable in their way. Others are not always based on the meticulous research in original sources and documents, without which definite results cannot be achieved.

By the very nature of the pioneer life of the early colonists such documents are scarce in America. The reconstruction of our early musical life, such as it was, presents a far more difficult problem than that which faces the European musical historian. State, city, village, church, and school records are comparatively copious in Europe, but not in America. Not until Oscar Sonneck made his notable and successful efforts to cast some light upon our own early history, chiefly by a minute study of the data provided by newspapers, was the situation in American musical historiography changed.

Dr. Louis Pichierri, in his *History of Music in New Hampshire, 1623-1800*, makes ample use of Sonneck's studies and likewise of the startling contributions of Percy Scholes in his writings about the Puritans and music. He also makes wise use of Sonneck's predecessors, where they are reliable, but he offers in his history a great deal that is new and hitherto unknown. Newspapers in America as used by Sonneck did not begin to be fruitful sources until about a decade or two before the middle of the eighteenth century. But Dr. Pichierri, in his researches in historical society archives and in state papers, brings to light, for example, facts about musical instruments in New Hampshire that may surprise us. An inventory made on July 1, 1633, in Newitchwannicke, ten years after its settlement, shows that "the Great House" possessed fifteen recorders and hoeboys. Another inventory in Piseataqua (July 2, 1633) lists twenty-six hoeboys and recorders and one drum. Another in Piscataqua (July, 1635) counts, among the arms and ammunition, two drums and fifteen recorders and hautboys.

Our author makes it quite clear that the economic, the political, and the ecclesiastical conditions that prevailed in the New Hampshire settlements differed greatly from those in nearby Massachusetts. New Hampshire seems never to have had any antimusical or antitheatrical blue laws. Its settlers were legally free to enjoy as much amusement of this kind as they chose, although tirades against this vice were not entirely lacking in New Hampshire.

At least one of the most popular psalm tune and anthem books, which provided the overwhelming majority of music published in the colonies and states from about 1770 to about 1830, was a New Hampshire product. *The Village Harmony* went through seventeen editions from 1795 to 1821. They were printed in Exeter. Editions one to seven (1806) were printed and published by Henry Ranlet, who, in the opinion of our author, was also the unnamed compiler. A whole chapter is devoted to a study of the history and the contents of this work.

In New Hampshire, as in other states, the teachers of instrumental music began to outnumber the teachers of vocal music toward the end of the eighteenth century. Dr. Pichierri accounts for a whole cohort of New Hampshire teachers. Some of them seemed to be very hopeful as to the eagerness of their prospective pupils. Mr. Francis Maurice, on March 18, 1797, announces that he proposes to open a Music School in Portsmouth, to teach ladies on the Fortepiano. "The school will be kept from six to twelve in the morning two days each week." Maurice taught gentlemen on the violin in the evening. The Portsmouth dancing master, Mr. Civil, announces in 1791 that he will teach French four mornings each week at six o'clock, and in 1792 he offers French four mornings from six to eight. Let us hope that his pupils were wide awake.

All in all, Dr. Pichierri gives us a lively and intimate view of early musical life in New Hampshire. He is well aware that he has not exhausted the subject, but he has made a valuable and most welcome contribution to the history of music in America.

OTTO KINKELDEY

Preface

MORE than forty years ago, Oscar G. Sonneck wrote in his *Suum Cuique: Essays in Music* that "literature on music in America is woefully inadequate both in quantity and quality.... There is not a city in this country that can point to a comprehensive, authoritative, scientific study of its musical life. . . . As to general histories of music in America, they plainly suffer from a dearth of local or otherwise specialized literature. . . . We can not do ourselves justice or expect justice at the hands of foreigners until we have produced a methodologically correct and abundant literature of city and state musical histories, on a critical digest of which the general historian may safely base his survey." [1]

In the decades that passed since Sonneck's great foundation studies, a number of books, periodicals, and monographs on America's music have been published, but not on a scale hoped for by Sonneck. In fact, it can be stated that we are still suffering from a "dearth of local or otherwise specialized literature."

The music history of New England, far from complete, has been largely written by a few individuals, the most distinguished perhaps being Gould, Hood, Ritter, Sonneck, Scholes, Pratt, Elson, and Foote. Their works, incidentally, reflect the musical interests of Boston rather than of New England as a whole. The output of these men, when placed beside the research in the field of the visual arts and literature, done in the New England area during the same period, remains comparatively small.

The lists of doctoral dissertations completed since 1934 show that but nineteen deal with the history of American musical development. Of these, seven relate to the period covered in this study, and only one is concerned exclusively with the New England area (Massachusetts).[2]

With Sonneck's idea in mind, the writer has attempted to provide a localized study of New Hampshire's music from its earliest settlement (1623) to the end of the eighteenth century. With the exception of occasional isolated references appearing in general and music histories, there has been no survey of early musical development in New Hampshire. This book is the first comprehensive record with respect to the state.

Originally, the purpose of the investigation was to evolve a history of music instruction. As the research progressed, it became increasingly evident that to treat the subject of music instruction without considering all the aspects of musical growth would have resulted in a skeletonlike survey, lacking a necessary frame of reference. Music education is usually rooted in musical life. It would be impracticable, for instance, to consider the teaching activities of Horatio Garnet, one of New Hampshire's early music teachers, without bringing to life his preoccupation with the theater, his performing and composing, and his achievements in presenting concerts of instrumental and vocal music to the inhabitants of Portsmouth.

It has been the intention of this study to bring into proper focus the development of music and music instruction in New Hampshire in relation to the other New England states and to Europe during the same period. Even for so limited an area as New Hampshire, this must be considered a first study, not a final one. The writer's primary concern has been to present a large body of data hitherto either unknown or unregarded by researchers in American music. He has attempted to present, in terms of the material itself, an objective picture of musical life in New Hampshire prior to 1800. For this reason, and because the material is not readily available, it has been necessary to quote extensively and generously. A further, more critically evaluative study of the music itself still remains as a future, and pleasantly anticipated, task.

The material in this history was derived chiefly from primary sources such as unpublished wills, legal documents, letters, diaries, contemporary newspapers, periodicals, and tune books. Secondary sources, especially the monumental works of Sonneck, were utilized for filling in gaps and for effecting relationships and perspectives.

While most of the information was gathered from the valuable archives of the New Hampshire Historical Society, it was frequently necessary to utilize the resources of the Portsmouth Athenaeum, Portsmouth Historical Society, New Hampshire State Library, Concord Public Library, Warner House of Portsmouth, Library of Congress, American Antiquarian Society, New York Historical Society, Boston Public Library, Newburyport Public Library, Widener Library of Harvard, University of New Hampshire Library, Dartmouth College Library, University of Vermont Library, and Syracuse University Library.

Acknowledgements too numerous to detail are in order to many individuals of these institutions. If one can be singled out among the many to whom the writer is indebted, it must be Miss Charlotte Conover, of the New Hampshire Historical Society, who undertook to read the manuscript and, with unusual kindness, to relieve him of many time-consuming details. The writer is also grateful to Dr. Otto Kinkeldey for reading the manuscript and offering some valuable suggestions, and to Dr. Harold Spivacke who was instrumental in the publication of this book.

Special acknowledgement is due to Professor Abraham Veinus of Syracuse University, who sympathetically and enthusiastically guided this book, originally a doctoral dissertation, from beginning to end, and to the writer's wife, whose assistance and enduring patience made it all possible.

Music in New Hampshire, 1623-1800

1. The Setting

TO comprehend the development of music and music instruction in New Hampshire from the earliest settlement of the
colony to the beginning of the nineteenth century, a brief
survey of a general historical nature is in order. Music, like
any other phase of civilization, cannot possibly be understood
as an isolated entity. For the broadest understanding of a
single aspect, some knowledge of the whole is required. Therefore, the purpose of this first chapter is to acquaint the reader
with the social, political, economic, and religious framework
within which the art developed in New Hampshire.

In 1622 Sir Ferdinando Gorges and Captain John Mason
received from King Charles I of England, the "Laconia" grant
of land in what was to become New Hampshire. The following
spring two expeditions arrived at the coast, one led by David
Thomson and the other by Edward and William Hilton.
Thomson and his party landed at Little Harbor, later to become
a part of the area of Portsmouth (at one time "Strawberry
Bank") but now in Rye; the Hiltons journeyed up the Piscataqua River and succeeded in establishing a settlement in New
Hampshire, later Dover.[1]

Unlike the Massachusetts Bay colonists who came to America
in quest of religious asylum, the primary objective of the first
Piscataqua settlers was the acquisition of wealth through fishing, fur-trapping, and trading with the Indians. They also
hoped to find gold and precious minerals.

Fifteen years after the founding of Portsmouth and Dover

the neighboring settlements of Exeter and Hampton had also developed into self-governing communities, these four towns practically constituting the entire province of New Hampshire for about forty years.[2] Each was a locally autonomous unit, self-sufficient and enacting its own laws.[3]

Meanwhile in 1631, John Winthrop, the governor of Massachusetts Bay Colony, anxious to extend his jurisdiction to include territories in New Hampshire and Maine, sent Captain Thomas Wiggin up to the Piscataqua settlement for the purpose of assuming control. Wiggin found himself challenged by Captain Walter Neal, and he retreated rather than risk bloodshed. In the ensuing year, however, Wiggin purchased the entire Hilton grant and endeavored to bring it under the control of Massachusetts.[4] The settlers, fearful of losing their lands, opposed the Bay leaders at first. By 1641, however, the Piscataqua inhabitants perceived the need of protection by a stronger neighbor and, being guaranteed the liberties they had always known, accepted the governmental guardianship of the Massachusetts Bay Colony.[5]

Unfortunately this union was not satisfactory. The freer thinking people, including the clergymen, of the Piscataqua settlements were in constant strife with the Puritans of the Bay Colony. Finally, in 1679, following two unsuccessful attempts to withdraw from Massachusetts control, the Piscataqua towns succeeded in separating themselves again and became a royal colony.[6]

In the same year, John Cutt, a wealthy merchant of Portsmouth, was commissioned the first president, as the chief magistrate was then called, of the province of New Hamsphire. He was appointed by the King, who simultaneously established an advisory council made up of prominent members of the province.[7] A second union with Massachusetts was effected in 1690, but this one lasted for only two years. New Hampshire's provincial government, re-established in 1692,[8] persisted until the Revolutionary War in 1775.

During the momentous period of the struggle for independence and briefly afterwards, a republican form of government was established for New Hampshire which functioned throughout the war. In 1784, the fifth provincial congress succeeded in framing a new constitution which has existed to the present with few changes.[9]

In the early years of the eighteenth century, New Hampshire began to expand and develop. Settlers from Massachusetts, offspring of the Puritans "who brought with them and transmitted to their descendants the republican principles of the Bay Colony," [10] established towns along the Merrimack. Meanwhile, groups of emigrants from western Massachusetts, Connecticut, and Rhode Island, followers of the more liberal tenets of Thomas Hooker and Roger Williams, made their way into the Connecticut Valley in the face of severe Indian attacks and founded many new communities in that area.[11] The northern part of the state remained largely unsettled until about 1760.

As already mentioned, the first commerce carried on in New Hampshire was fishing, fur-trapping, and trading with the Indians. In 1631, "eight Danish men and twenty-two women," [12] with other adventurers sent over by John Mason, settled in the vicinity of Portsmouth where the men were employed in sawing lumber and making potash. Along with a thriving lumber business developed the trade of shipbuilding, which eventually became and remains one of New Hampshire's most important industries. The earliest shipbuilders came from England and taught the settlers how to build vessels of all types. The celebrated frigate *Constitution* was a product of New Hampshire forests and New Hampshire craftsmen.[13]

A fondness for spirituous beverages was shared by the early settlers, be they lumbermen, fishmongers, magistrates, or members of the wealthy gentry. Wine and brandy flowed freely in the ordinaries and at investitures of ministers of the gospel. The demand for large supplies of liquor led to profitable trade with the Canary Islands, the Azores, and Spain. Saltfish and pipe staves were exchanged for Spanish wine and French brandy; rum was imported from the West Indies, while gin was brought in from Holland. The early colony derived much of its revenue from this liquor trade.[14]

Agriculture was considered relatively unimportant during the early years of the colony, but was developed to the extent that it would provide the basic needs for the maintenance of life.[15] By the end of the eighteenth century, however, farming had become one of the principal occupations in New Hampshire. In 1767 a group of Scotch-Irish who had made their homes in the Merrimack Valley, skilled in the culture of flax, commenced manufacturing linen, the beginning of New Hampshire's great textile industry.[16]

The entire population of New Hampshire in 1730, as reported to the home office, was about 10,200, of whom 200 were Negro slaves.[17] By 1775, according to a census of that year, the number of inhabitants had increased to 82,200.[18] Portsmouth, then regarded as the capital, was the largest town in the state, with a population of 4,590. Concord had 1,052 inhabitants, Exeter 1,741, Dover 1,666, Amherst 1,428, and Walpole 1,248.

Following the Revolution and the establishment of constitutional government under George Washington in 1787, the population climbed rapidly, and by the turn of the century New Hampshire numbered some 184,000 souls. Boston, then the largest city in New England, numbered 25,000 inhabitants, Salem had 8,000, and Providence, Rhode Island, 9,000.[19] Portsmouth in New Hampshire numbered 5,000, while in Connecticut, New Haven had 4,000 and Hartford, 3,000.[20]

The Congregational church organization was adopted by the majority of the Piscataqua settlers. They brought with them the King James version of the Bible and a religious tolerance unknown in the Plymouth and Massachusetts Bay Colonies. The first meeting house was built in Dover in 1633. In 1638, Reverend John Wheelwright, fellow-collegian of Oliver Cromwell, who had been ejected from the Bay Colony because of his nonconformist beliefs, established with his followers the town of Exeter.[21] And in the same year a church was organized at Hampton. By 1700 there were five Congregational churches in New Hampshire.[22]

The followers of the Church of England built an Episcopal chapel some time before 1638, and the Reverend Richard

Gibson was appointed to provide the pastoral leadership. "From 1642-1732 there was no Episcopal organization in Portsmouth nor in any of the Piscataqua settlements, although there were certain adherents of the Church of England among the officials and the populace." [23]

In 1701 a small group of Quakers built their first meeting house at Seabrook, and in 1719 the Scotch-Irish Presbyterians erected their first house of worship in Londonderry. In 1775 the first Baptist group under the pastorate of the Reverend Walter Powers organized a church in Newton. This denomination numbered nineteen churches by the year 1800.

Other religious sects which were established before the beginning of the nineteenth century were: the First Free Will Baptist in 1780; the First Methodist Society, whose membership numbered 171 by 1800; the Universalist at Portsmouth in 1781; and the Shakers in 1782. [24]

Generally speaking, the ministers of early New Hampshire were men of distinct erudition and scholarly attainment. Most of them were graduates of colleges that had been founded in New England for the "expressed purpose of providing an educated clergy," such as Harvard, Yale, and Dartmouth. [25] The minister performed a variety of employments: he was expected to assume the duties of both pastor and teacher in the community, and frequently he was called upon to act as lawyer and physician. This legitimate diversity of occupation made it possible for many clergymen to accumulate wealth and property; consequently, not a few of them built spacious homes, educated their children to become leaders in society and business, and achieved financial independence in old age. [26]

Between 1741 and 1767 when Benning Wentworth was provincial governor, New Hampshire was beginning to develop into a community of stature and influence. The capital of the province was Portsmouth, by the sea, a small aristocratic town of social and cultural eminence. "There were large fortunes made in Portsmouth, and the inhabitants imitated in splendor of living the mother country. Governor Wentworth, a man of most brilliant talents and accomplishments, with his enlarged

views, refined tastes, and elegant manners,—with the means
also of expense, receiving as he did a large salary (his salary,
besides his house-rent and farm, was fourteen hundred pounds
—a large sum previous to the Revolution) set the example of
social entertainments, and promoted every elegant amusement." [27]

Mary Rogers, in her *Glimpses of an Old Social Capital,* states:
"There were more private carriages and liveried servants in
Portsmouth in proportion to the number of inhabitants than in
any other place in New England. At the door of Queen's Chapel
were chariots with liveried footmen behind, waiting for the
gentry to come out. First the gentlemen—wearing immense
wigs white as snow, coats trimmed with gold lace, embroidered
waistcoats, ruffles of delicate lace, silk stockings, gold buckles
at knee and shoe, three-cornered hats, and carrying gold-headed
canes—and now the ladies come forth, stately, powdered, with
exquisite lace handkerchiefs folded over brocade dresses or
rare and beautiful mantles from over seas—and when they were
seated the pageant passed on." [28]

A conception of the elite circle which constituted Portsmouth
society before the Revolution is adequately described by Mayo
in his excellent biography of John Wentworth. He says: "Its
church was the church of England; its wealth came from ex-
porting lumber to the sugar islands and from importing rum in
return. But all the lumber in New Hampshire and all the rum
in the West Indies would not admit one to the charmed circle
of aristocracy unless the aspirant was otherwise acceptable." [29]

The architecture of Portsmouth manifested the unusual skill
of its early artisans in the delicate designs of the doorways, in
the symmetrical perfection and rare grace of the mantels, and
in the elaborate moldings of the majestic wooden mansions.

The vanity of Portsmouth's aristocrats provided a number of
colonial itinerant portrait painters with a ready market for their
talents. Joseph Blackburn, a prolific artist, whose background
still remains an historical puzzle, intermittently appeared in
Portsmouth from 1753 until about 1762 and placed his adroit
services at the disposal of many of the most prominent families

of the town. His patrons included such august names as Wentworth, Atkinson, Browne, Cutts, Warner, and others.[30] In 1765 John Singleton Copley, one of America's most celebrated colonial portrait painters, bequeathed to posterity the winsome countenance of Lady Frances Wentworth, one of the finest examples of his success with portraits of aristocratic beauties.[31] Other artists who visited Portsmouth were Trumbull and Stuart.

This New World magnificence was consistent with the real meaning and tone of Portsmouth society.[32] Here one witnessed an imitation of the rococo, graceful, formal, and essentially superficial, until brought to its tragic end with the events of the Revolution.

Throughout the entire colonial period the inhabitants of New Hampshire were seldom, if ever, subjected to those strict legal and religious restraints inflicted upon the Massachusetts Bay colonists. The Piscataqua settlers had come to America to fish and trade and in consequence would not submit to some of the fanatical laws of Calvinistic theology. This is not to suggest that the people of New Hampshire were not law-abiding citizens. On the contrary, they were aware of the fact that a society could not flourish without a well-defined system of jurisprudence. These inhabitants were more discriminating and cognizant of the practical value of common sense in the development of a suitable legal code. The separation of church and state here was therefore a reality.

Religious intolerance was mostly foreign to New Hampshire, partly because there was a mixture of members of the Anglican Church among the settlers, as well as of heretics and irreligious persons whom Massachusetts excluded.[33] There is no record of any person ever being put to death for witchcraft in New Hampshire, although a few charged with being witches suffered the indignities of public trial. In one instance, however, Eunice Cole of Hampton, New Hampshire, a town closely associated with the Massachusetts oligarchy where witchcraft delusions reached precarious bounds in 1692, was charged with being a witch, tried, and sentenced to life imprisonment. She served about twelve years of the sentence in a Boston prison, and after some further senseless legal jostling, was finally allowed to go free.[34]

A check of the laws of New Hampshire reveals no legal restrictions on music per se. However, when New Hampshire came under the dominance of the Bay Colony, the latter included in the *Colonial Laws of Massachusetts* a statute regulating "gaming & Dancing—in and about houses of common entertainment, whereby much precious time is spent unprofitably, and much waste of wine and beer occasioned." [35] (It is worth noting that the objection against dancing in New Hampshire was not predicated on religious grounds.) The law goes on to declare a penalty for keeping Christmas: "For preventing disorders arising in several places within this jurisdiction; by reason of some still observing such feastivals, as were superstitiously kept in other Countries, to the Great dishonour of God and Offence of others, It is therefore Ordered by this Court and the Authority thereof: That whosoever shall be found observing any such day, as Christmas or the like,—shall pay for every such Offence—." The law concludes with a "Penalty for playing at Cards & dice."

It is highly probable that the inhabitants of New Hampshire paid little heed to these legal restraints; furthermore, those vested with the authority to enforce these ordinances were undoubtedly occupied with more important civic duties. At any rate, this study has not produced sufficient evidence to support any case for concerted legal, religious, and social restrictions on the development of music in New Hampshire. Rather, its slow growth in this state, as was true throughout the rest of New England, can be generally attributed to the pressing demands of pioneer life. The development of culture in a community is usually commensurate with the amount of leisure time available. It was years before many of these New England towns achieved this leisure.

The legal and religious pronouncements of the Bay Colony's hierarchy have been taken far too seriously with respect to the actual development of secular music. Those who have been misled or have placed undue credence in the efficacy of these edicts would do well to read on this subject the works of Oscar Sonneck [36] and the illuminating study by Percy Scholes, *The Puritans and Music in England and New England.*[37]

Finally, it is generally supposed that what happened musically and otherwise in Boston, during its first two centuries of existence, happened also throughout the remainder of New England. Nothing could be further from the truth, and this fallacious notion should be forcefully and permanently eradicated. The inferences and conclusions contained in the following pages should make this point clear, at least in connection with Boston and Portsmouth. A similar study in a number of other New England communities of the same period would undoubtedly reveal like circumstances attending their perhaps more modest, but no less important and individual, musical development.

When, and only when, this research has become a *fait accompli,* and the data logically and scientifically assembled, will it be possible to distinguish, with clarity and finality, the differences between the musical development characteristic of Boston and the unique provincial music experiences of those towns outside of Boston.

II. Instruments in New Hampshire

THE cursory knowledge of the presence of musical instruments in New England during the seventeenth century is a veritable bane to the development of a sound history of music of the period. The truth, if ever disclosed, would certainly fill several volumes and make provocative reading. The research accomplished thus far can be considered, at best, meager; the investigator of early American music is, regrettably, still somewhat of a rarity. No doubt inquiry into the exciting circumstances surrounding the lives of the masters is infinitely more alluring than is the examination of the crude beginnings of American music.

Generally speaking, the music historian has disregarded the existence of musical instruments in New England before 1700.[1] One historian, W. Dermot Derby, has unequivocally stated that "there was not a musical instrument in New England before 1700."[2] Lamentably, these conclusions were not the results of step-by-step methodical and scrupulous research, but the outcome of the lack of scholarly research and of the indiscrimate quoting of statements, themselves predicated on flimsy evidence.[3] The fallacious notion persisted until 1934 when Percy Scholes published his monumental work, *The Puritans and Music in England and New England,* in which he included a stimulating chapter on "Instrumental Music and the New England Community." In this chapter Scholes produces evidence of "a treble viall"[4] owned by one Nathaniell Rogers. And by carefully examining the countless allusions to musical instruments in the works of Anne Bradstreet, the famous Puritan poetess, in Judge Sewall's *Diary*, and in other sources, Scholes postulates that many more musical instruments must have existed.

"I do not think that they possessed them in great quantities," Scholes says. "They were not common household objects, I suspect, but if a careful analysis of those inventories were to be made it would be found, I think, that there are objects often missing which every householder must have possessed." [5]

In spite of Mr. Scholes' brilliant research, his revelation that instruments did exist during the seventeenth century, and his success in dispelling the spurious notion that the Puritans "hated music," his audience has remained somewhat small. It is unfortunately true that our musical intelligentsia are still in the main ignorant of our American musical heritage, even though some valuable studies are readily accessible. In the last few years the situation has taken a turn for the better. Our scholars have begun to assume a greater interest in American studies, and in time we may hope for a profusion of detailed monographs and publications about music comparable to that which exists in the history of the visual arts and of literature in America.

Now to turn to New Hampshire. The first allusion to the presence of musical instruments in the state appears in the inventory at "Newitchwanicke, 1D, of Julie, 1633," ten years after the original settlement. It includes: "In the Great House, 15 recorders and hoeboys [hautboys]." [6] A similar reference occurs in the inventory "at Pascattaquack [Piscataqua] 2d Julie, 1633." This one includes no less than "hoeboys and recorders 26" and "1 drume." [7] Two years later in "An Inventory of the Goods and Implements belonging to the Plantation at Piscataway and Newichewanock, in New England, July, 1635" two other entries occur: "at Piscataway" among the "Arms and Ammunition" are listed "2 drums" and "15 recorders and hautboys"; and "at Newichewannock" also among "Arms and Ammunition" is listed "1 drum." [8]

The presence of drums in the early settlements is not unexpected, since it was the custom of the time to employ the drum as an instrument for calling the people together for religious worship or other assembly. "By an ancient law a penalty of forty shillings, by way of fine, was attacted to every town not provided with a drum to call the people to worship. In want of a bell a drum gave notice of the time of gathering for public worship." [9] The drum was gradually discarded as the bell made its appearance in the belfries of the meeting-houses.

As for the hautboys and recorders, they were apparently popular not only in New England but in the southern colonies as well. The hautboy or hoeboy was a seventeenth-century oboe —a double reed instrument, "long the nucleus of the military band and of great importance in the seventeenth and early eighteenth century orchestra." [10] The recorder was a "kind of flute" blown endways with a mouthpiece. It was the type of flute chiefly used in England until the middle of the eighteenth century; [11] it existed in a family which included discant, alto, tenor, and bass. Philip Alexander Bruce, in a valuable book on the *Social Life of Virginia in the Seventeenth Century*, notes: "For the amusement of the guests in the house as well as of the members of the family, musical instruments were to be found in nearly all the planters' residences: there are frequent references in the inventories to the virginal, the hand lyre, the fiddle, the violin, and also the recorder, flute and hautboy, as part of personal estates." [12]

And for New Hampshire, Brewster writes: "For music, there are two drums for the training days,—while no less than fifteen hautboys and soft recorders are provided to cheer the immigrants in their solitude." [13]

Since both the recorder and hautboy were well known in England,[14] it is entirely possible that some of the early settlers, having learned to play these instruments in the mother country, found an occasional moment from the rigorous travail of the day to amuse themselves with a tune on the "hoeboy" or recorder. The formidable number of hautboys and recorders, which by 1635 reckon to 56,[15] alone suggests a certain amount of musical activity in the early settlements. It is possible that the first New Hampshire inhabitants taught their offspring how to play these instruments, although there is no specific reference to such instruction in the seventeenth century.

The first colonists of New Hampshire must have attributed some importance to the hautboy and recorder, otherwise these instruments would not have been granted shipping space necessarily reserved for the transport of basic essentials. The viols were also currently popular in England, but the recorder and hautboy were easier to play and were smaller in size. Furthermore, the recorder needed no spare parts, while viol strings were, no doubt, a problem to keep in constant supply.

During the last decade of the seventeenth century Richard Chamberlain, the royal secretary (from 1680), when "attacked" by Lithobolia, "the stone throwing devil," at his house on Great Island (New Castle) just before he was to return to England, sought to ease his discomfort, caused by the witchcraft delusion, with a "little musical instrument." In his own words: "In the evening, as soon as I had sup'd in the outer room before mine, I took a little musical-Instrument and began to touch it, (the door indeed was then set open for Air) and a good big stone came rumbling in, and as it were to lead the dance but on a much different account than in the days of old, and of old fabulous Inchantments, my musick being none of the best." [16]

Sanborn suggests that the "little musical instrument" is perhaps a rebec.[17] But in our opinion, the lute would be a better guess since Chamberlain uses the expression "to touch," common for the lute as well as for keyboard instruments.[18] In Shakespeare's *Taming of the Shrew* (III.i. 63), for example, during Bianca's lute lesson Hortensio remarks:

> Maddam, before you touch the instrument, [lute]
> To learn the order of my fingering,
> I must begin with rudiments of art;
> To teach you gamut in a briefer sort.

From the English bard's *Two Gentlemen of Verona* (III.ii. 78) we extract the following quotation which also seems to strengthen this hypothesis:

> For Orpheus' lute was strung with poets' sinews,
> Whose golden touch could soften steel and stones.

The word "touch" comes both in meaning and form from the Italian toccare. In lute and in keyboard music, the phrase "to touch" was used technically and meant actually "to play on the instrument." [19]

The presence of the lute in New Hampshire at this time can hardly be considered remarkable, inasmuch as the instrument was common in England. Scholes lists no less than fourteen "English lutenist ayre composers" who were still alive in 1620. [20] To Judge Samuel Sewall of Boston "the lute was a familiar object" [21] and a ready point of reference: "When this was over, I desired the Governour's patience to speak a word: I said I had been concern'd about the Vote pass'd Nov. 1. At the Conference his Excellency was pleas'd to say, that everyone of the Council remain'd steady to their vote, and every word of it: This skrewing the Strings of your Lute to that height, has broken one of them; and I find myself under a necessity of with-drawing my vote." [22]

In the inventory of Edward Lyde, a son-in-law of Rev. Wheelwright, appears "a pair of virginals," notes Sanborn. [23] And in the diary of the inimitable Judge Samuel Seawall, that Puritan of Puritans, one encounters the following entry: "Sixth-day, Dec. 1, [1699.] Was at Mr. Hillers to enquire for my wives virginals." [24] Sewall's diary is small comfort to those who insist upon the myth that the Puritans hated music.

Two other references to the existence of musical instruments in New Hampshire before 1700 are contained in the manuscript "Probate Records of Rockingham County." In the will of Isaac Hanson dated September 17, 1683, "a trumpet" [25] is listed. The trumpet like the drum was employed to announce public assembly and also to sound the call to arms. "The governor . . . forthwith ordered the militia of the whole Province to be in arms, and understanding by the marshal that Gove could not be apprehended at Hampton, by himself and a constable, but was gone to his party at Exeter, from whence he suddenly returned with twelve men, belonging to that town, mounted and armed with swords, pistols and guns, a trumpet sounding, and Gove with his sword drawn, riding into Hampton ahead of them.—They were met withal, and taken by militia of that town, and secured with a guard; the trumpeter, forcing his way, escaped, after whom a hue and a cry was sent to all parts, but as yet he is not taken. [January, 1684.]" [26] Judge Sewall, in his diary, records that the trumpet was also used as an instrument for salutation: "Jan. 1 6th. day 1696. One with a Trumpet sounds a Levet [reveille] at our window just about break of day bid me good morrow and wishes health and happiness to attend me." [27]

It is reasonable to assume that the trumpet was in fairly common use in seventeenth-century New England, not only as an instrument for sounding public assembly and martial calls, but also occasionally for secular amusement. It is indeed difficult to imagine a trumpeter denying himself a few flourishes or the pleasure of a well-known tune.

To return to the "Probate Records," the second allusion to a musical instrument is an entry in the will of John Shipway, of Portsmouth, a wealthy merchant "as his father before him, and constable in 1688." His final testament dated January 29, 1690/ 91, lists "a treble viall" [28] which we place beside the one discovered by Percy Scholes. It is probably true that the treble viol and other instruments of the viol family were not present here in any great quantity; but it stands to reason that the instrument was known in the colonies. The discovery of only these two should justify the assumption that others were in the possession of some of the wealthier settlers and occasionally of a minister like Rev. Nathaniell Rogers of Ipswich. Frequently in the wills there is a blanket reference to "other goods" or "other goods in ye chamber." [29] It is possible that upon occasion a musical instrument was among the items unspecified.

To round out this picture it is worth recording that Foote has apparently tracked down another stringed instrument in the will of the Reverend Edmund Browne of Sudbury, Massachusetts, who died in 1678, leaving "a bass vyol, some books of music, and the reputation of being a good musician." [30]

John Josselyn, a visitor from England traveling in 1663 in the general area of Piscataqua and the Maine seacoast, reported that the Indians in this area were musical and could make "Kitts" [31] and play on them. He tells about it in his own words: "Musical too they be, having pretty odd barbarous tunes which they make use of vocally at marriages and feastings; but Instruments they had none before the English came amongst them, since they have imitated them and will make Kitts and string them as neatly and as Artifically as the best Fiddle-maker amongst us; and will play our plain lessons very exactly: the only Fidler that was in the Province of Meyn, when I was there, was an Indian called Scozway, whom the Fisherman and planters when they had a mind to be merry made use of." [32]

Inadvertently, Josselyn suggests that kits were fairly common among the early settlers and that some form of musical manuscript also existed. Obviously a certain amount of music was cultivated in those early days, though undoubtedly crude, as a release from the arduous daily tasks of building, fishing, and trading. It is not difficult to imagine the New Hampshire inhabitants of this time singing the ancient fishing songs and rustic ditties they had known in England and dancing to the lively meter of the country dance.

From 1756 to the turn of the century the search for references to musical instruments is facilitated by the columns and advertisements of the *New Hampshire Gazette* and other newspapers. The first allusion appears in the November 1757 issue of the *Gazette*.[33] Robert Trail, a Portsmouth merchant, advertises: "Just imported [listed among several hundred other items] best Italian violin strings, and silver bases." [34] By this time the violin was a commonplace musical instrument in the colonies. The mere fact that Mr. Trail includes the strings in such a comprehensive list supports this assumption. The numerous advertisements and teachers' notices contained in the newsfiles also attest to this fact. It is indeed impossible to imagine anyone living in the colonies during this period not being familiar with the secular sounds of the "fiddle." For instance, in the July, 1766, *Gazette* [35] is another advertisement bij Joseph Bass which includes, among other items, "violeins."

In December, 1767, through the medium of the *Gazette*,[36] Peter Curtis announced "that he will open a Dancing School— and will teach young Gentlemen and Ladies three Times a week.—Any Gentleman inclining to be instructed to play the Violin, shall be taught by the Lesson." Again in 1772 [37] another advertisement by Joseph Bass announces to the *Gazette* readers that "best Roman Violen [*sic*] Strings" can be purchased at his shop. W. S. Morgan notified the Portsmouth inhabitants in 1772 [38] that "Having been particularly requested," he intended "Instructing Ladies and Gentlemen on the Harpsichord, Violin etc. etc." On year later, in 1773,[39] William Crosbey advertised in the *Gazette* that he would teach the Violin, Flute, Harpsichord, and Organ.

From the versatile Horatio Garnet's notification in the March, 1789, *New Hampshire Spy*,[40] it can be taken for granted that the Portsmouth inhabitants were familiar with and were interested in acquiring some skill on the "Violin, Violincello, Guittar, Germ. [German] Flute, Clarionet, Hautboy, likewise the Harpsichord, Spinnet etc." John Latham Berkenhead, in 1793,[41] taught "the Organ, Harpsichord, Piano-Forte and other keyed instruments" to the "most respectable characters" of the town.

J. H. Smith, "Professor of Music," informed the readers of the *New Hampshire Gazette* on November 21, 1798, that he "teaches the Piano-Forte, Harpsichord, Spinnet, Singing, the Violin, Tenor, Bass Violin, and Flute."

Thus it is evident that by the year 1800 the New Hampshire inhabitants, and especially those who resided in Portsmouth and its vicinity, were familiar with the orchestra, band, and keyboard instruments of the day. This of course was true throughout the remainder of New England. To those disposed to think that early American music was confined to church psalmody this may come as a surprise. It is worth reiterating that despite the work of Sonneck and Scholes many misconceptions still persist.

Sonneck's well-documented conclusions in this connection are worth quoting: "The opinion has prevailed that the musical life of America was exceedingly primitive during the eighteenth century, but a few degrees less so in sacred music than in secular. To be sure our musical life had a rather provincial aspect if compared with that of London, Paris, Vienna or Rome, but it was by no means so primitive as historians usually picture it. As a rule they make the great mistake of observing things through a New England church window instead of studying more than superficially the secular music of ye olden time in the Middle and Southern Colonies. Their treatment of the subject did more harm than good. Our early musical life was provincial, but not so primitive as to deserve to be ridiculed. And if it is to be called primitive and crude, our early sacred music deserves this verdict more than the secular." [42]

A period of nearly fifty years has elapsed since Sonneck published his first book, *Early Concert-Life in America, 1731-1880*. This was followed by several other publications (see Bibliography) which attempted to discover the truth about our musical beginnings. A few researchers—evidently too few—spurred on by the spirit of Sonneck have endeavored to broaden his findings, but unfortunately the parade of ignorance, buttressed by mistaken ideas about the Puritans, still forcefully prevents the truth from asserting itself.

Returning to our quest for more musical instruments, we note in the July 6, 1779, *Gazette* another allusion to viols, in this case "a quantity of Viols, to be sold at Publick Vendue, on Tuesday the 13th Day of July next, at the house of James Thurston, Innholder in Exeter, at ten o'Clock A.M." These viols belonged to the estate of the Rev. John Tucke of Epsom who was ordained in that town "in the year of 1761 and dismissed in 1774" and who died while on his way to "join the revolutionary army, as chaplain." [43]

John Tucke was the son of Rev. John Tucke of Gosport (Isles of Shoals) and grandson of Robert Tucke of Hampton, who migrated from England before 1639. The latter was chosen town clerk of Hampton in 1647 and also kept "the first ordinary" in the town. Some few years before 1658, Robert Tucke "visited his native land" and on his return to Hampton "reopened his tavern." [44]

The *Gazette* advertisement is curious, for the viol is closely associated with the seventeenth and perhaps early eighteenth century. What could a "quantity of viols" be doing in Epsom, New Hampshire, at this late date? How did they get there? Where did they come from? These tantalizing questions sent us scurrying through church records, town reports, ministers' sermons, and wills but to no avail. Not one bit of solid evidence materialized that would in some small way assist us in developing a musical relationship between the viols and their owner or his family. Nevertheless, the fact remains that here is further evidence of the existence of the viol in America. Although our reference to these particular viols is dated 1779, one may not unreasonably conjecture that they were acquired by Robert Tucke (perhaps during his visit to England before 1658), used in his tavern, and handed down to his son, the Rev. John Tucke of Epsom, as an heirloom.

Finally, the reference to a "quantity of viols" suggests the plausibility of a "chest of viols," a seventeenth-century term for a complete set, or family, from treble to bass.

Exactly when the first organ made its appearance in New Hampshire is difficult to determine. However, when Samuel Sherburne, a wealthy unmarried merchant of Portsmouth died in 1765, "he gave a hansome legacy to the Episcopal Church in this town"[45] in the form of a "perpetual fund" of 2,000 pounds, to be used, "if necessary, for the support of an organist." [46] The entire "item," the initial one in the will, reads thus: "Item.—I give and bequeath to the Church of England as by law established in the town of Portsmouth and province aforesaid, £2000 of the present value of old Tenor, so called, to be under the care and direction of the Vestry and Church Wardens of the Queen's Chapel in said town for the time being; and this I give for a perpetual fund for that end, and the interest and income of the same to be appropriated and expended if necessary, for the support of an organist in said Church or Parish, without any diminution of the principal sum." [47]

If an organ did exist in Portsmouth before 1765, as the above item seems to certify, it was one of the very few in the country. The first organ in New England was the one procured by Thomas Brattle of Boston in 1711. When Brattle died in 1713 the organ was bequeathed to the Brattle Square Church, of which he was a leading member. The Brattle Square Church rejected the gift, and the will, having anticipated and provided for this eventuality, stipulated that it be given to the King's Chapel. In 1756, supplanted by a better organ, it was sold to St. Paul's Church in Newburyport, Massachusetts, and in 1836 it was moved to the St. John's Chapel in Portsmouth where it still exists. In 1736, Trinity Church and Christ Church in Boston each imported an organ. Newport, Rhode Island, installed its first organ in Trinity Church in 1733. It should be noted that the earliest organs in New England as well as outside of New England were installed in Episcopal churches.[48] Their congregations generally included a large proportion of newcomers from England, and their clergymen sought to introduce the latest Anglican practices. The increase in the number of organs, however, was slow, prohibited by cost and scarcity of organists.[49]

An interesting advertisement which appeared in the *Oracle of the Day* of December 25, 1793, presents some evidence on early organ manufacturing and selling in this country. It is noteworthy that Josiah Leavitt of Boston, the subscriber, considered Portsmouth a likely town for disposing of his wares. Leavitt advertises for sale a "Church-Organ" and curiously enough "an elegant House-Organ." Historically, the entire notice warrants quoting:

"Josiah Leavitt, Organ-Builder, Boston, Having a Church-Organ nearly completed, ... (except the Case and Pipes)—and whereas the price of said Organ when finished, will be greater, or less, in proportion to the number of pipes, and elegance of the case, which shall be made for the same, he begs leave to inform any Church or Society, that may wish to contract with him for the said Organ, that it shall be finished, in the above respect, as may be most agreeable, provided timely application be made.

"He likewise informs the public, that he has completed and for sale, an elegant House-Organ, with a Mahogany case, and which might be sufficient for a small Church or Society; which should it be purchased, and sound not large enough to answer their expectation, will be received by him, at any time within the course of one year from the delivery, in part pay for one of a larger size.

"He greatly acknowledges the several favours he has received from the public, by employing him in his line of business and assures them that he shall still endeavour to give the utmost satisfaction to those who have occasion to employ him."

If organs were still difficult to obtain during the autumnal years of the eighteenth century, the exact opposite prevailed with respect to the availability of other musical instruments and their accessories. In the January 9, 1789, *New Hampshire Spy* the following advertisement appeared: "To be Sold (opposite to the Post-Office) London-made Violins, German Flutes, Violin Strings, Lung Screw Bows, a very fine-ton'd Piano Forte, Books of Instruction for all these instruments, with a collection of the latest Concerts, Duets, Trios and Church Music—a variety of Country Dances for 1788, also, brass and iron barrel'd Pistols, suitable for the Cavalry.

"John G. Holland Ivory Turner from Boston," through the medium of the *Gazette* in September 20, 1792, "Informs the public that he has opened a shop, adjoining the office of the Town-Clerk's; where he makes and sells in the neatest and cheapest manner the following articles, viz.," the list including flutes, fifes, fiddle-bows, fiddle-pins and bridges.

One of the most engaging museum pieces in Portsmouth today is its celebrated eighteenth-century harpsichord.[50] For the present it is on display at the historic Warner House, having been only recently removed from its original residence, the "Old Wentworth Mansion" built by Benning Wentworth (circa 1750), one time wealthy, amusement-loving, theater-going [51] provincial governor of New Hampshire. Antiquarians point with ostentatious pride to this quaint prize possession, and several fascinating tales enliven its history.

The harpsichord has been associated by some with the luxurious old governor and his "romantic" residence at Little Harbor, consequently it has been assumed that the instrument was acquired in his lifetime. Other tales credit his wife Martha with the purchase. The few literary accounts that exist regarding the harpsichord tend to be elusive in matters of date and moreover manifest a striking similarity—evidently the result of compilation rather than investigation.

The initial assumption cannot be correct, for the manufacturer's label on the instrument reads:

Longman & Broderip
Musical Instrument Maker
No. 26 Cheapside & No. 13 Haymarket
London

In the latter part of 1771, notes the entry in Grove's *Dictionary of Music* under "Longman & Broderip," the house became known as Longman & Lukey, and this title remained until 1777 or 1778, when, Francis Broderip entering, it was styled Longman, Lukey & Broderip. In 1779 Lukey's name is absent, and the firm remained as Longman & Broderip until 1798. Before 1785 an additional address was at 13 Haymarket.[52]

From this it is evident that the harpsichord dates from between 1779 and 1785 and that Governor Benning Wentworth, who passed away in 1770, never saw the harpsichord.[53]

Those who credit Benning Wentworth's wife with the procurement of the harpsichord, on the other hand, may be nearer to the truth; however, this could only have occurred after Martha Wentworth, widow of Benning, became the wife of Colonel Michael Wentworth, a cousin of her former spouse, in 1770. The new couple made their home in the beautiful mansion at Little Harbor, where the Colonel, inclined toward elegant entertainments, held many grand *soirées*. According to Adams, Michael Wentworth "was remarkably fond of music and excelled in playing on the violin," [54] especially at the "assemblies" alongside Cuffee Whipple. Brewster describes the scene which may be imaginary as he gives no source for his information: "How often have the white teeth of Cuffee Whipple distinctly shown from its [the Assembly House] orchestra to the elite of the town on the floor below, as he labored with his violin to keep up the mazy dance! Cuffee was not alone, for sometimes that life of the Assemblies, Col. Michael Wentworth would stand by his side and as an amateur [fiddler] give his aid." [55]

When Michael Wentworth passed away in 1795 The New Hampshire *Oracle of the Day* stated that "music was his favorite amusement." [56]

Michael Wentworth's marriage to Benning's widow, their residence at Little Harbor, the acquisition of wealth through inheritance, his love of music (and probably hers also), the presence of the harpsichord in their home—all strongly suggest that the Michael Wentworths were responsible for purchasing the instrument.

The harpsichord [57] is about eight feet long. It stands on a four-legged trestle and is shaped like a modern grand piano, although it is considerably smaller in width. Made from rosewood and mahogany, it has thirty-five white keys and twenty-five black keys, with a range of about five octaves beginning with F (third octave below middle C) and extending to E (third octave above middle C). The entire frame is well preserved, and the instrument appears to have been a very expensive one.

III. Religious Music

MATERIAL evidence of religious music in seventeenth-century New Hampshire is indeed wanting. We can draw neither upon the more or less authentic jottings of a William Bradford, a John Winthrop, or a sanguine Samuel Sewall, nor have we been fortunate enough to stumble upon an intimate diary of some backwoods Samuel Pepys, in which might be found an occasional reference to the music of an almost-forgotten era.

There are no available records of the church service or the music in the service at the Piscataqua settlement, although there is reason to suppose that a church service with music consisting of congregational psalm-singing was then held. For instance, in the *Provincial Papers*, the following items necessary to Episcopal Church service are listed: one psalter (probably text only), one communion cup, one communion table cloth, and two service books.[1]

When the Massachusetts Bay Colony, in 1641, assumed the guardianship of the small New Hampshire colony, several of its clergy entered the area in the wake of the alliance in order to establish ministries. It is conceivable that they brought with them the *Bay Psalm Book* and the religious musical practices they had known at the Bay.

The *Bay Psalm Book* printed in Cambridge in 1640 was the "first book printed in the colonies."[2] The complete title was *"The whole Book of Psalmes Faithfully Translated into English Metre. Whereunto is prefixed a discourse declaring not only the lawfullness, but also the necessity of the heavenly Ordinance of Singing Scripture Psalms in the Churches of God."*[3]

The preface, long and involved, was written by Richard Mather, in which he gravely expounds upon the importance of psalm singing as a Christian duty and obligation:

"The singing of Psalmes, though it break forth nothing but holy harmony, and melody: yet such is the subtility of the enemie, and the enmity of our nature against the Lord, & his wayes, that our hearts can find matter of discord in this harmony and crochets of dirision in this holy melody. . . . There have been three questions especially stirring concerning singing. First, what psalmers are to be sung in churches? Whether Davids and other scripture psalmes, or the psalmes invented by the gifts of Godly men in every age of the church. Secondly, if scripture psalms, whether in their owne words, or in such meter as english poetry is wont to run in? Thirdly, by whom are they to be sung? Whether by the whole churches to gather with their voices? or by one man singing alone and the rest joying in silence, & in the close saying amen. . . .

"If therefore the verses are not always so smooth and elegant as some may desire or expect, let them consider that God's Altar needs not our pollishings:—for wee have respected rather a plaine translation, then to smooth our verses with the sweetness of paraphrase, and so have attended Conscience rather than Elegance, fidelity rather than poetry, in translating the hebrew words into english language, and Davids poetry into english meetre; that soe wee may sing in Zion the Lords songs of praise according to his owne will; until he takes us from hense, and wipe away all our teares, & bid us unter into our masters joy to sing eternall Halleluiahs." [4]

An instance of psalm singing, presumably from the *Bay Psalm Book*, is noted in the "Records of the First Church" with respect to an ordination in Portsmouth in the year of 1671: "Then ye Pastor ordained Sam. Haines, Deacon, with Imposition of Hand and prayer. A psalm was sung, and ye Congregation Dismissed by ye Pastor, with prayer and Blessing." [5]

The early editions of the *Bay Psalm Book* contained no music, but in the ninth edition, printed in 1698, at the back of the book, appeared thirteen crudely printed tunes, being the earliest example of music printing in the American colonies. The number of editions (in America, 70, the last in 1773, in England, 18, the last in 1754; and in Scotland, 22, the last in 1759) attests to its prodigious popularity on both sides of the ocean.[6] The *Bay Psalm Book* reigned supreme in the New England colonies until well into the eighteenth century, when it was gradually replaced by Tate and Brady's *New Version* of the psalms and by Watts' *Hymns*.[7] Both of these psalm books were used widely in New Hampshire.

The congregational singing of psalms, probably tedious and unmusical, was attended to with the utmost seriousness. The absence of music in the *Bay Psalm Book*, and the inability of many to read either words or music, led to a continuation of an earlier English practice of "lining-out" the psalms, which was done in the mother country by the parish clerk. In New England it was usually led by a deacon whose duty it was to read the psalm line by line while the congregation would sing each line as it was read.[8] Bouton gives us a description of this practice as carried on in Concord: "In the early period of the settlement, from 1730 till about the time of the Revolution, the singing on the Sabbath was led by someone appointed for the purpose; he giving out the tune and reading two lines at a time of the psalm or hymn which was to be sung—and the singers, with as many of the congregation as were able, joining in the service. What was called 'Tate & Brady's Collection' was then used." [9]

The first settlers of Boscawen knew very little in regard to music, says Coffin. It is probable that the best singer among them could not sing more than a dozen tunes, the *Old Hundredth* and *Windham* being two of the number. "We may think of Dea. George Jackman, or Dea. Jesse Flanders, as sitting in front of the pulpit in the old log meeting-house and reading a line of Ainsworth's *Paraphrase*, and the congregation singing it—the air. That finished, a second line is read and sung and so on through the psalm." [10]

And in Jaffrey, before the Revolution, "the singing was done by the congregation standing and facing the minister. The psalm was first read by him, and afterwards repeated line by line, and sung as read by the congregation. The deacon, instead of the minister, sometimes read or tuned the psalm; hence it was called 'deaconing the psalm.'" [11]

In 1778, prior to the incorporation of the church and the procurement of a pastor, "the town chose William Smiley and David Stanley to read the psalm, and Jonathan Priest, Abraham Bailey, and Daniel Stanley to tune the psalm." [12]

With the appearance of Reverend John Tufts's *A Very Plain and Easy Introduction to the Whole Art of Singing Psalm Tunes* [13] (circa 1712), the first instruction book in singing compiled in the English colonies, [14] the whole complexion of church music began to change. Ministers commenced to agitate for improvement of singing, recommending that the old way of lining out psalms give ground to the new way of reading by note. Tufts himself organized singing schools in Massachusetts and gave lectures on the subject. [15] Tufts's book, whose title suggests Thomas Morley's famous *Plaine and Easie Introduction* of 1597, ran through eleven editions. Early editions contained twenty-eight tunes, while the later ones had thirty-eight. The tunes were written in three parts, using letters, M, F, S, L (the initials of the solmisation syllables mi, fa, sol, la) in place of notes on a staff, with rhythm indicated by dots. The brief instructions in Tufts's booklet were derived from Thomas Ravenscroft and John Playford. [16]

A more detailed text than that of Tufts, using diamond-shaped notes with bar-lines, was published by Reverend Thomas Walter of Roxbury in 1721. *The Grounds and Rules of Musick Explained; or, an Introduction to the Art of Singing by Note,* as it was titled, included "A Recommendatory Preface" signed by Increase Mather and fourteen other leading divines of the past generation. [17] The rules for reading music were explained in the introduction. This work was very popular and continued in use for about forty years. Like Tufts, Walter also lectured and wrote on the necessity for better singing. [18]

Thus through the dedicated efforts of these two young ministers, the revival of singing spread rapidly throughout New

England. It is possible that those who left Newburyport to
establish communities along the Merrimack were acquainted
with Tufts's music book, since he was pastor of the Second
Church in Newburyport.[19]

In time some of the churches made provisions for reserving
the first seats in the gallery for the best singers, and from this
bold innovation the choir gradually evolved. However, ante-
diluvians did not abandon the venerated custom of lining the
psalms without a struggle, and more than one deacon had to be
forcefully "sung down by the congregation." [20] Bouton, in his
History of Concord, thus portrays the first change: "After Mr.
John Kimball, subsequently deacon, came into the town, some
innovations were introduced (at the First Congregational
Church). Being one of the singers, Mr. Kimball proposed to
Rev. Mr. Walker [21] to dispense with the lining of the hymns, as
it was called, on the Sabbath; but as Mr. Walker thought it not
prudent to attempt it first on the Sabbath, it was arranged
between them to make the change on Thanksgiving day. Accordingly, after a hymn had been given out, the leader, as usual,
read two lines; the singers struck in, but, instead of stopping at
the end of the two lines, kept, on, drowning the voice of the
leader, who persisted in his vocation of lining the hymn! This
was the first change." [22]

"Although some singers sat in the front seats in the neighborhood of the leader, the majority were scattered through the
congregation," writes Lyford, who continues the story of the
change: "Gradually it became apparent that the singing could
be more effective by collecting the singers in a compact body
and accordingly the choir was formed and a choir master was
chosen. When the meeting house was finished in 1784, it was
fitted with the singers' pew in the gallery opposite the pulpit.
There was a large square pew, with a box, or table, in the middle
on which the singers laid their books. In singing they rose and
faced one another, forming a hollow square. When the addition
was made to the meeting-house, the old square pew was taken
away, but seats were assigned to them in the same relative
position before the pulpit." [23]

The vexing problem of seating the singers in Jaffrey was evidently handled by due process of law via the annual town meeting. The mode of singing, in 1787, was transformed. Instead of being part of the congregation, the singers were "seated in one place by themselves." [24] The town at that time "voted to Grant the two middle body seats below, men and womens side, for the Singers. It also Voted to sing a Verse at a time, once in the forenoon and once in the afternoon after exercises. Voted that Jacob Baldwin assist Eleazer Spofford to tune the Psalm, and in his absence or inability to set it. In 1791 the singers were seated in the gallery, by vote of the town. March 1, 1791, the town Voted to grant half of the Front Gallery for the Singers and take it out of the Senter [center]. In 1792, March 6, the town Voted to annex the womans seats in the front of the Gallery to the Singers Seats." [25]

On March 2, 1802, the town of Jaffrey, compelled by the urgent need to further improve church music, "voted to raise forty dollars toward hiring a singing master for the purpose of instructing schools." A committee of three were voted "to expend the same." Samuel Dakin received "of the Selectmen, forty dollars in full for teaching singing school for the year of 1803." [26]

Twenty-nine individuals, in the small town of Dunstable (Nashua), proposed the establishment of a singing school for the advancement of church psalmody. Thus they expressed themselves in a pledge dated December 4, 1795: "We the subscribers being desirous of the Promotion of Good and Regular Singing in this Town and Especially that part of worship which Consists in singing Psalms Hymns and Spiritual Songs may be Performed in our Solemn Assemblies with greater decency and Regularity and more to edification Do Promise and Engage to give the Several Sums affixed to our Respective names for the Purpose of maintaining a Singing School for the benefit of Such of the inhabitants of this town as Shall be dispos'd to attend the same at the dwelling House of Mr. Thomas Lund So long a term as the whole Sum that shall be Subscribed Shall be sufficient for the s'd school to be Subject to Such rules and regulations as the Instructor Shall See fit to institute and in Case Mr. Aaron Brown shall Procure Mr. Redfield for the Instructor of s'd School and it Shall be opned [sic] about the Middle of this month above mentioned we Promise to deliver the Sums Subscribed by us Respectively to him the S'd Aaron Brown three weeks from the time Said School shall be opned." [27]

In the town of Stratham, during the ministry of the Reverend Joseph Adams (1745-1783), a difficulty occurred with respect to the singing in the church. Desirous of perpetuating a current trend, the singers wished to "break up the old habit of lining, as it was called." The entire matter was finally settled by compromise, the town voting that the deacon should line "half the time." [28]

During his ministry at the First Parish in Dover, Jeremy Belknap, author of the *Sacred Poetry consisting of Psalms and Hymns*,[29] which ran into several editions, and of the first *History of New Hampshire*, recorded in his diary, March 23, 1767, that "At a Chh & Congrega: meeting Dec^n Ham refus'd to sett ye Psalm & Capt Evens was chose for ye Business." On June 21, 1767, he notes: "Voted to sing Watts' Psalms in Congregation." And on June 28 he adds: "Sung them ye 1st Time." [30]

On March 3, 1772, it was "voted that the two hind seats of mens on the floor be built for Singing seats." Twenty years later, on August 17, 1792, the congregation voted: "To build a Pew for the Singers to project from the front of the front Gallery as far forward as the Committee shall think convenient, and that they proceed to do it as soon as may be." [31] The pew was completed "before 8 September following." [32] According to Quint, it extended "nearly into the centre of the house, was over the center aisle, and stood upon pillars." [33]

In town after town throughout New Hampshire, as well as the remainder of New England, the same story was repeated with occasional variations. By the end of the eighteenth century, with the gradual development of the church choirs resulting from the efforts of the singing schools and musical societies, most of the deacons had been finally and forcefully "sung down" by one method or another, and the time-honored custom of lining the psalm passed into history.

Not everyone acquiesced to the inevitable changes. The February 8, 1792, issue of the *New Hampshire Spy* carried an editorial entitled "On Psalm Singing" in which the author expounds on the significance of preserving "free from interruption" the revered institution of church psalmody while looking distrustfully upon the intrusion of the choir in the worship service:

"No part of public worship is more difficult to be preserved free from interuption than that of psalm singing. Various and constant endeavours must be made, to retain any tolerable music, even after a great expense in instructing youth in that pleasing art. In Europe they too often depend upon hired choirs (persons paid by the parish for their constant attendance). Some parts of our country have made amends for this, by making singing in public respectable and proper employment for youth and others of both sexes, and all ranks in life. The rich set the example; and one of the best ornaments in a christian congregation is now the whole front galleries, filled with singers.

"Singing pews below are almost intirely out of use, even in country places. . . . The singing of no congregations is so much admired, or even envyed, as those who constantly follow the practice of their youth in general. . . . So varied are the opinions formed by custom, that to set below is esteemed as arising from want of voice, knowledge, or inclination as prudish, and mark of antiquity."

This communication with its obvious ambiguities suggests that the writer wistfully longed for the good old days. It is evident, however, that public opinion and the tides of progress conspired against him.

The second innovation which swept the churches of New Hampshire during the latter part of the eighteenth century was the introduction of musical instruments into the worship service as an aid to the choir and the congregation. Before the advent of instruments, the pitch-pipe was used to "set" the tune. The introduction of string and wind instruments produced an excite-

ment akin to that which agitated the meeting-houses a few
years previous. Coffin points out that "those who had the
hardihood to play a viol were contemptuously called fiddlers."
Doctor Eaton, an eccentric citizen of Boscawen, "never became
reconciled to their use. . . . He called them wooden and catgut
gods, and they who used them were serving the devil!" [34]

In Concord instruments were first introduced under the
ministry of the Reverend Israel Evans (1789-1797), who was
"very fond of music." [35] He was a native of Pennsylvania and
a graduate of Princeton in the same class as Aaron Burr.[36]
Bouton explains that "according to tradition some persons left
the meeting-house rather than hear the profane sounds of the
fiddle and flute." [37] One of the defiant deacons in Stratham,
in describing the acquisition of a bass-viol, said, "they had got
a fiddle into the church as big as a hogs-trough." [38]

The introduction of instruments in Jaffrey was not at the
outset very favorably received by the older members of the
congregation, "but time and the influence of the younger
portion overruled and at length they became very acceptable." [39]
The "flute, clarionette [sic], bassoon, trombone, and violin"
were the first to be used, followed by the "bass-viol, by some
called Dagon [40] by others the Lord's fiddle." [41]

An article appearing in the New Hampshire Spy of February
20, 1789, discusses the spiritual effect of musical instruments
in the church worship and the important role played by the
musical instrument manufacturers. The brief essay follows
in full:

From The Mechanics Lecture
By Absalom Aimwell, Esq.
Musical Instrument Makers.

"Jubal, one of the grandsons of Adam, was the first inventor
of musical instruments, and father of all such as 'play on the
harp and organ.'

"If David with his jewsharp alone, could drive the devil out
of Saul and restore his wandering sense;—if the soft breathing
flute can sooth us to pleasure; if the cheerful violin can raise

our spirits up to joy; if the solemn sounds of the church organ can raise our spirits to heavenly meditations, and fit our hearts for sacred devotion—how much are we indebted to those promoters of harmony, and rational delight, the musical instrument makers.

"It is said that musick hath charms to sooth the savage breast, to soften rocks and bend the stubborn oak, etc. Timotheos with his music raised a mortal to the skies and Cecilia drew an angel down; and by musick Orpheus charmed his wife from hell.—Yet not withstanding all these wonderful effects, there are three kinds of animals which hate musick;—a hog, an ass and the devil. This we see in part verified in our churches: For when good musick, whether vocal or instrumental, is introduced into the Church there are always a number of people who are possessed of the spirit of one of the above animals, to such a degree, that they immediately, at the sound thereof, go away, just as the evil spirit did from Saul, when David played before him.—In short it will always drive the devil out of them, or drive them out of the church."

Thus, in spite of the sometimes bitter opposition against the introduction of musical instruments in the church service, the tenacious persistence of the more progressive elements of each community ultimately emerged triumphant.

By 1800 the existing musical forces in many of the New England churches were of considerable consequence. A glance at the number of vocal and instrumental performers in the Congregational Church in the small village of Hopkinton, New Hampshire, during that year, gives the present day choir director and organist reason for envy. This church choir, by no means unique, sometimes included as many as fifty voices, and the instrumental section comprised four bass-viols (cellos) to say nothing of violins, clarinets, or other instruments.[42]

Neither the *Bay Psalm Book* nor the small works of Tufts and Walter, however, could have sustained the awakening musical interest of choirs and singing schools. By the end of the colonial period, a number of improved collections had appeared in the wake of James Lyon's famous Philadelphia publication of

1761,[43] which included six original pieces by Lyon in addition to English staples selected from Arnold, Green, Knapp, and Evison. It would seem reasonable, in view of its large circulation, to suppose that Lyon's *Urania* was known and used in New Hampshire. In any case, Obadiah Noble, pastor of the Congregational Church in Orford, New Hampshire, was among the subscribers to the volume. Not to be outdone by Philadelphia, its cultural rival, Boston soon followed (1764) with Josiah Flagg's collection of psalm tunes [44] chosen from "the most approved Authors." And in the same year Daniel Bayley (1729-1792), potter, publisher, and organist of St. Paul's Church in Newburyport, Massachusetts, contributed a small instruction book based on Tans'ur and likewise insisting that its tunes were "from the most approved Masters." Since Bayley's volume is much less celebrated than either Lyon's or Flagg's often mentioned collections, and since it is comparable in date to these two important publications, we give its title in full:

"A new and complete introduction to the Grounds and Rules of Music, in two books.

Book I.

"Containing the Grounds and Rules of Music; or an introduction to the art of singing by note, taken from Thomas Walter, A.M.

Book II.

"Containing a new and correct introduction to the Grounds of Music, rudimental and practical; from William Tans'ur's Royal Melody; the whole being a collection of a variety of the choicest tunes from the most approved Masters." [45]

This work contains thirty-four melodies, neatly engraved, utilizing diamond-shaped notes. The tunes are arranged in three parts: bass, treble, and tenor, as in Walter's book, and, with the exception of three, are similar. It is a matter of historical interest, relevant to this study, to point out that Daniel Bayley's instruction book was engraved in Exeter, New Hampshire, by John W. Gilman (1741-1823), a native of the town and postmaster for forty years.[46]

These publications were the obvious signs of a ferment in

church music which agitated New Hampshire as well as the remainder of New England and the mother country. With the encouragement that publication offered potentially to new composition, new tunes were in the air, and a rising generation of largely self-taught composers were soon elaborating fresh techniques derived both from their own practical experience, and from an old tradition of the itinerant peddlers of psalm tunes in the rural villages of England. These fresh tunes and techniques, as popular as they apparently were, also provoked much embittered comment from that sector of the congregation for whom a familiar tune in a familiar setting constituted the essence of church music. The lively delight of the younger generation in "fuging a tune," for example, was as roundly condemned by at least one New Hampshire die-hard, as this practice in the rural areas of England had been by the Bishop of London.[47] Thus in 1764, when Josiah Flagg and Daniel Bayley brought out their tune books, a provocative communication appeared in the January 13, 1764, *New Hampshire Gazette* in which the writer, an uncompromising, irate scribe, caustically derides the use of the fuging tune in religious worship. The letter was submitted to the newspaper as a reply to the "young and gay" who had previously written on the "new Method" of psalmody:

"To the Printers

"As you some Time since favoured your Readers with some Pieces from the young and gay on the New Method of Psalmody, you will be so impartial as to oblidge several of the ancient Customers to the [Boston] News Letter, by inserting the following.

"There are a set of Geniuses, who stick themselves up in a Gallery, and seem to think that they have a Priviledge of engrossing all the singing to themselves; and truely they take away a very effectual Method to secure this Priviledge, namely by singing such Tunes, as is impossible for the Congregation to join in. Whom they get to compose for them, or whether they compose for themselves, I will not pretend to determine; but, instead of those plain and easy Compositions which are essential to the Awful Solemnity of Church Music, away they get off, one after another, in a light, airy, jiggish Tune, better adapted to a Country Dance, than the awful Business of Chanting forth the Praises of the King of Kings:—A Clergyman of my Acquaintance, at my Desire, presumed once to beg the Favour of these Gentlemen, to sing the Old Hundredth Psalm. Was his Request granted Think you? By no Means. After looking upon him with a smile of Pity for his want of Taste, they told him that was out of Date but they would give him the new Tune to the same Words, which was much better for that it consisted of four or five Parts, and had many Fuges. Imagine to yourself, that you are hearing ten or a dozen Ballad-singers bawling out Ally-Croaker one after another, Line after Line, and it will give you some faint Idea of our Entertainment.

"Now who will wonder, after this true Representation of the Matter, that the Congregation, not being able to accompany these Connoisseurs, should by Degrees look upon themselves as unconcerned in the Duty, and consider it in the Light of an Amusement (such amusement as it is!) rather than a Part of Divine Service? They think they may as well sit down as stand up, to hear these Gentlemen shew their Talents in Music, which seems to be (and I fear, too often is) their sole View in singing. They are so much taken up in beating Time, and endeavouring to execute the Fuges as they are pleased to call them) properly, that the Matter of the Psalm has very little Share in their Attention. How much better it is calculated to answer the Purposes of Devotion, when the Psalms are sung in such an easy and plain Stile, as that the whole Congregation may with one Heart and Voice, join to-gether to celebrate the Praises of their Creator?

F.B.

"(The foregoing is published only to satisfy the Desire of some of our good old Customers; this is tho't necessary to be mentioned lest Offence should be taken at the Publishers, by the Gentlemen who practice the present Method.)"

The remarkably rich development of original compositions in church music in the four decades between Lyon's *Urania* and the turn of the century have been ably treated in recent years by Foote and Ellinwood.[48] It is not the point of this study to recapitulate the achievements of well-known figures like Billings, or Swan, or Law, but to call attention to the worthy, if modest, share which New Hampshire composers had in this development and which has hitherto escaped the attention of researchers. At least two deserve to be added to the list of those whose reputation has already justly been established. The first is Richard Merrill of Hopkinton, who in 1797 published a psalm book of original compositions. The title page follows:

"The Musical Practitioner or American Psalmody, In Two Parts. Containing, I. A number of Psalm, Hymn Tunes, and Anthems. II. A number of the most Modern and Celebrated American and English Songs. The whole Entirely New. Composed by Richard Merrill of Hopkinton, (N.H.). Printed Typographically at Newburyport, By William Barrett, Market-Square, Jan. 1797. Sold by the Author in Hopkinton, and at Barrett's Bookstore, Market-Square, and by many other Booksellers."

A copy of the work, which appears to be the only one available,[49] is in the library of the New Hampshire Historical Society. It numbers more than fifty-four pages, the last one or two being missing. It includes thirty-nine tunes and two anthems, in the main employing the metrical versions of Watts's psalms. The harmony, typical of the unschooled composer of American psalmody, spills over with what the nineteenth-century conservatory-trained church musician would consider glaring imperfections: an abundance of parallel fifths and octaves, triads with three roots, omitted thirds, sudden unprepared modulations, incorrect resolutions, and abrupt rhythmic changes. In accordance with the taste of the day, Merrill's book contains several fuging pieces. The tunes are written in two, three, and four parts. Merrill's talent for melody, however, distinguishes the work. In tune after tune this characteristic is strikingly noticeable. The melodic style, simple and modal, suggests an ear tuned to the familiar folk music of the Elizabethan period. Some of the melodies display virility and strength, and others exhibit a tender, subtle quality of the unskilled novice.

The Musical Practitioner furnishes further insight into the musical circumstances of the period, especially within the church, allowing a more intimate glimpse of the person or persons who set down naively and enthusiastically the very heartbeat of an emerging republic. Here are to be found genuine indigenous harmonies proclaiming the new independence.

"If this work should meet with encouragement," writes Merrill in the advertisement, "it may be an inducement to the Author to publish another, consisting of Psalm and Hymn Tunes, Anthems, Odes, and Chorus's of his own composition." [50]

It is worthy of note that Merrill titles his psalm book the *Musical Practitioner* and in the advertisement he states deliberately: "Perhaps it may be expected by some, that I should say something concerning the Rules for Composition, to which I answer, that Nature is the best dictator: Nature must lay the foundation, Nature must inspire the thought. Though in some sorts of composition dry study is required, and are very requisite."

Merrill's indebtedness to the *New England Psalm Singer* of William Billings is obvious. Billings's explanation being much longer, we extract only the portion utilized by Merrill: "To all Musical Practitioners: [This is undoubtedly where Merrill got the idea for his title.] Perhaps it may be expected by some, that I should say something concerning the Rules for Composition; to these I answer that Nature is the best Dictator. . . . Nature must lay the foundation, Nature must inspire the Thought."

Evidently Richard Merrill was well acquainted with the works of Billings, and it is even reasonable to presume that he might have been in attendance at one of the famed singing master's schools. For this possibility, however, there is no proof, since thus far it has been even impossible to trace any biographical background.

The preface commences with a gentle admonition to the "critical to be tender." We quote in full:

"Notwithstanding this composition has cost me much time

and pains, still I little thought of exposing it to the Public: But being importuned by my friends, I determined to commit it to the Press. If this work should meet with a favourable reception, it would be equivalent to all the trouble I have been at, and the time I have spent in the performance and prosecution of it.

"Perhaps there may appear in the eyes of some, much inaccuracy which I was not able to discern: I would beg the critical to be tender, and rectify those errors which through inexperience may escape the notice of youth. Nevertheless, such as it is, I now offer it to the Public, under a humble persuasion that it will be an inducement to the unskilled in Music to prosecute the study of it, and an entertainment to those who are more experienced in it.

"Hopkinton, Nov. 1796."

This is followed by:

> "The Power of Music—
> Music, how pow'rful is thy charm!
> That can the fiercest rage disarm,
> Calm passions in a human breast,
> And lull ev'n jealousy to rest;
> With Am'rous thoughts the soul inspire,
> Or kindle up a warlike fire.
> Inflam'd by music soldiers fight,
> Inspired by music poets write;
> Music can heal the lover's wounds,
> And calm fierce rage by gentle sounds;
> Philosophy attempts in vain,
> What music can with ease attain.
> So great is music's power."

Customarily the early New England repositories of music contained a section with several pages of instruction, but for one reason or another Merrill dispenses with it. However, he does include "An Explanation of the most Useful Terms that are used in Music—set down in alphabetical order," which is reproduced in full:

Adagio, the slowest movement of time.
Allegro, as quick again as Adagio.
Affectuoso, tender and affectionate.
Bass, the lowest foundational part, and generally confined to the F. Cliff.

Cliff, the key to open a piece of music.
Cadence, all parts making a close.
Chorus, all parts moving together.
Divoto, in a devout manner.
Echo, soft like an echo.
Forte, loud, strong.
Fortissimo, very loud.
Gravasonus, very grave and solid.
Moderato, of a moderate strength.
Maestuoso, with majesty grand.
Octave, a perfect eight.
Replica, let it be repeated.
Piano, soft and sweet like an echo.
Presto, quick.
Solo, either part alone.
Syncopation, sounds driven through the bars.
Vivace, gay, quick, lively.
Vigeroso, with life and spirit.
Voce solo, a solo to be performed by a single voice.
Vibration, shaking or trembling.
Veloce, very quick.

The Musical Practitioner, according to the index, contains the following tunes:

Albany	Chelmsford	Grafton	Malden
Aleppo	Corinth	Greenland	Meditation
A Morning Hymn	Danbury	Hamilton	New West
	Divinity	Harvard	Plainfield
Attraction	Easter	Iberia	Petition
Beverly	Freedom	Jersey	Salvation
Bradford	Funeral	Liberty	Sandwich
Cambridge	Thought	Majorca	Sardinia

Shoreham	Stillwater	Vienna	Waltham
Silesia	Syria	Wallingsford	Wilmington
Solitude			

In addition to the psalm tunes there are two anthems:

"The Lord reigneth
The voice of my beloved"

Most of the pieces are written in three parts. Twelve, however, include four parts:

Danbury	Majorca	Plainfield	Silesia
Easter	Malden	Sandwich	Vienna
Harvard	Petition	Sardinia	Wilmington

Of two-part settings there is only one: "Shoreham."

The four-part settings are written for treble, counter, tenor, and bass; the three-part settings for treble, tenor, and bass; and the single two-part setting for tenor and bass. Musical indications like "Piano," "Forte," "Vivace," "Vigoroso," "Divoto," "Affetuoso" occur but seldom. The text in the majority of the tunes appears only in part and in two cases it does not appear at all. The texts to "Wallingsford," "Solitude," and to the anthem, "The voice of my beloved" are decidedly secular.

The second New Hampshire contributor to the literature of psalmody was David Merrill, "Philo Musica" of Exeter.[51] His psalm tune collection, unlisted in any of the present bibliographies, is entitled *Psalmodist's Best Companion*. The work, a copy of which is in the New Hampshire Historical Society, comprises six original compositions by the author. Attempts to bring to light biographical data concerning Merrill have thus far proved futile.[52] The title page of this work reads as follows:

"The Psalmodist's Best Companion, being an Extract of many approved Authors: containing A brief Introduction to the Grounds of Music, with a Collection of Psalm Tunes and Anthems which are suitable for Divine Worship, with a number never before published. Sing unto the Lord a new Song, and his Praise in the Congregation of Saints, Psalms, etc. By David Merrill, Philo, Musica. Exeter, New Hampshire, Printed Typographically by Henry Ranlet for the Author, 1799—— where music of all kinds, Books, Blanks and Hand bills are printed on low terms for cash."

The book includes seventy-two pages: title page, preface, five pages of instructional material, sixty-four pages of tunes and an index.

In the preface, Merrill expresses his ideas on the improvement of psalmody and how he hopes his book will bring this about. He writes:

"The advantages for studying the principles of Harmony are so extensively limited that it can not be expected that any Book whatever can be thoroughly criticised and permanently agreed to by all perusers. But I have endeavored as far as possible to fit a book suitable for the new beginner, and to assist the more accomplished singer in performing with ease and accuracy.

"It may be thought strange by some perhaps that I have inserted some new characters and omited [sic] others which were before in use, many characters which were used for artificial graces and others which I have inserted in the rules, and tunes I conclude highly necessary, and for proof I submit to the candid peruser.

"Tradition has caused many characters to have been continued in books for tradition sake only, which are of no service, but puzzling to the learner; therefore I would wish to drop tradition and follow the best rules. Several years study and practice in vocal Music has at last brought me to determination to publish this smal [sic] Book, consisting of Tunes and Anthems of an approved quality, in which I have endeavored to insert nothing but what is profitable to learn, so that a singing society may learn the whole book and have no unprofitable pages in it.

"I have spared no labor nor pains in rendering this work as correct as possible, but if critics should find any errors I humbly entreat them to look upon them with tenderness. I am the public's humble servant,

"Exeter, July 24th, 1799.   D.M."

The brief introduction includes five pages of instructional material. It treats the "Scale of Music or Gamut. . . . The Names

and Proportion of Notes used in Music, with their Rests . . .
Modes of Time . . . Triple Time Modes . . . Compound Time
Modes . . . Musical Characters and their Uses . . . Of Tuneing
the Voice . . . Change of the Key . . . General Observations. . . ."

A few quotations will afford some idea of the width and
depth of musical theory. We read on page seven:

Of the Keys Used in Music

"There are only two natural or primitive keys used in music,
viz. the cheerful or lively, called the Major or Sharp Key, and
the melancoly or mournful, called the Minor or Flat Key—C is
the sharp, and A is the flat key. The last note in the Bass is
always the key note, and is fa, or la; if the key be sharp, it is fa,
if flat, la. The key note is the foundation of the tune, and from
it all other parts are derived. In the sharp key, every 3d, 6th,
and 7th, is half a tone higher than in the flat. When flats or
sharps are placed at the beginning of a tune, they form what
are called Artificial Keys, which have the same effect as the
natural keys. The key note will not always be on C, or A.

Change of the Key

"In some tunes, or anthems, the key alters one or more times,
in consequence of the stile of the words altering. Sometimes
the key is altered by the transposition of the me, by flats, sharps,
or naturals, and sometimes by the principle or longest notes in
the tune being altered from fa to la, or from la to fa. But when
flats, sharps, or naturals, are inserted in the middle of a tune;
they have the same influence through the tune, as though they
were at the beginning; unless contradicted by a reserve.

General Observations

"When a tune is well learnt by note, it may be sung in words,
and every word should not only be pronounced according to
the best rules of Grammar, but spoken plainly and distinctly.
Singers often fail in this point, by which means half the beauty
of the music is lost the words not being understood.

"High notes in every part, should in general, be sung softer
than the low. The tone of the bass should be full and majestic;

of the tenor, bold and manly; of the counter, soft, yet firm and round; of the treble, smooth and delicate.

"Suitable attention should be paid to the Directory Terms soft loud, etc. a good tune performed with no variation will appear dull and insipid. In a company of singers it would have a good effect for some of the performers on each part to be silent when passages marked soft, occur; the additional strength of their voices in the loud, which generally precedes or succeeds the soft, would mark the contrast more distinctly, and give peculiar force and energy to the performance. A becoming manner of conduct in a collection of singers, will greatly increase the agreeable sensations which naturally arise from good performances. Above all, let a suitable attention be paid to the important truths offered in singing, that the great judge of quick and dead may be praised with reverence and solemnity."

According to the index, the *Psalmodist's Best Companion* contains the following tunes anthems:

Ashby	Kimball	Judgement	
Arnheim	Holyoke	Anthem	
Amherst	Billings	Judgement	Belknap
Alfred	Merrill	Lynnfield	Billings
Amity	Temple & M.	Lena	
Anthem for		Majesty	
Easter		Mirando	Merrill
Anthem for		Mortality	Ingalls
Thanksgiving	Merrill	Mount Vernon	
Claremont	Temple & M.	Pennsylvania	
Denmark	Madan	Psalm 49th	
Enfield	Chandler	Plymouth	
Edom		Repentance	
Exeter	Smith	Solitude-New	
Emanuel	Fasset	Truro	Merrill
Funeral-		The Farewell	Merrill
Thought	Williams	Unity	Reed
Friendship		Vermont	Kimball

Windham	Merrill	Winter	Reed
Woburn	Smith	Yarmouth	Kimball
Gilmanton	Billings		
Hiding-Place			
Jordan			
Jerusalem			

"Norwich," the first tune in the book, is not listed in the index. Without exception the settings are in four parts. Of the works "never before published," the following six are listed in the index as Merrill's own: "Alfred," "Anthem for Thanksgiving," "Gilmanton," "Mount Vernon," "Unity," and "Vermont." Two ("Amity" and "Claremont") are attributed to "Temple & M." (perhaps Merrill). For the three remaining new works ("Friendship," "Mirando," and "Repentance") no composer is given:

The Psalm tunes are written for treble, counter, tenor, and bass, with the exception of the "Judgement Anthem" and "Lynnfield," in which the counter is replaced by a second treble. "This counter and some others in this Book," writes Merrill at the outset of the "Judgement Anthem," "are put an octave below what is commonly, and must be performed in a Treble voice." This anthem is a fairly long, elaborate composition involving a number of solo passages.

David Merrill's own compositions manifest a healthy attitude toward fuging music. Of the six works definitely ascribed to him, four, "Vermont," "Unity," "Mount Vernon," and "Alfred," fall into the typical American fuging tune pattern, while "Gilmanton" is essentially homophonic. His "Anthem for Thanksgiving," a lengthier setting, alternates between homophonic passages harmonized in plain choral style and passages which show attempts at imitation.

The work of the Merrills indicates that musicians in New Hampshire were not content simply to perform the music emanating from the main centers like Boston and Philadelphia, but were also interested in contributing creatively to the growth of the choral repertoire. It would be a mistake, however, to imagine that their work developed in the isolation of backwater communities. New Hampshire was well aware of the latest publications and the newest advances. Richard Merrill's indebtedness to Billings has already been noted. A check of the "for sale" advertissement in the New Hampshire press shows that musicians in that area had readily available to them the work of Tans'ur, Billings, Holyoke, Kimball, Belcher, and many others. By way of example, we excerpt a few such press entries:

New Hampshire Gazette
May 26, 1769
"Just imported from London by William Appleton and to be sold at his Store in Portsmouth, a very large and compleat [*sic*] Assortment of Books. Tans'ur's Singing Book, Williams' Psalmody . . . the Vocal Companion."
January 18, 1783
"A few of the Singing Masters' Assistant, or Key to Practical Music, Composed by William Billings: To be sold by William Appleton of Portsmouth."
February 25, 1785
"To be sold by Alfred Buttler, William's Psalmody."
January 13, 1787
"For sale at Benjamin Dearborn's Shop in Market Street; Worchester Collection of Sacred Music, Law's Collection of Sacred Music."
December 7, 1793
"For Sale by J. Melcher at his Printing-Office. New Musical Publication by Andrew Law M.A. The Musical Primer, Containing a concise and comprehensive system of rules, together with a number of plain lessons and tunes—designed expressly for beginners. . . . The Federal Harmony, The Worcester Collection & Holyoke's Collection."

Oracle of the Day
November 21, 1795
"New Singing-Book. Just Published, and to be sold by the quantity [*sic*] or single, at C. Peirce's Book-Store, in Court-Street, Portsmouth, The Village Harmony, or Youth's Assistant to Sacred Music,—Containing a concise Introduction to the

Grounds of Music, with such a collection of the most approved Psalm Tunes, Anthems, and other Pieces, in three and four parts, as are most suitable for divine worship Designed for the use of Schools & Singing Societies."

December 21, 1799

"For sale, Charles Peirce, At the Columbian Book-Store & Oracle Printing-office. Village Harmony, Worchester Collection, Rural Harmony, Continental Harmony, Harmony of Maine, Harmonia America."

Concord Herald

November 8, 1792

"New Music. Just published and for sale at the store of William A. Kent,The American Harmony, Containing a number of Odes, Anthems, and plain Psalm Tunes, composed for performance on Thanksgiving, Ordinations, Christmas, Fasts, Funerals etc. by Oliver Holden Teacher of Music in Charlestown."

October 4, 1800

"William A. Kent . . . the fifth edition of the Village Harmony, just published, is received for sale. Singing Societies, and others, may be supplied by the dozen, or less, as low as of the publisher."

Walpole Museum

November 20, 1797

SACRED VOCAL MUSICK

"Just published, price 5s 3 single, and 9 dols. pr. doz.

"The Worcester Collection of Sacred Harmony—containing the Rules of Vocal Musick, in a concise and plain manner. Also, A large and choice collection of Psalm Tunes, Anthems & c. proper for Divine Worship; many of which are entirely new. Compiled for the use of Singing Schools and Musical Societies. Being the Sixth Edition, altered corrected and revised, with Additions. This work is so well known as not to need a recommendation to this Sixth Edition."

"Also, price 4s 6 single and 8 dols. by the doz.

"The Union Harmony, or Universal Collection of Sacred Music, in two vols.—Vol. first contains a valuable collection of Tunes, many of which were never before published. Vol. two contains a large collection of Anthems, Odes, &c. many of which are entirely new. By OLIVER HOLDEN."

"This valuable work has met with great encouragement—a 2d Edition has been published in two years from its first appearance. It is sold in separate vols. or both vols. bound together as purchasers wish. The price of the 1st vol. which is more particularly adapted to schools, is 4s 6 single, and 8 dols. per doz. The price of the 2d vol. containing Anthems, Odes &c. is one dol. single, and 10 1/2 dols. pr. doz. The price of the two vols. bound together which are valuable as a School Book, or for private use, is 10s 6 retail and 18 dols. pr. doz."

"Also, price 5s 3 single, and 9 dols. pr. doz.

"Harmonia Americana, containing a concise Introduction to Musick, with a variety of Airs, suitable for Divine Worship, and the use of Musical Societies. By SAMUEL HOLYOKE A.B."

"Also, price 4s 6 single, and 8 dols. pr. doz.

The Rural Harmony, being an original composition, in three and four parts—for the use of singing schools, and musical societies. By JACOB KIMBALL, Jun. A.B.

"This is a work of great merit, and stands first in the list of American musical composition. It is well calculated for a school book; and every encourager of American musick should become a purchaser."

"Also, price 4s 6 retail, and 8 dols. pr. doz.

The Harmony of Maine, being an original composition, containing an introduction to Musick, with Psalm Tunes, Fuging Pieces and Anthems. Calculated for schools and societies. By S. BELCHER.

"This is also a valuable American composition, and deserves the patronage of the lovers of musick, particularly those in the district whose name it bears."

"Also, price 6s single, and ten dols. fifty cents pr. doz.

"The Continental Harmony, containing a number of Tunes, Anthems, Fuges and Chorusses, [sic] all entirely new—with an Introduction &c. By WILLIAM BILLINGS."

"Also, price 10s 6 single, 9s [dollars?] pr. doz.

The Massachusetts Compiler of Theoretical and Practical Elements of sacred vocal Musick. Together with a Musical Dictionary, and a variety of Psalm Tunes, Chorusses, &c. chiefly selected or adapted from modern European publications. By H. GRAM, S. HOLYOKE, and O. HOLDEN.

"This is a most valuable and use Musical publication, more particularly for those who wish to become complete masters of the science, and to be able to write musick grammatically. It is highly approved and recommended by many good judges. It is in a quarto vol."

"Also, price 40 cents retail, and 4 dols. pr. doz.

"Middlesex Harmony. By SAMUEL BABCOCK. Also Sundry Anthems, &c., calculated for Thanksgiving days, and other publick occasions. By COOPER CRAM. &c."

"All the above valuable Musical Publications, are printed by THOMAS and ANDREWS, and sold, wholesale and retail, at their Book store, No. 45, Newbury street, Boston."

By way of epilogue to this survey of religious music, we append a few brief notes on a development that deserves to be more thoroughly investigated. The various enthusiastical sects employed music as an adjunct to their revival meetings. Formal publications of this music are, for obvious reasons, rather uncommon, but some knowledge of the effects of music upon the "awakened" ones can be gathered from memoirs.

The "Great Awakening" swept the colonies from 1734 to 1744. This extraordinary evangelical movement which had been started by Jonathan Edwards of Northampton, Massachusetts, from 1739 to 1741, came under the leadership of Reverend George Whitefield, the zealous and fiery English preacher. Whitefield was active in promoting the use of Watts' *Hymns and Psalms*, "which he greatly admired." Foote asserts that he placed considerable faith in the value of singing as part of the worship service.[53]

During his famous tour of New England, Whitefield visited Portsmouth in 1740, where he taught the Calvinistic doctrines to the inhabitants of the town. The Reverend William Shurtleff, pastor of the Second Church there at that time, records the visit and refers to the music in a letter to Reverend William Cooper, dated June 1, 1743. Shurtleff first writes of the character of the residents: "You are doubtless in some Measure acquainted with the Character, which the People of this Town have heretofore generally sustained. They have I think been remark'd by strangers for their Politeness in Dress and Behaviour; have been thought to go beyond most others in equal Circumstances, if not to exceed themselves, in their sumptuous and elegant Living, and Things of a like Nature: and while they have been justly in Repute for their generous and hospitable Disposition, and for many social virtues; Diversions of various Kinds have been much in Fashion, and the Vices that have been usual in a Sea-Port and trading Places, have been common and prevalent among us." [54] Regarding the music he says: "Music and Dancing seems to be wholly laid aside. Where you might formerly have heard jovial, and it may be profane and obscene Songs; you may now hear Psalms and Hymns of Praise Sung to God, and to our Lord Jesus Christ." [55]

A curious discussion in connection with abnormal manifestations of religious enthusiasm which appears in the *History of Durham*, provides some unusual references to singing and dancing in that town in 1746. The entry is extracted from the diary of Rev. Samuel Chandler dated August 20, 1746: "Then we went into the house & were entertained. Mr. Gilman came in and after him a number of those high flyers, raving like mad men, reproaching, reflecting. One Hannah Huckins in a boasting air said she had gone through adoption, justification & santification & perfection & perseverance. She said she had attained perfection & yet had a bad memory: I reasoned the point with her, but presently she broke out into exclamations, Blessed be the Lord, who had redeemed me, Glory, glory, glory, etc. fell to dancing around the room, singing some dancing tunes, jiggs, minuets, & kept the time exactly with her feet. Presently two or three more fell in with her & the room was filled with applauders, people of the same stamp crying out in effect Great is Diana of the Ephesians. One of these danced up to Mr. Gilman & said, Dear man of God, do you approve of these things? Yes, said he, I do approve of them. Then they began to increase and the house was full of confusion, some singing bawdy songs, others dancing to them & all under a pretence of religion. It is all to praise God in the dance and tabret." [56]

Such extreme use of music as a religious utterance, once very common, is still known in some communities. As a folk expression it is a valid part of the American scene, a vehicle through which a rather special aspect of the American character has revealed itself (and still continues to do so) with great fervor and conviction.

iv. Secular Music

IF records of religious music during the early period of the New Hampshire settlement are meager, a detailed account of secular music is also difficult to document. It is necessary to emphasize, nevertheless, that the England that these early settlers left behind at the beginning of the seventeenth century "was at the very height of her musicianship—a height she has perhaps never reached before or since." [1] The wonderful English madrigal school had reached its zenith; the equally remarkable virginal school had already matured; the country abounded in lutenists and lute ayre composers, and some of its most brilliant musicians were contributing to an increasing popular chamber music repertoire.

This study has already cast some light on a goodly number of musical instruments extant in New Hampshire during the seventeenth century, doubtless imported in the main from England. Along with these musical instruments, the first-generation settlers brought with them mentally at least if not in written form, many of the secular songs of the mother country.

Prior to 1640 the "Eastern people," as the inhabitants of New Hampshire and Maine were then known, were "thorough-paced Episcopalians, or conformists to the Established Church of England." According to John S. Jenness, the historian, the Anglican Church, at that time, upheld a "genial patronage of gaiety and merriment." It encouraged "maypoles, morris dances, wassails and junketings of all sorts; it smiled approvingly upon mince pies, cakes and ale, bone lace and tiffany hoodes, and all manner of bravery of apparel." [2]

Taverns and ale houses abounded in the settlements and, to be sure, their walls "echoed with the hoarse hilarity of the outlandish company." As they tipped their tankards of ale and other liquors, some weather-beaten salt would relate a marvelous yarn. A moment later, "one of the chanters of the fishermen would pipe up, in high key, some old forecastle ditty, or some ancient fishing song, that he learned in England." [3] On the bare tavern floor the young men and women would dance the brantle, the fore-and-aft reel, or the boisterous old country dance of England revived by Charles II, called cuckholds all awry,[4] accompanied by the scratchy tones of a fiddle.

Secular music in those settlements along the Merrimack and Connecticut rivers during the second quarter of the eighteenth century, when most of them came into being, arose from the need for social commingling. For instance, a "raising" usually furnished an excellent opportunity for satisfying the universal desire for sociability. When Jeremiah Story of Hopkinton built the frame of his two-storied dwelling house, the younger people in the neighborhood held a grand party and some of them "danced all night till broad day-light." [5] Husking was another form of social intercourse which usually terminated in a dance to the music of the violin. When instrumental music was wanting, "dancing was kept up to the jingling melody of the best singers in the company." [6]

Most of the towns of any consequence usually had access to some rustic fiddler who turned out to be the life of the party. When some damsel in the neighborhood was about to be married, the young men would engage the services of "some broken-down fiddler, who, for a few coppers, would scrape his fiddle till chanticleer warned him of the rising sun." [7]

Colonel Archelaus Moore of Canterbury was the master of a noted Negro fiddler whom he ultimately set free for fighting in the Revolutionary War. Sampson, as he was known, "was a famous fiddler and for many years afforded fine fun for frolicsome fellows in Concord with his fiddle on election days." [8]

Sir John Wentworth, provincial governor of New Hampshire between 1767 and 1775, generous country gentleman, benevolent administrator of the Crown, and skilled equestrian, was also fond of music. In a letter to William Bayard dated July 3, 1767, Wentworth recalled his pleasant visit with the family and particularly Miss Bayard's "harpsichord and voice." He wrote: "I wish to God that I was escaped from all this dust, parade, show and ceremony to your piazza at Greenwich, remarking the pleasant views over to Hoebuck [Hoboken] . . . or turning over the music while Miss Bayard's harpsichord and voice call all our pleased attention from delightful scenes to better harmony." [9]

The forty-foot-long ballroom in the spacious Wentworth mansion at Wolfeborough fifty miles north of Portsmouth must have been the scene of many festive occasions, balls and musicals.[10] Lady Wentworth, in a letter to Mrs. Langdon of Portsmouth written in October, 1770, informed the latter that "the great dancing-room is nearly completed, with the drawing room, and begins to make a very pretty appearance." [11] Compelled by the exigencies of her husband's duties as "Surveyor General of His Magesty's Woods" to reside in the country, Lady Frances Wentworth, "who was never happier nor more at home than in a ballroom," [12] probably took every opportunity to put her "great dancing-room" to use as compensation for the rural tranquility for which she expressed a measure of well-bred contempt.[13]

A year earlier Governor Wentworth had written to Paul Wentworth, a relative in England, inquiring for domestics who were also musicians. The letter is quoted in part from the manuscript: "The servants (I brought out of England) are married and well provided for that I want two good men as footmen. As you have connections abroad will you give me leave to ask your assistance to send me two that can play well on a French horn also if they can, or one of them play on a violin; and will also serve me five years faithfully in my family. I will besides the wages you recommend, at the expiration of their time, give them each one hundred acres of good land in a settled country, and give them some little Government place of profit as they may be capable of. If you should meet with one or two of such men, Mr. Inman, my tailor, will clothe them in my livery; and the mast ship or any other ship to this port will bring them out to me. It is not of any consideration to me what country or religion. If they are good, well tempered, honest, capable men. I will do more for them than they can ever expect in Europe. Neither is it essential that their musical execution should be of the first rate, as we are not great Connosseurs in that way. Pardon me, my dear sir, for giving you this request, and be assured that I shall be unfeignedly happy in every opportunity of approving myself with the highest gratitude and esteem my dear kinsman, your cordially obliged and most sincere Friend,

J. WENTWORTH." [14]

It is interesting to compare this with Thomas Jefferson's more famous request for musician-domestics. In 1778, nine years after Wentworth's letter, Jefferson addressed himself to a friend in Paris, setting forth more explicitly than Wentworth the restrictions imposed by domestic economy upon a passion for music:

"If there is a gratification which I envy any people in this world, it is to your country its music. This is the favorite passion of my soul & fortune has cast my lot in a country where it is in a state of deplorable barbarism. I shall ask your assistance in procuring a substitute, who may be proficient in singing & on the Harpsichord. I should be contented to receive such a one two or three years hense when it is hoped he may come more safely and find here a greater plenty of those useful things which commerce alone can furnish.

"The bounds of an American fortune will not admit the indulgence of a domestic band of musicians, yet I have thought that a passion for music might be reconciled with that economy which we are obliged to observe. I retain, for instance, among my domestic servants a gardner, a weaver, a cabinet-maker and a stone cutter, to which, I would add a vigneron. In a country where like yours, music is cultivated and practiced by every class of men, I suppose there might be found persons of these trades who could perform on the French horn, clarionet, or hautboy, and bassoon, without enlarging his domestic expenses. A certainty of employment for a half dozen years, and at the end of that time, to find them, if they chose, a conveyance to their own country, might induce them to come here on reasonable wages. Without meaning to give you trouble, perhaps it might be practicable for you—to find out such men disposed to come to America. Sobriety and good nature would be desirable parts of their characters. If you think such a plan practicable and will be so kind as to inform me what will be necessary to be done on my part, I will take care that it shall be done." [15]

The growing interest in secular music reflected, for example, in the attention of the psalmodists to secular part songs (Billings' "Modern Music," "Consonance"), was manifest also in the growing demand for patriotic airs, English ballad opera tunes, and songs "satyrical" and sentimental. Publishing was still in its infancy, and much of the published music was imported from England. However, some printing was being done in New Hampshire by the various newspaper establishments. The New Hampshire newspaper of the period provides some measure of the diversity of and interest in secular music, either published domestically or imported.

The first notice which attracts our attention is found in the October 6, 1758, *New Hampshire Gazette*. It reads: "An Old Song, wrote by one of our first New England Planters, on the management in those good Old Times; To the Tune of Cobbler there was, & Poor Richard's Description of his Country Wife Joan, and a Song to the Tune of the Hounds are all out, &. (Price Six Coppers.)" A year later, the *Gazette* carried the following: "This Day is Publish'd Sold at the Printing-Office in this Town, printed on a large Derry Paper, (Price 12s. old Tenor). A New Song on the Successes of the Year past, against the French, more particularly in America,—Also a new Thanksgiving Song. Together with another on the Reduction of Quebeck [*sic*] Ticonderoga, Niagara, Crown Point etc." [16]

The *Gazette* of June 21, 1765, lists "a very large assortment of Pamphlets and Songs," and on May 26, 1769, an advertisement calls attention to "The Mask, a Collection of excellent new songs," as well as to a large stock of psalm books. In 1788, the *Gazette* announced "A New Periodical Work to be entitled, the Massachusetts Magazine or Monthly Museum of Knowledge and rational Entertainment." Each issue was to contain a section of music. The advertisement continues: "In each Number will be presented one Copperplate Engraving—together with some favorite Piece of Vocal or Instrumental Music printed typographically. Should we at any time neglect giving a Copperplate, eight pages of Letter Press shall be added in lieu of it, or an additional piece of Musick; and if it should so happen that the Copperplate and Music should both fail, than there should of sixteen pages of Letter Press, for the Magazine of that month wherein the failure happens.[17]

The initial issue of the magazine was dated January, 1789. Evans's *American Bibliography* gives the title page:

"The Massachusetts Magazine; or, Monthly Museum of Knowledge and Rational Entertainment. Containing, Poetry, Musick, Biography, History, Physick, Geography, Morality, Criticism, Philosophy, Mathematics, Agriculture, Architecture, Chymistry, Novels, Tales, Romances, Translations, News, Marriages, Deaths, Meteorological Observations, etc. etc. . . . [January] 1789.

"Printed at Boston, by Isaiah Thomas and Ebenezer T. Andrews. Sold at their Bookstore, No. 45, Newbury Street, and by said Thomas, at his Bookstore in Worcester, by whom subscription for this work are still received." [18]

Andrews, in a brief note to Thomas, conveys some idea of the quality of the music printed in the *Massachusetts Magazine:* "Gram [19] says he will engage to furnish the Musick for our Magazine for one dollar per month, that it shall be always good and adapted to the season." [20] Among the list of contributors appeared such names as William Billings, Samuel Holyoke, Jacob Kimball, and Horatio Garnet (see Chapter X) as well as Gram. The *Massachusetts Magazine* expired in 1796.

Joseph Melcher, "Printer and Bookseller" in Portsmouth, advertised several song books for sale in 1792. They were:

"Ramsay's Songs, American Songster, London Songster, Steavens Songs, Several New Song Books." [21] About a year later Melcher put up for sale "Cheats of London (A Song-Book); Cheerful Companion (A Song-Book); Kitty Fisher's Song-Book; Songs, comic, satyrical and sentimental; Sky-Lark, being an elegant collection of Songs; Songster's Companion: Roundelay, or the New Syren (a collection of choice Songs); and Buck's Delight (Song-book)." [22]

In April, 1798, Samuel Larkin, publisher and bookseller, announced through the *Gazette* that he had: "Just Published And for Sale at the Portsmouth Book-Store the Columbian Songster, and Freemason's Pocket Companion, A collection of the newest & most celebrated Sentimental, Convivial, Humour-ous, Satirical, Pastoral, Hunting, Sea, and Masonic Songs, Being the largest and best Collection ever published in America. To which is added, Monsieur Tonson a Tale. Subscribers are requested to call or send for the books." [23]

The "Book Store and Stationery Shop" in Washington Street owned by Charles Peirce was obviously a fine place to shop for all sorts of musical materials during the last decade of the eighteenth century. The proprietor included in his stock most of the well known psalm books of the day, religious instruction manuals (see Chapter III), songs, song, collections, dances, in-strumental and vocal "preceptors" (instruction manuals), operas, farces, and a selection of Shakespeare and Goldsmith. [24] Ostensi-bly, the wide assortment of music at Peirce's establishment attests to the keen interest in and demand for these products.

In 1793, Charles Peirce announced that he had "Just Received a few Musical Books, containing Directions and the newest Tunes for the Flute, Fife, and Violin." [25] Less than a year later Peirce, also the publisher of the *Oracle of the Day*, had moved his establishment to Court Street, announcing for sale at his new address "The Farmer; a Comic Opera, in two Acts, by John O'Keefe, Esq.—the Quaker; a Comic Opera, in two Acts.—All as performed at the Theatre in Boston, 9d each." [26] A few years later, Peirce advertised a "New Song-Book, To which is added the Figures of 24 new Country Dances," as just published and for sale at 1s 6. The name of Peirce's shop was changed from "Book Store and Stationery Shop" to the "Columbian-Bookstore" and the address to No. 5 Daniel Street.[27] It would be pleasant to think that the latest change was motivated by the needs of an ever-expanding business.

On December 21, 1799, the *Oracle of the Day* advertised:

The Columbian Songster   6s
New-Philadelphia song book   4s 6
Sky-Lark   4s, [or gentlemen and ladies' complete songster][28]
Humming-Bird   3s and 3s 9, [or New American Songster . . . With modern toasts and sentiments] [29]
Vocal Companion   3s & 1s 6
The Social companion   1s 6

In the December 7, 1799, *Oracle*, Peirce's advertisement announced for sale the "Musical Magazine, Musical Primmer, Art of Singing and Instructions for the Guitar," while an advertisement in the columns of the June 7, 1800, *Oracle* listed no less than eight "Plays and Farces" for sale by the Columbian Bookstore, among which are to be found several librettos of the currently popular operas, some of which had already been performed in the town of Portsmouth. For the benefit of the reader we cite them and include the composers and the dates of publication: [30]

Highland Reel	William Shield	1799
Jew [and the Doctor]	Thomas Dibdin	?
No Song No Supper	Stephen Storace	1792
Gentle Shepherd	Allan Ramsay	1795
Prisoner	Thomas Attwood	?
Mountaineers	Samuel Arnold	1795
Children in the Wood	Samuel Arnold	1795
Romp	Thomas Dibdin	1792
Poor Soldier	William Shield	1787
Robin Hood	William Shield	?

Elsewhere in the state newspaper advertisements likewise offer evidence of a lively interest in secular music. In Walpole, for instance, the June 26, 1798, *Farmer's Weekly Museum* announced a large number of plays and farces for sale. A few comic opera librettos are listed as well: [31]

Love in A Village,		
a comic opera	25 cents. Thomas Arne	1794
Highland Reel,		
a comic opera	25 cents. William Shield	1794
The Woodman,		
a comic opera	25 cents. William Shield	1794
Slaves in Algiers, or a struggle for Freedom, interspersed with songs by Mrs. Rowson	25 cents. Alexander Reinagle	1794
Mountaineers,		
a comic opera	25 cents. Samuel Arnold	1795
The Lord of the Manor,		
a comic opera	20 cents. William Jackson	1790
The Quaker,		
a comic opera	25 cents. Charles Dibdin	1794
The Governess,		
a comic opera		
Lionel and Clarissa,		
a comic opera	25 cents. Charles Dibdin	1794

On November 5, 1798, the same weekly advertised for sale to the Walpole inhabitants the two patriotic songs, "Hail Columbia" and "Adams and Liberty," "now sung with increasing applause throughout the United States." The "favorite song" of "Heaving the Lead" was likewise available; and also a new song book, "the Echo; or Federal Songster, being a collection of the most celebrated Songs, now in vogue; consisting of Patriotic, Bacchanalian & Sentimental etc. etc." [32]

The New Hampshire press is also a convenient source for the texts of songs popular in the state. Many are of a patriotic nature and were adapted to tunes already popular. Some are importations from abroad; for example, Dibdin's "Nancy" and "Neighbour Sly." In the case of the adaptations, the newspaper noted, for its readers' convenience, the old tune to which the new text was to be sung.

New Hampshire Gazette

May 26, 1775: "A song To the Tune of The Echoing Horn." [A Revolutionary War pharaphrase.]

May 25, 1776: "A Song, from a new musical interlude called the Election."

June 1, 1776: "Ode to Independence."

April 12, 1777: "A song, just came to hand which was sung before General Sullivan, and a Number of respectable Inhabitants of this Town." To the tune of "Eugene's March."

November 17, 1781: "New Song Occasioned by the Surrender of Cornwallis and his whole army to General Washington." To the tune of "Derrydown etc."

June 12, 1798: "Adams and Liberty. The Boston Patriotic Song. Written by Thomas Paine A.M."

July 23, 1799: "Song, For the celebration of the 17th July, 1799." Composed by J. M. Sewall, Esq. Tune "Rule Britannia."

The Oracle of the Day

July 6, 1793: "The following Ode was composed by a young Gentleman of this town, for the 4th of July, 1793—and sung at one of the parties assembled to celebrate the Anniversay of the Day."

September 7, 1793: "Neighbour Sly: A New Song-By Dibdin."

April 4, 1795: "A Song written by J. M. Sewall. First line: "Columbia's sons in Songs proclaim."

March 22, 1797: "Nancy; or, the Sailor's Journal, A favorite Song; written by Mr. Dibdin. Sung by Mr. Williamson at the Haymarket Theatre, Boston."

New Hampshire Spy

March 31, 1789: "Song. From a new American Farce, entitled the Better Sort; or, The Girl of Spirit; lately published in Boston."

July 7, 1789: "The two following Odes (wrote for the occasion) were sung Saturday last by the gentlemen assembled at the Globe Tavern, [in Portsmouth] to celebrate the glorious

era-American Independence." [Both odes were written to the
tune of "God Save the King."]

July 11, 1789: "An Ode For Independence, July 4th 1789 by
Daniel George." The music to this ode was written by Horatio
Garnet [see chapter X] and published in the *Massachusetts
Magazine*, Boston, July, 1789, pp. 452-453.

We conclude this chapter with a rather interesting reference
to secular music which occurs in the accounts of Major General
Marquis de Chastellux's visit to Portsmouth in October, 1782.
The Marquis, one of the forty members of the French Academy,
was "distinguished not only in the character of an amateur, but
for his scientific knowledge of music." [33] He was present in
Portsmouth at the same time as the French regiment of Viennois, whose music he enjoyed. Chastellux recalls the circum--
stances: "I proposed on the morning of the 11th, to make a tour
among the islands in the harbour, but some snow having fallen,
and the weather being by no means inviting, I contented myself with paying visits to some officers of the navy, and among
others to the Comte de Vaudreuil, who had slept on the shore
the preceding night; after which we again met at dinner at Mr.
Albert's, a point of union which was always agreeable. M.
d'Hizeures had ordered the music of the regiment of Viennois
to attend, and I found with pleasure, that the taste for music,
which I had inspired into that corps, still subsisted and that
the ancient musicians had been judiciously replaced." [34]

French as well as English bands were fairly common in the
colonies during and after the Revolution. The bands attached
to Rochambeau's forces which landed in Rhode Island in 1780
were, according to Fitzpatrick, "more showy" than the drum
and fife units of the Continental Army. [35] The British Guard
Regiments customarily boasted of bands whose instrumentation
included oboes, clarinets, horns, and bassoons, in addition to
the traditional drums and fifes. [36] In 1771, Josiah Flagg conducted a program of "vocal and instrumental musick accompanied by French horns, hautboys etc. by the band of the 64th
Regiment," [37] a British organization. It is also known that Flagg
"founded and drilled the first real militia band of Boston." [38]

v. Music for Public Occasions

IT is a commonplace in a society's conduct of its public ceremonial and celebration that the festivity should be marked by
music. That "a decent ball" [1] should have been featured in
Concord's recognition of George Washington's sixty-fifth birthday, or that the festivities for Independence Day that same
year (1797) should have "closed with harmony & song" [2] indicates that social usage, at least in this respect, was in essence
no different in New Hampshire from elsewhere. Newspapers
are the most obvious source for information about such public
celebrations, and for this reason we are better informed from
the seventeen-sixties on than for the period prior to newspaper
publication. However, there is no reason to suppose the public
ceremonial and music appropriate for it was unknown in New
Hampshire before the earliest newspaper reference to such an
affair. A few examples from newspaper sources will suffice to
illustrate the social tone of such celebrations and the manner
in which music played its part.

For the celebration of the repeal of the Stamp Act in 1766
the ships in Portsmouth harbor "were decorated with their
Colours, the Bells rang an incessant Peal, Drums and Music
contributed to make the Harmony of Sounds concordant to
the apparent Tempor and Disposition of the People." [3] A music,
more sedate and gallant, concordant with the temper and disposition of the ladies and gentlemen invited by Governor John
Wentworth and his Lady, probably marked the ball given in
1772 in honor of Queen Charlotte's birthday. "The Splendor
and Brilliancy of the Ladies, the Grandeur and Elegance of the
Room, and the Harmony and Festivity which reign'd among

the numerous joyful Guests, all conspired to give this Entertainment the Preference to any of the kind given in this Province." [4] Later that year, on September 22, the anniversary of the coronation of King George III was observed in the "usual manner"—that is, by the firing of the guns at Castle William and Mary. In the evening the "Gentlemen of the Town gave a genteel Ball at the Assembly-Room, at which were present a number of Strangers." [5]

College commencements, no less than birthdays of queens, had their appropriate music. As the *Gazette* notes, when Dartmouth College granted Governor John Wentworth, one of its benefactors, an honorary Doctor of Laws, both morning and afternoon exercises were "closed with an Anthem suitable to the Occasion." [6] This may suggest a rather perfunctory use of music, but for the observance of Dartmouth's twentieth anniversary commencement of its founding (August 24, 1791) the musical portion of the program was quite substantial. The ceremonies of the day began with a procession which included faculty, students, and visiting dignitaries. "On entering the College Chapel, they were entertained with a concert of musick vocal and instrumental amidst a brilliant concourse of spectators." [7] Following the president's address, an "Ode to commencement" was performed, set to music by John Hubbard, A.M., professor of mathematics at the college and "a man of superior talent, knowledge and taste, in the science of music," [8] which (so the *Concord Herald* reports) "most delightfully prepared the mind" for the ensuing exercises. The morning observances concluded with "musick," followed by an intermission of two hours during which all present repaired to the College Hall, where they "partook of an elegant repast." [9]

In the afternoon the exercises were resumed with the rendition of a chorus from Handel (not specifically identified in the *Concord Herald's* account) and, following the last dialogue before the degrees were granted, still more "musick" was performed. After the "valedictory Oration, the musicians performed Champlain, from Mr. Holyoke's valuable publication [10] of musick in a manner that showed the sublimity of the art." [11]

Samuel Holyoke was present and received an honorary degree, the nature of which is obscure in the *Concord Herald*'s account. Although music was not a regular part of the curriculum at Dartmouth, the commencement exercises indicate that it may well have been a strong extracurricular activity. If so, it would be difficult to imagine that secular music was studiously avoided and that the rehearsing of a commencement anthem was the student body's total musical nourishment.

Patriotic celebrations called inevitably for music. Independence Day was usually ushered in with the ringing of bells and the discharge of cannon from various parts of the town. Mid-morning the citizenry attended worship service and then repaired to "elegant dinners" marked by the drinking of an impressive number of toasts. The eventful day customarily culminated with fireworks and a "genteel" ball in the evening. The music heard during the day ranged from dance music and patriotic songs to the "sublime anthems" of the church service. Accounts of typical Independence Day celebrations in Portsmouth can be found in the May 3, 1783, and July 9, 1789, issues of the *New Hampshire Gazette*. In the former issue, "several sublime anthems . . . suited to the joyful occasion" were noted as following upon Rev. Mr. Buckminster's prayer. In the evening a "beautifully illuminated" ball, at which the ladies were "numerous and brilliant," was given by a "number of gentlemen of the town." In the latter issue, the account of Portsmouth's celebration of the thirteenth anniversary of American Independence includes a reference to the singing of "several excellent songs, accompanied by instrumental musick." [12]

There was apparently a considerable amount of music, and all of it exuberant, during the festivities that broke out in Portsmouth upon the news that the Federal Constitution had been ratified. Our account is taken from the *New Hampshire Gazette* of June 26, 1788. The news reached the port city on Sunday June 22, 1788: "Mutual congratulations took place, and public thanks was returned in all the churches." It being the Lord's Day, all further testimonials were postponed until

Monday morning, at which time the bells rang a joyful peal while several citizens "paraded the streets with music."

On Thursday of that week the planned celebration took place. The extended procession was led by "A Band of Music in an open Coach and six horses decorated." Pressmen, with Mr. Benjamin Dearborn's "new invented Printing-Press (named the American Press), employ'd during the whole processsion in striking off and distributing among the surrounding multitude songs in celebration of the ratification of the Federal Constitution by the State of New Hampshire." The procession moved on through all the main avenues of the town, the band playing and singing the federal song "It comes! It comes!" to the tune of "He comes, he comes."

> It comes! It comes! high raise the song
> The bright procession moves along
> From pole to pole resound the Nine [states]
> And distant worlds the chorus join.

> In vain did Britain forge the chain
> While countless squadrons hid the plain
> Hantonia,[13] foremost of the Nine
> Defy'd their force, and took Burgoyne.

Following the parade, a "cold Collation" was provided, during which "the Band of Music" played. Immediately after the firing of a nine-gun salute, which was reciprocated with three cheers, "three songs were sung, accompanied by the band."

The day was climaxed with a concert, the *Gazette* describing it thus: "In the evening the State-House was beautifully illuminated with nine candles in each window, while a large company of ladies and gentlemen, formed in a semi-circle, were entertained by the Band from the Balcony." [14]

The federal songs "sung at the procession, after dinner and in the evening," were especially written for the occasion and set to the tunes of "He Comes, He Comes," "Smile, Smile, Britannia," "When Britains first, etc.," and "Union." [15]

George Washington's arrival in Portsmouth was an opportunity for an especially lavish outpouring of music and poetry.[16]

The illustrious visitor pronounced himself "sensibly impressed" by the welcome accorded him in the "metropolis of New Hampshire." Upon his appearance, he was greeted by a salute of cannon fire, ringing of bells, and repeated shouts from grateful thousands. Arriving at the State House, he took his place on the balcony. Then from a stage erected for the purpose, three odes, composed by a "gentleman in this town,"[17] were sung by a prepared group, accompanied by the band.[18] As a sample of the affected public poetry sung upon such occasions, we reproduce in full one of the odes set to the melody of "God Save the King":

I

Long may the Trumpet, Fame,
Let echo waft the Name,
   Of WASHINGTON:
O'er all the world around,
Far as earth's utmost bound,
Thy equal is not found,
   Columbia's Son.

II

Ye blest of Human kind,
Columbians, call to mind,
   The deeds he's done:
Hark! Hark! those shouts declare,
That Heaven's peculiar care,
The matchless Hero's here,

   Great WASHINGTON.

III

Hantonia's sons rejoice,
Welcome with heart and voice,
   Your country's pride:
On this auspicious day,
Drive sorrow far away,
And sing in rapt'rous lay,
   Let joy preside.

IV

Rejoice—let all rejoice
And with united voice
    The HERO hail;
He stem'd oppression's tide,
And humbled Britain's pride,
Is still your matchless guide
    That will not fail.

The following morning, Sunday, Washington attended divine services at Queen's Chapel, and in the afternoon at the First Congregational Church. At Queen's Chapel, "several pieces of sacred musick, were performed, suited to the ... occasion." Most probably the President heard some "sacred vocal and instrumental musick" at the Congregational Church, although the *Gazette* makes no mention of it.

On Monday, Washington, accompanied by President Sullivan, the Hon. Mr. Langdon, the Marshall of the district, the Consul of France and his two secretaries, went on an excursion down the harbor on a barge "rowed by seamen dressed in white frocks followed by music." As the *Gazette* explained: "A number of young gentlemen who compose the band in this town, anxious to afford our illustrious and beloved president, all the entertainment in their power, followed him in a barge, and performed several pieces of music on the water, we hope to his acceptance." [19]

George Washington's visit to Portsmouth was brought to a close with a ball in his honor on Tuesday evening. "In the evening an elegant ball was given by the Gentlemen of Portsmouth, which the President honored with his preference, when he was introduced to a brilliant circle of more than seventy ladies. The president being seated, an excellent song was sung accompanied by the band; after which the dances began and the evening passed away with all the joy and good humor which the occasion naturally inspired."

In subsequent years Washington's birthday was marked in New Hampshire by special festivities. *The Courier of New*

Hampshire for February 19, 1797, notes that in Concord, "a decent ball was given in the evening" to celebrate the event. And in the *Oracle of the Day* of Portsmouth for February 23, 1799, we read that for Washington's birthday, "The felicities of the occasion [were] greatly augmented by an incomparable Song, the handy work of that celebrated genius J. M. Sewall, Esq. who amid the avocations of the bar and press of clients, devoted a few pleasing moments to celebrate the praises of Washington."

In Exeter "a splendid ball was given" to commemorate the day.[20] Sewall's talent may appear questionable to us, but his services for these patriotic occasions were much appreciated and extravagantly praised. We encounter him giving "spirited performances" of his bombastic verses (which, it would seem, he adapted to already famous melodies) not only on Washington's birthday but on John Adams's as well. For the latter occasion, he sang his verse, of course, to the tune of "Adams and Liberty." The *Oracle of the Day* hails him in one issue (July 6, 1799) as the "American Apollo and poet of the day" and in another (November 2, 1799) as the patriot

> Whose lyre to raptures extatic [*sic*] is strung,
> When Adams, when Washington, dwells on his tongue.

If Washington's birthday evoked great public rejoicing, his death produced an equally intense public grief. In Portsmouth the formal observances commemorating his passing began with a procession, including "drums muffled and Music in crape," playing the "Dead March" from *Saul*.[21] When the funeral cortege entered the church, "a most solemn piece of sacred music was performed on the organ." The meeting house was "elegantly habited in full mourning;—the pulpit, organ-loft, orchestra, alter [*sic*], etc. claimed particular notice." Jonathan M. Sewall, chosen to pronounce the eulogium, spoke on "The Pride of eloquence, & the power of Verse." [22] A select group of vocal performers from all the different religious societies in the town under the immediate direction of Captain Gookins,[23] "as senior Church chorister," performed the "National Dirge,"

"Masonic Ode," and "Christian Hymn." The correspondent to the *Oracle* observed that "The performers were excellent. The soul was melted and the eye dissolved. Mr. [Isaac] Stanwood [24] played the Organ with astonishing effect; it was indeed, the pealing Anthem on the deep ton'd Organ." [25]

The text to the dirge composed [26] by Reverend George Richards gives some idea of the patriotic sorrow which swept the nation on the death of its first president:

> Columbia, Virtue, Freedom, rise!
>   And sweep the plaintive chords of woe;
> A Nation's tears; am Empire's sighs,
>   Mourn Washington, by death, laid low.
>
> The Patriot, Hero, Sage, combin'd;
>   The Good, the Great, the Brave, the Just;
> The sire, and Friend of human Kind;
>   Of men the Best, of Men the First.
>
> 'This Washington who bows the head!
>   His Virtues tow'r above the grave;
> The Hero, Patriot, Sage, is dead;
>   George Washington, the Good, the Brave.
>
> A Washington can never die;
>   The Good, the Great, the godlike Brave,
> In ev'ry tear, in ev'ry sigh
>   Shall live, and triumph o'er the grave.
>
> The world's vast round is Virtue's urn;
>   But all our Hearts shall be his grave;
> There, Love's eternal lamp shall burn;
>   And Life entomb the Good, the Brave.
>
> Columbia, Virtue, Freedom, Fame,
>   Shall twine the Laurel, Civic wreath;
> And Angels bear th' Immortal Name
>   Above;—beyond the grasp of death.[27]

As elsewhere in the new republic, the revolution in France evoked great enthusiasm in New Hampshire. As part of the anniversary celebration in 1793, "a number of songs, several of which were composed on the occasion, were sung . . . accompanied with instrumental music. To heighten the scene, in the midst of music, entered the room in exactest order a beautiful procession of Boys wearing caps inscribed with the words Liberty and Equality." [28]

In 1795 the celebration of the "brilliant and unexampled successes" of the French, in the "compleat conquest" of Holland, and the freeing of that nation from the "chains of despotism," included the drinking of toasts accompanied by a number of patriotic songs, sung by "Several French and other gentlemen of the Company." [29] One of the songs, "Columbia's sons in songs proclaim" was sung by Jonathan M. Sewall, and perhaps composed by him.[30] Another sample of Sewall's rhymed bombast, the first two of the eight verses of this song, are here given: [31]

> Columbia's sons in song proclaim
>   Our brave Allies, in union join'd!
> The noblest wreaths your skill can frame,
>   On Holland's brows, & Gallia's bind!
>
> Chorus
>
>> The foes of liberty restor'd,
>> By reason conquer'd, sheathe the sword.
>
> When France shook off oppressions chain,
>   And Mad'ning despots rush'd to arms,
> Deluded Holland took the plain,
>   While Europe thundered with alarms.
>
>> They thought their cause (infatuate blind!)
>> The cause of justice and mankind.

Masonic celebrations were apparently as elaborate and impressive in Concord as in any of the large New England cities. From the *New Hampshire Gazette's* account (May 14, 1799) of the installation ceremony of the Blazing Star Masonic Lodge in Concord we learn that the solemnities were introduced by a prayer, succeeded by a "very elegant piece of sacred harmony." Later in the day, during the parade, "A most capital band of instrumental performers, placed exactly at the center, enlivened the line of march, on the length and breadth of the oblong square." The divine worship, following the parade, was held at Rev. Asa McFarland's meeting house: "It is supposed that little short of 1500 spectators were present. . . . The orchestra was filled, by a select band of vocal and instrumental performers, the exquisite harmony of whose sweetly melodious tones, are yet vibrating on the ear of music: Every amature [sic] of the sacred art spoke in rapture of the concluding hymn: It was one of those irresistible energies of composition and execution which might have sooth dispair and calmed outrageous prhenzy [sic]."

In conclusion, comments the Gazette, "the musical society and vocal choristers are sincerely tendered all possible acknowledgements for the generous assistance which they so readily afforded."

As for the Rev. McFarland, whose meeting house was used for this impressive occasion, his own ordination in Concord on March 7, 1798, was also marked by a most enthusiastic and unsolemn style of rejoicing. Tradition has it that there was a plentiful supply of refreshments, including "spiritous liquors," and it may be judged that general conviviality was the order of the day. Music played a major role in the entire proceedings. "The procession of the ordaining council, from the town house to the meeting-house, was attended by a band of music." [32] The ordination service itself included the singing of "Champlain," "Chelhunt," and "Easter Anthem." In its account, the Courier of New Hampshire reported that "much praise is due to the musicians in particular for the accurate and judicious performance." [33] The festivities were crowned with a "splendid ball in the evening at Stickney's celebrated tavern." [34]

The installation of ministers in Concord was, however, not always as elaborate nor as enthusiastic as Rev. McFarland's.

Some years earlier, for Rev. Israel Evans's installation in July of 1789, "several pieces of music ... performed in a masterly manner" were apparently regarded as sufficient for the occasion.[35]

The material contained in this brief review is by no means exhaustive, but has been selected to illustrate the various types of public ceremonial (other than worship service) for which music was regarded as indispensable.

VI. Opera before the Revolution

THE history of opera and the history of the theater in America during the closing years of the eighteenth century are so closely allied that it is impossible, as well as impractical, to study one to the exclusion of the other. At the outset, the operatic repertoire was chiefly devoted to performances of English-ballad opera by such favorite composers as Thomas Arne, Samuel Arnold, Charles Dibdin, Stephen Storace, and William Shield. The "pasticcio" was another favorite type of musical theater, and it is worth noting that it included not only music of English origin, but music from the finest Italian, German, and French sources as well.[1] Toward the end of the century, the operas of a few American composers like Benjamin Carr, Victor Pelissier, Alexander Reinagle, and James Hewitt began to appear on the theater boards.

The peculiarities of the American stage in the latter part of the eighteenth century merit a moment's attention. The popular ballad-operas, pantomimes, harlequinades, farces, and ballets as well as plays were, for the most part, introduced in this country by traveling professional theatrical companies from England and the West Indies. It is at least possible that their productions compared favorably with the European presentations of the day. The ability both to sing and act was a necessary prerequisite for a member of one of these itinerant troupes. The actor-singer, as a player was known, performed in a Shakespearean tragedy or Garrick comedy on one night and sang his way through a fashion-ballad-opera the next, or even the same evening if the occasion warranted it. Between acts, the inclusion of "favourite songs" and "patriotic airs" was common practice and, when available, an orchestra would also provide music. "Consequently," writes Sonneck, "nobody with ears to hear could escape music if he ventured into the theatre."[2]

Although the development of opera in Portsmouth was not without its vicissitudes, it encountered nothing comparable to the antitheater blue law which prevailed in Boston from 1750 until its repeal in 1797.[3] As early as 1762, the citizens of Portsmouth indicated their desire for "theatrical entertainments," in a petition dated June 3rd of that year to the governor proposing the erection of a playhouse. The petition, signed by forty-five persons of the town, largely representing the wealthy leisure classes, included such familiar family names as Wentworth, Warner, Livermore, Atkinson, Rindge, and others. The proposal for the playhouse had come from one of the actors of the plays, "sometime since at Newport, but lately at New York," who intended presenting "no obscene or immoral plays, but such as tend to the improvement of the mind." As a matter of historical interest the document is here quoted in its entirety:

"Petition for a Play-house at Portsmouth.

"*Province of New Hampshire*

"To his Excellency BENNING WENTWORTH Esq. Governor and Commander-in-Chief in and over his Majesty's Province of New Hampshire: The Petition of sundry of the Inhabitants of Portsmouth, in the Province of New Hampshire—*Humbly Shews*: That the Subscribers understand that there has been a proposal made by one of the actors of the plays, sometime since at Newport, but more lately at New York, to erect a play-house here sometime hence; and that there is a petition presented to your Excellency to inhibit and prevent the same.

"Now your petitioners, being informed that the said actors act no obscene or immoral plays, but such as tend to the improvement of the mind and informing the judgment in things proper to be known, in a civil and well regulated society: Your Petitioners pray your Excellency not to discourage, but rather

forward the same; and your petitioners as in duty bound shall
ever pray, &c. Signed June 3d, 1762." [4]

On the succeeding day two hundred and twenty-three
citizens countered with two separate petitions against the
exhibiting of plays, adding among other things that the stage
"would bring on so many burthens and difficulties, and as the
poor will always imitate the richer, every servant in town will
soon turn player." The opposition used for argument the hard-
ships of the times and the "pernicious consequences" to the
morals of young people. The first petition reads:

"Petition against a Play-house, &c.

"To his Excellency BENNING WENTWORTH, Esq. Governor and
Commander in Chief in and over his Majesty's Province of New
Hampshire, and the Honorable his Majesty's Council of said
Province:

"*Humbly shews,* sundry of the freeholders and other Inhabitants of the Town of Portsmouth, in said Province—That your
petitioners have been informed that a motion has been made
for liberty for a number of plays to exhibit sundry entertainments of the stage in this town, which your petitioners
apprehend would be of very pernicious consequences, not only
to the morals of the young people, (even if there should be no
immoral exhibitions) by dissipating their minds, and giving
them an idle turn of attachment to pleasure and amusement,
with other ill effects, which there is the greatest reason to fear
from such entertainments in a place where they are a novelty.
Add to this, that such a time of general distress, where in [*sic*]
the people here have lately suffered for want of the necessaries
of life, and which is not yet entirely over, is more peculiarly
improper for such amusements, which are always destructive
to a new country, but especially at a season when there is the
utmost need to raise and promote a spirit of industry:

"Wherefore, for these and many other reasons, your petitioners humbly pray that no such liberty may be granted: and
if assumed, that they may be restrained, and your petitioners
shall ever pray, &c." [5]

The second follows:

"To his Excellency BENNING WENTWORTH, Esq. Governor and Commander-in-Chief in and over his Majesty's Province of New Hampshire:

"We, the subscribers, inhabitants of the town of Portsmouth, humbly pray your Excellency to prohibit the acting and exhibiting of plays in this town, especially as it would bring on so many burthens and difficulties in addition to those we have so lately suffered for want of the necessaries of life, and carry off the little remaining silver and gold there is in the town; and when people make such difficulties in paying the common and ordinary taxes and charges of government, that the taxes are seldom collected within the year, through the pretence of poverty, with other objections, too obvious to be mentioned to your Excellency; but especially considering every mouthful of bread we have eat, has been for many months past, and what we shall use must be for many yet to come, Imported, we apprehend it would be destructive to the circumstances of the people, as well as their morals: and as the poor will always imitate the richer, every servant in town will soon turn player. For these and other reasons, which your Excellency knows better than we do, being better acquainted with things of this kind, we humbly pray no liberty for this purpose may be granted at such a remarkable season and time as this.   June 4, 1762." [6]

On Saturday, June 5, 1762, the House of Representatives voted to address the Governor, protesting against the proposed playhouse on the grounds that such entertainments would influence the minds of young people, endanger morals, and foster idleness. Furthermore, because of the effects of both famine and war, the introduction of such a plan was considered "improper and extraordinary." The recommendation to the governor read as follows:

"Whereas this house has been Informed that an application has been made to his Excellency the Governor of this Province for Liberty to Exhibit plays & Theatrical Entertainments in the Town of Portsmo in said Province, which is yet under consideration, & as this house apprehends such Liberty would great effect the Interest as well as morals of the people they represent, Therefore,

"Voted, That an Address & Request of this house be presented to his Excelly that he would be pleased to discountenance & deny all such proposals at least at this time, for the following reasons, viz:

"Because where such Entertainments are a novelty they have a moar [sic] peculiar influence on the minds of young people, greatly Indanger their morals by giving them a turn for Intriguing amusements and pleasure, even upon the best and most favourable supposition that nothing contrary to Decency & Good manners is Exhibited yet ye strong Impressions made by the Gallantries Amours & other moveing Representations with which the best Plays about will dissipate & indispose the minds of youth not used to them, to every thing Important & serious, & as their is a General Complaint of a prevailing turn to pleasure & Idleness in most young people among us, which is too well grounded, the Entertainments of the stage would Inflaim that temper; all young countries have much more occasion to Incourage a spirit of Industry & application to business than to countenance Schemes of amusement and allurements to pleasure.

"That it would be more especially Improper & Extraordinary that such Entertainments should be first introduced when the people are labouring under the calamities of a famine (for such the late scarcity upon the whole may justly be Estimated) the effects of which will be felt for years to come, and though there is at present some Relief, yet as that is only by Importation & on which we must depend for months to come, the distress is far from being removed: Add to this that we are still deeply Ingaged in an Expensive war from which there is no present prospect of Deliverance & that curiosity will tempt the youth in the remotest parts of this Province to take a journey to Portsmouth to see such rarities, & those who lately begged a Dollar to buy a little Bread will purchase more for a sight of them, by wch means all the valuable part of our Cash will have another way of exportation besides the purchase of provisions, for these and many other Reasons, this House prays your Excellency's negation upon this motion." [7]

The Portsmouth aristocracy eventually obtained their playhouse, but on this occasion the Governor, Benning Wentworth, held with the opposition. Presumably, however, plays were sold even if they were not acted, for in the *New Hampshire Gazette* for July 19, 1765, the "Beggers Opera in two acts" is advertised as for sale. Four years later [8] the same newspaper announced: "By Authority this Evening at Mr. Staver's large Room Mr. Douglas will deliver a lecture on Heads, Coats of Arms, Ladies Head Dresses, etc. etc. etc. in three parts. To conclude with Alexander's Feast or the Power of Music, an Ode written by Mr. Dryden, and the first Act of Love-a-la-Mode. To begin exactly at seven o'clock. Tickets for Admission to be had at Mess'rs Fowle's Printing-Office, and at Mr. Staver's Tavern, in Pitt-Street, Portsmouth, at Half a Dollar Each."

On November 3, 1769, a number of Portsmouth citizenry were entertained with a reading of the currently popular *Love in a Village* at Staver's Long Room. The *Gazette* [9] stated that "the Songs will be Sung By a Person [10] who has read and Sung in most of the great towns of America. He personates all the Characters, and enters into the different Humors and Passions, as they change from one to another throughout the opera. The Songs in this Opera (of which there are Sixty-Nine) are set to Musick by the Greatest Masters. Tickets for admission, Price Half a Dollar, each."

What appears to have been Portsmouth's first theatrical season extended from September 1772 to January 1773. The "exhibitions," as they were then known, were directed by Mr. W. S. Morgan, a violinist, conductor, composer, and teacher, who had introduced himself to Boston as a "pupil of Signior Giardini" [11] and who, after some professional difficulties with one William Turner of that city, repaired to Portsmouth to conduct his "weekly exhibitions" and instruct ladies and gentlemen on the "Harpsichord and Violin etc. etc." [12]

Morgan's small entourage included a Mr. Foster and a Mrs. Foster, a Mr. Deacon, as well as "Mr. Deacon the Minor" for whom a benefit was held on December 12. There is no allusion to the accompaniment employed for these exhibitions, but it is fair to assume that at least a harpsichord was used.

In the *New Hampshire Gazette* of August 21, 1772, Mr. Morgan advertised a series of theatrical exhibitions on a subscription plan: "Mr. Morgan begs leave to inform his subscribers and the Public in general, that the 2nd week in September his Exhibition will begin with a Benefit Night for the Poor of the Town,—and the Subscribers Nights will commence the ensuing Evenings."

Either a new place was built or an old one remodeled for these exhibitions. In any case, judging from the information at hand, the "Oratorical Academy Room" included a pit and a gallery. On September 25, 1792, the *Gazette* announced that "the Oratorical Academy Room in Pitt Street is nearly finish'd and will be open'd very soon, with a Charity Night for the benefit of the Poor of the town, when the following Exhibitions will be deliver'd." The program included:

1. A Prologue in Praise of Charity.
2. The Politicians, or What News, a Dramatic Satire.
3. A Comic Dance, called Irish Lilt.
4. A Pantomimical Entertainment in Grotesque Characters call'd the Escape of Harlequin turn'd Doctor, To Conclude with an address.

Tickets were at 3 pistereens, 2 pistereens, and 1 pistereen each, "to be had at Mr. Steven's Tavern, Mr. Tilton's Tavern, Mr. Appleton's Store, the Printing Office and Mr. Morgan."

On October 9th a notice appeared explaining that the exhibition had been postponed by reason of bad weather, but that "By particular Desire of the Subscribers," the doors were to be opened at three o'clock, and the curtain to be drawn up exactly at four, on the Monday following (October 12, 1772).

This particular exhibition was the first in a series which ran to December of that year. The *Gazette* makes no reference either to the content or quality of these entertainments. This practice seems to be characteristic of the papers of the time, which were preoccupied with "foreign intelligence." As Sonneck observed, this absence of detail does not imply that the program was not worth mentioning, "for it should be remembered that in Europe, too, the custom prevailed to observe silence in the advertisements as to the program." [13]

In the *Gazette* of October 23, 1772, W. S. Morgan, "Musico Theorico," announced that his second exhibition of the season would be held "Tuesday next the 27th Inst," at which time "will be performed the following Pieces":

1. A New Prologue.
2. A Song.
3. The Devil and the Doctor, or, a hint to the College of Physicians.
4. An Interlude of Singing & Dancing Call'd Navel Glory; or, The British Tars Triumph.
5. A Pantomimical Entertainment in Grotesque Characters, call'd Win Her and Wear Her; or, Harloquin Skeleton.
6. To Conclude with an Epilogue Addres'd to Everybody, not meant at Anybody, to be spoke by Somebody, in the Character of Nobody.

The theatrical exhibition was scheduled for six o'clock, while the doors to the Academy Room were to be opened at five. Mr. Morgan, in reply to several complaints that the gallery "was very In-commodious, takes this opportunity of informing the town, that he has alter'd it as much for the better as the House will allow, in order to do which he has been oblig'd to take away the upper Gallery intirely." [14] Repeat performances of this entertainment were advertised in the *New Hampshire Gazette* on October 30th and November 6, 1772.

A similar program was presented on November 13, "by Desire of the Right Worshipful the Master and Brethren of the New Hampshire Lodge of Free and Accepted Masons," [15] the oldest established Masonic Lodge in the state and one of the oldest in the country. On this program Morgan included, among other things, "A Masonic Song," "A Horn Pipe," and (for the last time)

Harlequin Turn'd Doctor. The whole concluded, appropriately enough, with an "Address on Masonry."

These theatrical exhibitions were attended not only by residents of Portsmouth, but also by many people from the country, and when occasionally a performance was postponed without advance notice, the stranded country folk expressed justified resentment. In the November 27, 1772, *Gazette,* along with the announcement of an exhibition, Morgan attempted to mollify his grumbling clientele: "As many Complaints have been made by persons from the Country, being disappointed at there being no Performance, on account of Extremity of Weather, Mr. Morgan gives this Public Assurance that nothing of the nature shall happen again, but will positively Exhibit on Mondays, Wednesdays, and Fridays, till Notice is given in the Paper, for a stop to prepare something new."

Several new works made their appearance on this program which we reprint in full:

1st.   A Prologue in the Character of a drunken Sailor

2d.   An Oration on the Origin, Progress, and Utility of the Stage

3rd.   An Entertainment Call'd Lethe; [16] or Aesop in the Shades

Aesop	By Mr. Foster
Mercury (with a Song) Frenchman, and Snip the Taylor	By Mr. Deacon
And the old Man and drunken Man	By Mr. Morgan

4th.   An Entertainment of Dancing and Singing, in Grotesque Characters, call'd the Witches; or Harlequin Mercury

The Character of Harlequin	By Mr. Morgan
Don Choleric Snap Shorto de Testy	By Mr. Deacon
Lumberhead	By Mr. Foster
Colombine	By Mrs. Foster

To conclude with a Hornpipe.[17]

The same exhibition was "perform'd as usual with Alterations" on the 4th of December.[18] Concerning these repeat performances and unspecified alterations, one wonders why Morgan did not find it necessary to change the theatrical fare much more frequently in order to hold his public. It is unlikely that, for over a period of three months, he played to a different audience each evening. The combined population of the town and vicinity was not large enough to warrant this possibility. Reattendance, however, may have been encouraged by a variety of entertainments customarily included on each program but which, according to current newspaper practices, were not always advertised in advance.

On December 12th, Morgan advertised a benefit for Mr. Deacon the Minor, at which time "will be exhibited a new Pantomime Entertainment. The Particulars will be inserted in the Bills." Between the 12th and 25th of December the music master must have been involved in preparations for a new series of exhibitions, for a notice in the *Gazette* on the 25th of the month announced that "At the Academy-Room in Pitt-Street, on Wednesday Evening next, will be performed a new comedy call'd the Register-Office and a new Pantomime Entertainment call'd the Elopement; or Harlequin's Court. The Scenes and Machines intirely new."

The pantomime was a type of dramatic entertainment which necessarily called for music, for the characters expressed themselves by gestures, dancing, and vocal rendition. This form of theater, enormously popular in eighteenth-century England, found an appreciative audience also in the colonies. The stock pantomime characters were an old man, his pretty daughter, or ward, her poor and favored lover, a wealthy but unwise suitor, and the old man's knave. The girl and her lover were protected by a fairy, while the old man and his favorite were abetted by a malevolent spirit. To evade the machinations of the evil one, the fairy transformed her protégés for a probationary period into Harlequin and Colombine. The evil spirit countered by transforming the old man and his servant into a Pantaloon and a Clown, and the wealthy suitor into a Dandy Lover. The two lovers are pursued through a variety of adventures and finally the fairy, as *deus ex machina,* reappears and brings the piece to a close by proclaiming the success of the lovers.

The finest English theater composers of the day, such as

Arne, Dibdin, Battishill, Linley, Shield, and Attwood, composed music for these pantomimes. Many of the English ballad-operas performed on the American continent during the eighteenth century were frequently turned into pantomime "pasticcios." [19]

It is curious to note that Morgan presented pantomimes and other theatrical selections in Portsmouth, but not in Boston. According to Sonneck, Morgan appeared before the Boston public as a violin soloist, conductor, and composer, as these four references from *Early Concert-Life* show:

1. "Mr. Morgan begs leave to acquaint his subscribers and the public in general that his first evening's entertainment will be on Tuesday the 11 instant; when will be performed a Concert of Vocal and Instrumental Music." [20]

2. "In a concert given October 3, 1771, according to the *Massachusetts Gazette*, Morgan 'conducted. (And a solo on the violin) by Morgan, organist of Newport.' " [21]

3. "A concert program published in the *Boston Evening Post*, May 13, 1771, included 'A new Hunting Song, set to music by Mr. Morgan.' " [22]

4. "At a concert presented on April 20, 1774 at Concert Hall, Morgan appeared as a composer of 'a grand Military Simphony accompanied by kettle drums, etc. compos'd by Mr. Morgan.' " [23]

Boston's ban on theater entertainment apparently effectively dissuaded Morgan from staging his theatricals there. If he counted on complete lack of opposition in Portsmouth he was mistaken, for in the *New Hampshire Town Papers* is a petition of January 11, 1773, with sixty-one signatures to it, protesting the performances. The grounds for protest were much the same as in 1762. Theater entertainments, declared the petitioners, were a waste of time and money, all the more reprehensible since times were bad and "Diligence and Good Economy" more than ever necessary. They would impede progress in "Learning both in our Schools and among our Handicrafts" and expose the young to "Temptation and youthful Lusts" when their attention should be given to the Holy Scriptures and to serious concern "for Death and the World to come." [24] The petition mentions Morgan by name:

"That your petitioners have accordingly observed with concern the Encouragement one Mr. Morgan has obtained in his Weekly Exhibitions in the Town, and apprehend that some of the above mentioned ill Consequences resulting from the free Toleration of such Theatrical Exhibitions are already too plainly seen among us.

"That if he and his Fellow Actors after having attempted to set up their Business in other parts of New England and being universally refused should settle themselves in this Town in said Business, We may Expect beside the great Expense of maintaining him and them, We shall have others of like Character and for the same purpose Crowding in upon us to the no Small Detriment of the Town and the State." [25]

The reference to Mr. Morgan being "universally refused" in other parts of New England leads one to believe that the petition was directed against him personally. Sonneck notes that except as a musician of considerable ability he was *persona non grata* in most other circumstances. Moreover, his "path in the Colonies was not to be strewn with roses and for this he had nobody to blame but himself. Mr. W. S. Morgan seems to have been somewhat of an adventurer, spendthrift, drunkard, and all-around rascal." [26]

William Turner, who had befriended Morgan when he first arrived in Boston and who was largely responsible for sending him to Portsmouth, refers to Morgan's difficulties there in a letter to the *Boston Gazette*, dated April 26, 1773. Turner writes: "He [Morgan] again got into good business and might have continued so till this day, if he had behav'd like a gentleman." [27]

The attitude of the petitioners is therefore understandable. On January 13, 1773, they were given permission to bring in a bill: "Petition Ag^t Theatrical exhibitions—Ag^t allowing exhibitions which being Read Voted unanimously that the prayer of said petition be granted & that the Petitioners have leave to bring in a Bill accordingly." [28]

There appears to be no evidence of the bill being presented to the Assembly or acted upon. Morgan returned to Boston in April of the same year seeking professional employment from

Turner, but upon being rejected, threatened to "lead Mr. Propert's Concert against him." Turner describes the meeting: "Being obliged to quit that place [Portsmouth], he once more return'd here, and call'd at my house in the evening and told me, if I did not employ him he should lead Mr. Propert's Concert against me; I having company, and finding him not in a capacity to talk with, desir'd he would let me know where he lodg'd, and I'd call and talk with him in the morning. This he declined and went off leaveing me in the dark. This happen'd on Friday Evening and I never heard anything of him 'till I read Monday's paper and found he'd come to assist Mr. Propert against me although he had repeatedly declar'd he never wou'd perform against me on account of my great friendship towards him." [29]

Morgan's collaboration with David Propert against Turner resulted in a "grand concert" in which Morgan was advertised to play the violin and Propert the harpsichord. The concert was originally scheduled for April 22, 1773, but was postponed to April 26 owing to difficulties with Turner.[30] Shortly following this episode, Morgan returned to Portsmouth to teach "Musick and Dancing," according to a notice in the August 6, 1773, *New Hampshire Gazette,* which reads thus: "Mr. Morgan Takes this Method of informing the Public that on Tuesday last at three o'clock P.M. he opened his Academy for Musick and Dancing, at the Assembly House; and purposes attending there Tuesdays and Fridays. Those Ladies and Gentlemen who chuse to also honor him with the Care of their Children may depend on the utmost exertion of his Abilities in the Cultivation of their Education."

The *Gazette* of August 20, 1773, carries another advertisement concerning Morgan's teaching activities in the town:

"Mr. Morgan Begs leave to inform the Public that he has open'd his Academy for Music and Dancing, at the Assembly-House—Music at a Pistole a Month, and Dancing at Four Dollars the Quarter, two to be paid at Entrance, and purposes attending Tuesday and Friday Afternoon at present, and oftner as the School encreases [sic]."

"He likewise on Tuesday next shall open an Evening School, from Seven o'clock 'till Nine, for the Instruction of those whose Avocations prevent their attending in the Day-Time.

An announcement which appeared in the *New Hampshire Gazette* a week later on August 27, 1773, is the last reference to Morgan's presence in Portsmouth. Two months later, on October 28, he conducted a "Grand Concert of vocal and instrumental music" at Faneuil Hall which "partook of the character of a testimonial concert" for Josiah Flagg.[31] Morgan's final public appearance seems to have been in a concert given at Boston on February 2, 1775.[32]

VII. Opera after the Revolution

THE adversities and privations generated by the revolution were anything but sympathetic to musical development in any form. As previously noted, newspapers were frequently smaller in size and the columnists devoted their attention, in the main, to the more critical matters of foreign and domestic politics. Moreover, there is a decided absence of musical advertisement. A turn for the better is evident early in the ensuing decade when the names of teachers once again begin to appear in the pages of the austere *New Hampshire Gazette*.

Theatrical notifications, on the other hand, are conspicuously absent until late in 1787. On January 23, 1788, however, the *New Hampshire Mercury* contained a critique of Shakespeare's *Othello*, in which the author could not "praise the presentation too highly." Regarding the actors he continued: "All seemed designed for the parts they supported and repeated applause testified the enjoyment the spectators received from the exhibition,—the characters of Othello and Iago were supported in a manner that vied with the best in European representation." Apparently a relatively small town like Portsmouth (population less than five thousand) possessed the cultural background to sustain such ponderous drama as *Othello*. This striking aesthetic tendency will become increasingly evident in the succeeding pages.

The *Mercury* also noted that the tragedy of "Douglass" and a farce, the "Citizen," were to be acted on the following Friday evening. Regrettably, this is all the information we have on what may perhaps have been a theatrical season. The *New Hampshire Gazette* does not give recognition to this new invasion of the community by an itinerant troupe of players. Although no reference to music appears in the advertisement, perhaps, as usual, a number of "favourite songs" were interpolated as part of the evening's entertainment.

The year following (1789) "An Attic Entertainment" or a "Lecture on Heads" was presented on July 13 and 16 [1] at the "Assembly Room." Mr. McPherson,[2] a former member of The American Company, a theatrical group which held forth in New York, Philadelphia, and Baltimore, finding his talents appreciated, repeated the performance on September 1 [3] and 7 [4] with slight alterations. Programs of exceptional length included "The Better Sort; or, The Girl of Spirit," an "operatical comical farce," and a generous offering of entr'acte musical diversions. In the meantime, on August 1 the inhabitants of Portsmouth turned to more plebeian amusements when Donegani, the celebrated Italian Balance Master, displayed his virtuosity by performing tumbling feats on the slack rope as well as playing on different musical instruments.[5]

At this juncture, a period of over two years passes without any reference to the theater either in newspaper files or other available sources. Late in 1791, however, the *Gazette* informed the public that Mr. Civil,[6] a local teacher of "Dancing and the French language," who also did miniature painting "in the most elegant manner," and Horatio Garnet "return their sincere thanks to the Gentlemen of this town; for their generous and spirited exertions in assisting them to establish a Theatre." The Portsmouth impresarios, having already moved into the new Bow Street Theatre, reported that it would "be finished as soon as possible." Anyone who wished to subscribe was requested to do so immediately, "as no subscription can be taken after the first play." [7]

In advance of opening night at the Bow Street Theatre, the *New Hampshire Spy* supplied its readers with a series of quaint informative notices heralding the auspicious event; publicity and advertising happily were not spared in this case. The initial notification in this propaganda campaign, appearing in the December 14, 1791, *Spy*, announced the contemplated performance of the "Comedy of the West Indian," to be preceded by an "Occasional Prologue, On opening the Theatre in this town," [8] written by Portsmouth's "favourite bard," Jonathan M. Sewall, Esquire. "At the intervals," continued the newspaper, "several select pieces of music will be performed by a number of Gentlemen," and following "Act the 3rd, a Clarinet Concerto composed and to be performed by Mr. Garnet" was to be included on the program.

The gentlemen who comprised the band (orchestra) in Portsmouth at this time were in all probability pupils of Horatio Garnet, the "Superintendent of Music." From the information we have assembled on Garnet, it seems fair to say that Portsmouth's musical life was definitively enhanced by his presence as a teacher in the town.

Jonathan M. Sewall, with customary poetical poignancy, describes Garnet's duties as one of the managers of the Bow Street Theatre. He likens him to the "giant Handel":

> "Next for the Managers (you know the men,)
> One guides the music, and one forms the scene;
> Here is their station—here in frugal way
> They paint, rehearse, eat, sleep and play, and pray.
> With nicest touches of their several arts,
> How they have labour'd to attract your hearts.
> When the play paus'd the one with pleasing sounds
> Has chear'd, or sooth'd your souls, and heal'd its wounds;
> Like giant Handel, with his youthful band,
> Taught by his skill, and guided by his hand." [9]

The Bow Street Theatre, by no means an elaborate structure, had a pit and a gallery,[10] with a combined seating capacity said to be four hundred. On one occasion, when the musical farce Lethe was being presented, "the audience was large, and nothing prevented it from being larger, but the circumscribed place of exhibition." [11] Sewall describes poetically how the building had been transformed from a warehouse:

"The other manager, the courteous Civil—[12]
Say, is he a magician, or the D---l?
Methinks I see him with his magic wand,
Like some old necromancer circled stand:
He strikes the warehouse, and the fabric to!
Turns to a theatre beneath the blow.
Where hogsheads, bales, were once promiscuous seen
Here frowns a Monarch and there walks a Queen:
That wood, that mountain, and that beauteous valley
Was where the worthy owner once kept tally;
Where porter men with muddy hoofs once flock'd
Great Chrononhotonthologos has stalk'd
And where you beauteous forms attract your love
Dry goods, teer, over teer, were pil'd above:
Then Oh! this conjurer favour with your nod,
If you refuse—that self same potent rod
That from a ware house—rear'd this magick scene
Shall turn all to a paltry store again." [13]

The presence of unwelcome visitors in the rear of the stage was evidently a source of constant consternation to eighteenth-century theatrical management.[14] In this connection, the December 31 issue of the *Spy* reminded its readers that at one of the previous performances "there were several intruders on the stage both during and after the Play who were not at all welcome" and consequently, "we are sorry to repeat 'No persons what ever to be admitted behind the scenes.' " The same issue announced that "A few tickets will be sold by Dr. C. Storer and as (through the inattention of the door-keeper) many were admitted without a Ticket—the ones made use of that evening will not be received without the Managers signatures." [15]

Also on the same day the ladies of the town were "respectfully" informed "that the gentlemen, out of complaisance to them, intend to appear at the Theatre uncovered, all they hope in return, is that the head dress of the Fair may be comprised within moderate bounds, and that the hoops may be dispensed with." [16]

The cast, made up of local talent, is discussed in the following news item. "The young gentlemen who are to support the several characters," writes the correspondent to the *Spy*, "have gone thro' rehearsal, and, if we may hazard a judgment, will do themselves honor in the performance." Noting that the *West-Indian* had been performed heretofore in Portsmouth, the correspondent continues: "Several of the characters, are filled by the same gentlemen who appeared on the stage when the comedy was last acted in this town, and who then received the most flattering applause from a well informed audience." Focusing attention once again on Sewall and Garnet, the writer concludes: "The Prologue is to be spoken by a gentleman who has more than once borne the laurels from the stage. As to the music, we only observe, that that part of the entertainment will be under the direction of Signior Garnet." [17]

Traffic difficulties are not peculiar to the twentieth century: "It is requested that all carriages in going to the Theatre, be ordered to proceed by the way of Market-Street and return by the way of Chapil [Chapel] Street, in order to prevent difficulties which may arise from their meeting in the night." [18]

Whether opening night was a huge success or a failure, we shall probably never know. At any rate, the *Spy*, seemingly cautious of any rhetorical display, merely informs us that "the President of the State, the Treasurer, Secretary, several of the hon. Senate and House of Representatives, and some of the Rev. Clergy" were in attendance at the exhibition. [19] By this time, theater was clearly respectable entertainment.

Civil and Garnet launched their carefully planned theatrical enterprise in Portsmouth with a season of "eight Subscription Plays." [20] To those not interested in subscribing for the entire season, tickets for single performances were available. "Tickets for non subscribers," announced the *Spy*, "will be sold at Osbornes office." [21]

In early January, the company admitted through the *Spy* that "The very great expense attending the fitting up the Theatre, and the subscribers' money already advanced not being sufficient to support it in the style we wish, renders it

necessary for us to make this a 'stock [nonsubscription] play'."
The notice continues: "Different tickets from the former ones
will be issued, and sold at the Spy Printing Office, or by the
Managers. . . . As this is not a subscription play, the subscribers'
tickets will not be delivered 'till the next." In the same announcement, Mr. Civil and Mr. Garnet took the opportunity to
sincerely thank the "gentlemen performers" who assisted at the
exhibitions.

The admission fee to these entertainments was: pit, 3 shillings
(6 shillings to a dollar) and gallery, 2 shillings. This price seems
to have survived the season with the exception of a "benefit
night" for Messrs Civil and Garnet at which time the general
admission was a flat two shillings for either pit or gallery.[22] The
doors opened for each performance at six o'clock in the evening,
and the program began precisely at seven.

The first season of the Bow Street Theatre extended to the
end of July, 1792. Its repertoire was largely confined to
comedies and farces with an occasional tragedy. The usual
entr'acte music included among other things the performance
of "Fisher's Minuet with Variations," probably on the harpsichord by Mr. Garnet.[23] Once again, the inimitable J. M.
Sewall, with the aid of the heroic couplet, gives lyrical expression to this practice in his "Introductory Prologue":

While Music, at each pause, exalts, inspires,
Or ravishes with all Apollo's fires.[24]

Four popular musical entertainments, in addition, were presented in Portsmouth during the theatrical season of early
1792, according to the *Spy*. The works performed were:

March 13,[25] April 17: [26] *The Spanish Miller*
(Harlequin pantomime)
May 4: [27] *The Friar Metamorphosd*   (Harlequin pantomime)
May 23: [28] *The Waterman* (a comic opera by Charles Dibdin)
July 31: [29] *Lethe* (a musical entertainment)

Judging from a lengthy, florid, and sympathetic critique which
appeared in the April 18, 1792, *Spy*, the efforts of Mr. Civil and
Mr. Garnet were deeply appreciated in Portsmouth. All con-

cerned were heartily lauded by the correspondent: "Last evening was performed (by particular desire) the 'Clandestine Marriage,' a comedy, after which was presented a Pantomime Entertainment, called the 'Spanish Miller,' we are happy to add—the young gentlemen who supported the several characters, both in comedy and pantomime, did them the greatest justice and gained to themselves lasting honor, if we may be permitted to judge from the countenances and repeated plaudits of a numerous and brilliant audience: such was the entertainment of the evening, that gentlemen acquainted with and who have visited the British Theatres declare it equal to any they ever saw exhibited; from those who have been entertained with the theatrical exhibitions during the winter, when the beauties of Nature (which now begin afresh to open on us) were fled and nought but dreary prospects appeared to view— greatful acknowledgements are due to those young gentlemen who voluntarily stepped forth and have by their unremitted exertions on the stage endeavoured at once to please and entertain them, not from mercenary views but from hearts possessed of that which must and will endear them to those who have been partakers, that is, a delight in the happiness of their fellow citizens—the managers Messrs Civil and Garnet, for their indefatigable endeavours in procuring accomodations, which was an arduous undertaking, entitled them to a share of our thanks, but this is not all, the scenery thro the season, executed by Mr. Civil has been elegant and served for a repast to the eye—Mr. Garnet, superintendent of music, has displayed not a small specimen of his abilities in that most enchanting part which has contributed greatly towards completing and setting off to advantage the entertainments we have been pleased with; to unite the whole we must say, the scenery fed the eye—music reasted [rested] the ear—tragedy served (for those who relished it) to feast the love-sick heart, and comedy, to those merrily inclined, a most delicious repast." [30]

In the meantime, a company of comedians headed by Mr. Watts,[31] "a vulgar fellow with the wry neck," [32] appeared in Portsmouth during April and May of 1792, at the very time that

Messrs. Civil and Garnet were endeavoring to expand and promote their modest theatrical enterprise. Mr. Watts and his professionally trained and more adroit thespians exhibited for the divertissement of the interested populace seven works—all but one being operas—in a brief six-week span. At a time when nearby Boston was still chained to the ridiculous antitheater act of 1750,[33] the music-lovers of Portsmouth were treated to the following operas by the Watts troupe:

April 23: [34] *Provok'd Husband* or the *Reform'd Wife* [35]
          Poor Soldier (William Shield)
May 11: [36] *Beggars Opera*
May 25: [37] *Beggars Opera*
          Lethe (Musical entertainment)
June 1: [38] *Elopement* (pantomime by Demarque)
          Romp [39] (Charles Dibdin)

The *Spy* notified prospective patrons that tickets would sell at three shillings each "to be had of Mr. Stavers—and at either of the Printing Offices." [40] As for the popular and patriotic airs to be sung between the acts, the *Spy* advertised four selections in advance:

"The favourite Song of heaving the anchor short—called 'Heo! Hoe!'—in the character of a sailor, by Mr. Solomon.

"The favourite hunting Song of 'The Twins of Latona,' by Mr. Murry.

" 'The Greenwich Pensioner,' by Mr. Solomon.

"The Picture of a Play House or 'Bucks have at ye all,' by Mr. Watts." [41]

Following the performance of the "Poor Soldier," [42] the evening concluded with a "dissertation on Jealousy" and "the comic song call'd the Four and Twenty Fiddlers" rendered by the *prima donna* of Watts' entourage, Mrs. Solomon.

No contention seems to have arisen from the commercial rivalry between the home-town troupe and the traveling actors. In fact, a pastoral dance by Mr. Civil and Mrs. Solomon occurring after the "Beggars Opera" on May 11 would seem to indicate that relations were fairly friendly.[43] Eight days later

(May 19) Watts himself, according to the *Spy*, was advertised to sing "the favorite song called the Watry God." More than likely Mr. Watts took part in *The Waterman*, "a comic opera" scheduled for the same evening.[44]

The Watts company brought its theatrical season to a close on June 1, 1792, with the performance of the *Elopement* and the *Romp*. Mrs. Solomon also entertained with "a favorite Scotch Song" called "To the Green Woods gang with me" and concluded with "a farewell address to the ladies and gentlemen of Portsmouth." [45]

Following the end of the theatrical season, Watts did not leave Portsmouth immediately but stayed on to aid Messrs. Civil and Garnet with their local productions, which were still flourishing. A theatrical critique in the August 1, 1792, *Spy* expresses in glowing terms the excellence of Watts's direction of and acting in the *Absent Man* and *Lethe* the previous evening: "To particularize on such an occasion would be invidious; but as Mr. Watts had the principal direction of the whole and took the most conspicuous characters in both plays, it would be doing him the greatest injustices not to take particular notice of his performances. Suffice it to say that in the opnion [*sic*] of the most experienced judges, they both never had more justice done them."

After this event, nine months expired before Portsmouth had occasion to enjoy further operatic treats. In April, 1794, Mr. Watts returned after having performed "with universal applause in Newport, Salem and Glocester." [46] To his theatrical staff he had added Mrs. Mechtler, "nee Fanny Storer, a popular soubrette." [47] On the evening of April 21 the company presented Dryden's *The Tempest*, probably with incidental music by Henry Purcell,[48] and a favorite musical entertainment by Dibdin called *The Padlock*, which, in the words of Sonneck, "seems to have been considered an especially difficult and complicated opera." [49] The lengthy advertisement, as it appears in the April 19, 1794, *Oracle*, is reproduced in its entirety:

"Theatre Assembly Room—On Monday Evening next will be presented (for that night only) a celebrated Comedy. which has been performed by this Company with universal applause in Newport, Salem, and Glocester—called

The Tempest, or the Enchanted Island

Prospero,	Mr. Adams
Lypolito, (A man that never saw a woman)	Mr. Watts
Alonzo, Ganzalo,	Mr. Solomon
Ferdinand,	Mr. Redfield
Dorinda,	Mrs. Solomon
Miranda,	Mrs. Watts
Ariel, (An airy spirit with the original songs)	Mrs. Metchler
Sailors, etc.	
Stephano, master of the ship,	Mr. Solomon
Mustacho, mate of the ship,	Mr. Redfield
Caliban, a monster of the isle,	Mr. Watts
Trinculo, a drunken boatswain,	Mr. Adams

"The first act will open with a shipwreck and a grand shower of fire—a ship in distress.

"The piece concludes with a beautiful view of a calm sea, and Neptune and Amphitrite, in a sea chariot.

Neptune and	Mr. Solomon
Amphitrite with original duet	Mrs. Metchler

"With new machinery, scenery and decorations.

"To which will be added a favorite musical entertainment called,

The Padlock

Don Diego	Mr. Watts
Leander	Mr. Solomon
Scholar	Mr. Redfield
Mungo	Mr. Adams
Ursula	Mrs. Watts
Leonora	Mrs. Metchler

"Tickets may be had at Mr. Melcher's and Mr. Pierce's Bookstore—at Mr. Walden's near the sign of the Sun—and the Theatre the evening of the performance—3s. each.

"The doors will be opened at half-past 5 o'clock, and the performance will begin at 7."

The Assembly House where Watts exhibited was considerably more elaborate than the old Bow Street Theatre. George Washington considered it "one of the best I have ever seen anywhere in the United States." [50] The builder and owner of this imposing edifice, which probably came into being *circa* 1772,[51] was Mr. Michael Whidden.[52] According to a firsthand account written by Mrs. Ichabod Goodwin in 1870 and quoted in *The Portsmouth Book*: "The house was of wood, large, long and painted white. There were on the lower floor three great parlors, a kitchen, and an immense hall and staircase. This hall ran through the house and opened upon a garden, decorated by a summer-house, octagon in shape, of two stories, with large glass windows. . . . Perhaps the most remarkable feature of the Assembly House was the abundance and variety of wood carvings. The facade was decorated in festoons of flowers over the windows, and every imaginable figure proper to external ornamentation was there." [53] The Assembly Room itself, continues Mrs. Goodwin, "took the whole front of the second story, and was about sixty by thirty feet, with large windows and an orchestra over the entrance. Back of it were two dressing-rooms. There were three chandeliers for wax candles, and branches from the walls also for candles. In the Assembly-Room the cornices were beautifully carved, and in all the rooms the carving was richly gilded." [54]

The only other reference to opera in Portsmouth that year (1794) is to a brief summer theatrical season which ran from August 27 through September 8, when the music lovers of the town heard Samuel Arnold's *Inkle & Yarico* (September 3),[55] William Shield's *The Farmer* (September 8),[56] a "Musical Interlude" called the *Humours of Billy Bristle* (August 27),[57] and a "favorite Interlude" called *Dr. Last's Examination* (August 30).[58] Tickets for these performances sold for three shillings each and were "to be had at Peirce's Bookstore, and at the Assembly-House" where the exhibitions were held. No mention is made in the advertisements concerning the performing troupe, although it is reasonable to guess from the repertoire that it was an itinerant group.

The succeeding two years passed into history apparently without a renewal of operatic features, judging from an absence of any such advertisements in the newspaper files and other sources. In the fall of 1796, however, one Mrs. Arnold, having just recently introduced herself to Portsmouth by presenting two concerts of vocal music (to be discussed in the next chapter), informed the people there through the September 3, 1796, *Gazette* that "she had filled up a compleat theatre, assures them nothing will be wanting on her part to render the performance such as shall gratify the audience. Flatters herself those who favor her with their company will find themselves pleasantly accomodated. Mrs. Arnold requests leave to thank those Ladies and Gentlemen who honored her with their attendance at her Concerts, and hopes to merit a continuance of their favors. It is requested Ladies and Gentlemen will if possible purchase their tickets from eleven in the morning till three in the afternoon."

Mrs. Arnold's theatrical retinue included her nine-year-old daughter Elizabeth Arnold, destined to become the mother of Edgar Allan Poe, Miss Green "of the Boston Theatre," and several "gentlemen of Portsmouth" as well as "a lady of Portsmouth" [59] and "a celebrated performer." [60] Charles Clapham, Esq., from Dover, New Hampshire, who had played at the Federal Street Theatre in Boston [61] obligingly consented" to take part in the opera *Devil to Pay* scheduled for October 28 and other performances.[62] In all probability, Mrs. Arnold spent the month between her first concert and the first opera in preparation for opening night (September 5) and the season which was to follow, fusing the talents of the amateur thespians with those of the professionals. The operas and other musical entertainments offered at this time by Mrs. Arnold's company were:

September   5: [63] *Spoil'd Child*
            14: [64] *Mountaineers* (Arnold)
                     Lethe
            19: [65] *Devil to Pay*
            26: [66] *Rosina* (Shield)

October 19: [67] *Devil to Pay*
   28: [68] *Devil to Pay*
   31: [69] *Devil to Pay*

"In *Lethe*," said the *Gazette*, "will be introduced a Mock Italian Duet by Mrs. Arnold and a gentleman." [70] During the intermissions vocal selections, such as the duet "Conzonet of Time has not thin'd my Flowing Hair" and others,[71] were performed. The admission fee was initially advertised as "First seats half a dollar, second seats quarter dollar." [72] In a subsequent press notice the "first" and "second" seats are discovered to be the pit and the gallery respectively.[73]

The cast of the *Devil to Pay* will give a good idea of how Mrs. Arnold combined the local performers with those outside of Portsmouth. Unfortunately, the newspaper did not print the names of the amateurs:

Conjuror Butler Cook Coachman	By gentlemen of Portsmouth
Jobson (the Cobler)	By Charles Clapham Esq.
Lady Loverule	By a gentleman
Lucy (the Maid)	Miss Arnold
Nell (Cobler's wife)	Mrs. Arnold [74]

Regarding the music and the acting, the newspaper, characteristically, made no critical observations. It may be assumed, nevertheless, that Mrs. Arnold was more than gratified with her Portsmouth reception for in the October 29, 1796, *Gazette* [75] she submitted a proposition for erecting a theater in the town at a cost of fifteen hundred dollars where good performers were to play twice or oftener in every week during the summer months. The entire proposal makes interesting reading:

"Mrs. Arnold's engagement calling her away, she begs leave to offer to the gentlemen of the town of Portsmouth and its vicinity the following proposals, and from their liberality doubts not of carrying into effect, the building of a Theatre in this town. She conceives 1500 dollars will be sufficient to defray the expense, to be raised by 30 shares of 50 dollars each, by installments as the work may require. As committee of the subscribers to superintend the place & the building. To regulate all disbursements. The Theatre to consist of boxes, pit and gallery. The proprietors to lease the theatre for five or more years, at a rent to be agreed on. Mrs. Arnold giving security to engage good performers, and to play twice or oftener in every week during the summer months. The Theatre to be begun immediately, so as to open the latter end of May. The ground to be purchased or leased, and the situation chosen by the determination of the committee. Mrs. Arnold intreats their liberal support and speedy exertions.

"Subscription paper with Mrs. Arnold at the Assembly Room October 29, 1796."

What became of this quixotic plan is not known, for neither the *Oracle* nor the *Gazette* make any further reference to it.

Mrs. Arnold could not have left Portsmouth immediately, for a week later, on November 9, the troupe presented "by particular desire, one night more" *Polly Honeycombe,* a comedy, and *The King,* a farce. Between the two performances, Mr. C. Clapham, Esq., entertained with the "Song of the Vicar and Moses" followed by Mrs. Arnold's "The Song of Ellen, or the Richmond Primrose Girl." [76]

On November 23, 1796, Portsmouth turned to the more platitudinous amusements of the "slack rope" and "a great variety of extraordinary tumbling feats" at the Assembly Room. The diversion also included the "Spanish fandango," a favorite dwarf dance and a horn pipe "which is danced in the first theatres in Europe." The evening was brought to a close with a celebrated horn pipe, "never before danced in this country."

In January, 1797, Mrs. Arnold, who had become Mrs.Tubbs,[77] returned to Portsmouth as a member of a theatrical company under the management of a Mr. Harper and her husband, Mr. Tubbs. The troupe had just spent several weeks entertaining a Portland, Maine, audience.[78] The personnel of this company included Mr. Tubbs "late of London, but for the moment connected with the Boston stage," [79] who performed well on the piano-forte but who could not sing,[80] and Mr. Harper, Boston's first theater manager.[81] The organization, of course, included Mrs. Tubbs, the star of the company,[82] and her charming daughter, Elizabeth. The other members were Mr. King and Mr. Peters, two young men of Portland, Mr. Charles Clapham, and Mrs. Harper.[83]

A notice in the January 28, 1797, *Gazette* informed its readers that "Messrs. Harper & Tubbs Propose (on their way to Providence) fitting up the Assembly-Room For 3 nights only." The group exhibited four nights instead, and was responsible for the presentation of the following:

February   6: [84] *Spoil'd Child*
            15: [85] *Mountaineers* (Arnold)
                     Spoil'd Child
            27: [86] *Battle of Hexham* (Arnold)
March   1: [87] *Shipwrecked Sailor* (pantomime by Taylor)

Thanks to the discerning interest of a correspondent to the *Eastern Herald & Gazette of Maine*, we are provided with some notion of the vocal abilities of Mrs. Tubbs and her daughter, Elizabeth: "Mrs. Tubbs always does well. Her vocal powers we believe are equal to any of her sex who have appeared in this country. But the powers of her daughter, Miss Arnold, astonish us. Add to these her youth, her beauty, her innocence, and a character is composed which has not, and perhaps will not again be found on any Theatre.—Lovely child! thy youth we know will not long continue; thy beauty soon will fade; but thy Innocence! May it continue with and support thee in every character while on the theatre of this world." [88]

A plentiful supply of incidental amusements occurred during the run of the company. In addition, a benefit night was held for Mrs. Harper on February 27, followed immediately by a second benefit on March 1 for Mrs. Tubbs. The latter's benefit evolved into a fairly pretentious endeavor; nothing was spared, judging from the notice in the March 1, 1797, *Oracle*: "Positively for the last Night. The rest of the Company being sent forward to Providence. For the benefit of Mrs. Tubbs who respectfully informs her friends, her indisposition on Friday evening, obliged her to postpone the Entertainment Till This Evening, Wednesday, March 1. When will be presented an entertainment in two parts. Part 1st. A lecture on Heads, or The Gallery of Portraits, with the remarkable case of "Daniel against Dishclout," the whole to be interspersed with Songs by Mrs. Tubbs and Miss Arnold. End of Part First, Fencing, by Messrs. Tubbs and Harper. Act 2d. A pantomimical Ballet now performing at the Hay-market Theatre, Boston, called the "Shipwrecked Sailor" or, the "Generous American Tar." To conclude with a Double Hornpipe by Messrs. Harper and Tubbs. After the Entertainment, a Farewell Epilogue is to be spoken by Miss Arnold."

Allowing no distinction between the pit and gallery seats, tickets of admission, a half a dollar each, were to be procured at the Assembly Room, or at Mr. Peirce's Bookstore.

Following Harper's and Tubbs' departure, no operas were staged in Portsmouth for the remainder of the year. In December, however, Mr. Evonet from Europe set up his "Entertaining Museum" at the Assembly Room. "He has also a beautiful new organ," notes the December 23, 1797, *Oracle*, "with which he will entertain the company with many new and pleasant tunes."

The year of 1798 was a quiet one in terms of operatic exhibitions. For want of something finer, Portsmouth turned to more "innocent amusements" by Mr. Maginnis, a ventriloquist, who performed with a set of artificial comedians; John Hodgkinson's comic piece, *The Launch; or, Huzza for the Constitution* on March 14; [89] *Babes in the Wood* and *Noah's Ark*, March 21; [90] and again *The Launch* on March 28, [91] along with the feats on wire of Don Pedro Cloris.

The seaport town audience may have displayed considerable interest in Hodgkinson's American potboiler because of its historical reference to the shipbuilding industry in Portsmouth. *The Launch*, originally a musical piece in one act, was a patriotic trifle in honor of the frigate *Constitution*, "as performed in Boston eleven nights, to crouded [sic] houses, and universal

applause." The whole was to conclude with a "striking representation of the late launching—boats passing and repassing on
the water, a view of the river of Charlestown, and the
neighbouring country, taken correctly from Jeffry and Russel's
wharf." [92]

Other amusements of the evening were a figure of a country
girl, "as natural as life" dancing a jig, while another figure in
the character of an "American Tar" performed a hornpipe.
The "much admired Italian Scaramouch" rendered a fandango.
As an added attraction, "Mr. Maginnis will sing the favourite
song called the Hobbies." [93]

The next year (1799) seemingly passed without theatrical
incident in Portsmouth, judging from the news files. In May
of 1800, however, Charles Stuart Powell announced in the press
"that he has fitted up Capt. Whidden's Assembly-Room, like a
regular Theatre, and will open (with entire new scenery etc.)
on Monday evening next, May 12th 1800." [94]

Powell was the well-known manager of Boston's first theater,
the Federal Street Theatre established in 1792. [95] He was also
responsible for advertising in 1796 [96] "proposals for erecting a
new theater near the corner of Tremont and Boylston Streets,"
which he called the Haymarket. Mr. Powell's long experience
as an executive and his versatility as an actor promised Portsmouth an unusual theatrical treat. The season, which lasted
about six weeks, included a wide variety of music and drama.
We quote not only the operatic repertoire, but also the dramatic
fare advertised by the Boston Company:

May 12:	Wives as They Were	*Oracle*, May 10
	All the World's A Stage	
14:	She Stoops to Conquer	*Gazette*, May 13
	An Entertainment, as will be ex- pressed in the bills for the day	
19:	The Stranger	*Oracle*, May 17
	Widow	
20:	King Richard the Third	*Gazette*, May 20
	Mad-Cap (Female Madcap) "A fa- vourite [musical] entertainment" [97]	

26:	The Jew	*Oracle,* May 24
	Village Lawyer	
June 2:	Bunker Hill	*Oracle,* May 31
	Castle Spectre [98] (Michael Kelly)	
4:	Bunker Hill (John Burk)	*Gazette,* June 3
	Castle Spectre	
9:	Castle Spectre "A farce"	*Oracle,* June 7
11:	Romeo and Juliet	*Gazette,* June 10
	"End of Act 4th: The Funeral Procession of Juliet to the Monument of the Capulets, and a Solemn Dirge" [99]	
	Plymouth Rock; or Harlequin released from Bondage. (pantomime)	
16:	Self-Immolation	*Oracle,* June 16
	Jew and Doctor (Opera by Dibdin)	
23:	Inkle and Yarico (Opera by Arnold)	*Oracle,* June 21
	Self Immolation	
25:	Battle of Hexham (Opera by Arnold)	*Gazette,* June 24
	Botheration or Ten Years Blunder	
	"performed at Boston last season with universal applause" (a musical entertainment) [100]	

At the commencement of the season, a reporter for the *Oracle,* having attended several performances, praised them as "masterly" and expressed regret at seeing "the house so thin of good company." The scribe added: "The plays certainly are moral, instructive entertaining, and useful; and it hoped that the performers will not have reason to regret their coming to this town to pas a few weeks. Sentimental amusements are the most innocent of any we can participate in, and while they are conducted on moral principles, they merit the smiles and claim the cash of a virtuous community. Compare a theatre with many fashionable places of resort, and estimate the difference." [101]

Attendance was vastly improved about two weeks later when

Bunker Hill, a tragedy calculated to arouse the patriotic emotions of the auditor, was performed to overflowing houses, according to the June 7, 1800, *Oracle.* "The glorious characters who figured in the important drama of the auspicious day, were most ably supported by the several capital performers. who represented the heroes of America." The article emphasizes the importance of theatrical amusements and also describes the merit of Powell's troupe:

"It has been a general complaint that the inhabitants of Portsmouth, were insensible to the charms of theatrical amusements. In fact they are as tremblingly alive to the impulse of nature and of art, as any in existence. The truth is, they were never favored before with a Powell, a Harper, a Villiers, and a Dickinson, to call their dormant feelings into life. With such performances a house will always be crouded. They merit the homage of public sentiment, and it has done honor to the taste of the Town, in doing honor to them. We hope that they will favour us with their company and talents in every recess from the labours of Boston; and that their moral influence will abolish the love of billiards, and every other species of play.

"The Castle Spectre was performed last evening to the universal applause of a crouded audience—and we are happy to hear that it is to be repeated on Monday evening."

The Boston Company, under Powell, having survived the trials of repeated reorganization and other theatrical vicissitudes, seems to have attained a remarkable height of achievement by the end of the century. The case of Arnold's opera *Inkle & Yarico* will afford a glimpse of the most "capital performers" Powell assembled in Portsmouth, all of whom were well known on the Boston stage:

Inkle	Mr. Happer
Sir Christopher Curry	Mr. Baker
Medium	Mr. Kenny
Camply	Mr. Usher
And Trudge	Mr. Villiers
Wowski	Mrs. Harper

Narcissa	Mrs. Dickinson
Patty	Mrs. Baker
And Yarico	Mrs. Powell [102]

As usual, a number of extradramatic incidents were included in the bills of the day, which reflect further light on contemporary tastes and social customs. At the performance of the drama *Self-Immolation* and the opera the *Jew and the Doctor,* Mr. Villiers, according to the *Oracle,* was scheduled to sing the comic song of "John Bull's Trip to France, or Monsieur Nong Tong Paw." Following the first act of the opera, Mr. Dickenson was to sing Dibdin's "Comic Song of the Country Club" or "Here's to Ye Neighbour Spriggins." [103]

The familiar benefit nights for the various members of the company were begun on June 11. A notice in the June 10, 1800, *Gazette* announced "that the first is fixed for Mr. Powell who hopes for the honor of their patronage and support." [140] On Wednesday, June 18, a benefit was held for Mr. Harper. The correspondent to the *Oracle* "observed with regret the small number who were present" for the occasion. He suggested that another evening be devoted for the purpose, being "confident that many gentlemen with their families would attend to testify to Mr. Harper the high sense they entertain of his theatrical abilities." [105]

Again *Self-Immolation* and Arnold's *Inkle & Yarico* were the musical fare of June 23, when a benefit night was staged for Mrs. Powell. Her "celebrity as an actress merits a dintinguished reward," commented the *Oracle,* "and on the final occasion, the Ladies of Portsmouth will interest themselves in the felicities of a very amiable woman, not only by their personal attendance, but by a fascinating appeal to the Gentlemen, who cannot deny the solicitations of the fair, in behalf of one of the softer sex." [106] It was likewise announced that "Several comic Songs" were to be sung by Mr. Villiers between the play and the opera.[107]

The final night of the season, June 25, was turned into a benefit for Messrs. Usher and Kenny. During the second act of the *Battle of Hexham* by Arnold, a celebrated glee,[108] "When

Arthur first at Court began" was sung by Dickinson, Usher, and Villiers. Several other miscellaneous selections were presented that evening, and the seasonal curtain closed with the singing of the farce *Botheration*.[109]

Mr. Powell's apparent success in Portsmouth encouraged him to revisit the town following the turn of the century. An examination of the newspapers reveals that he chose the years of 1801, 1802, and 1805, at which time the operatic fare included such well-known current successes as Arnold's *The Mountaineers*, Stephen Storace's *No Song No Supper*, William Reeve's *The Purse*, Arnold's *Inkle & Yarico*, Dibdin's *The Romp*, Shield's *Rosina*, Shield's *Rival Soldiers*, and Dibdin's *Quaker*.

Elsewhere in the state, the inhabitants were not yet prepared for the engaging humors and passions of the stage. As has been pointed out, the cultural development of most of the communities outside of Portsmouth, toward the end of the century, was still in a period of relative infancy.

Dover, however, had a theater as early as 1792, and according to a notice in the *Phoenix*, the friends of drama in the town had occasion to hear at least two operas, and undoubtedly more before the beginning of the nineteenth century. The advertisement, as quoted in the *History of Dover*, reads thus: "Theatre—At the Theatre in Dover, on Friday evening the 8th inst. will be presented an Opera, called the Beggars Opera. To which will be added Garrick's Satyrical Farce called Lethe or Aesop in the Shades. Tickets 1s6 may be had at this office." [110]

Perhaps "Charles Clapham, Esq. from Dover," already mentioned in connection with Mrs. Arnold's company, and who had sung not only in Portsmouth but also in Portland,[111] Boston,[112] and Providence,[113] had a hand in the theatrical excursions of his native village.

Our final reference to opera performed before 1800 outside of Portsmouth is to be found in the literary *Farmer's Weekly Museum* of Walpole. The notice refers to a contemplated presentation of Dibdin's "comic opera" *Lionel and Clarissa* and Michael Arne's "musical entertainment" *Cymon* by a local group of actor-singers:

Mr. Hubbard's [114] Exhibition

"On the afternoon and evening of Wednesday next, the public will be gratified by Mr. Hubbards Exhibition. We understand that the performance will consist of the comic opera of 'Lionel and Clarissa' and the musical entertainment of 'Cymon.' Both these plays are remarkably interesting, elegant and chaste. From the industry and professional talents of the preceptor, and from the ambition of the performers, we may expect a very agreeable display of theatrical elocution. The vocal powers and graceful forms of the young ladies, who are concerned, must add much to the interest of the occasion." [115]

It was well into the nineteenth century before the New Hampshire communities outside of Portsmouth had the opportunity to enjoy opera and other musical entertainments on a large scale. Portsmouth, on the other hand, because of its strategic position as a seacoast town, heard during the last quarter of the eighteenth century perhaps as many performances of operas as any other town of its size in America.

VIII. Concert Life

CONCERT life, in the strict sense of the term, commences in Portsmouth, New Hampshire in 1783. It is possible, however, that (as in Salem,[1] Massachusetts) public concerts with programs of hymns and anthems were also given in the town before the war, inasmuch as singing schools were in evidence at a very early date.

The first real public concert recorded in New Hampshire was advertised in the *New Hampshire Gazette* of August 17, 1783, in the town of Portsmouth. It was performed at the Assembly Room by the "Band of Music" belonging to Col. Crane's Regiment of Artillery. This does not necessarily imply that it was the first concert given in Portsmouth or even in the state, although it is the initial notification of a concert which has come to our attention. We have already mentioned Marquis de Chastellux's reference to enjoying the music of the regiment of Viennois. The engaging notice as published in the *Gazette* of February 15, 1783, reads: "The Band of Music belonging to Col. Crane's Regiment of Artillery, propose to give a Public Concert, on Monday Evening next, at the Assembly-Room in this town: Where will be performed several pieces of Music—consisting of several Overtures, Symphonies, Military Music, several Songs, and several Duettoes on the French Horns. Tickets, at Six Shillings each, may be had at the Printing Office. The Concert will begin at Seven o'clock."

A similar concert had been presented at Salem a month earlier.[2] It is interesting to note how mistaken was the universal belief "that the bands of the Continental Army consisted merely of few fifes and drums and were incapable of playing none but fife and drum music." [3] The program of "Overtures, Symphonies, Military Music, several Songs, and several Duettoes on the French Horns" naturally disproves this notion.

Some time before Horatio Garnet, already mentioned in the previous chapter, became involved in his theatrical enterprise; he was responsible for providing Portsmouth with a series of concerts. A number of the performances were restricted to instrumental music, while others included both vocal and instrumental offerings. His concert debut occurred on October 23, 1788, according to a notice in the *Gazette* of the same day:

"This Evening Concert. Mr. Garnet, Respectfully informs the Ladies and Gentlemen of Portsmouth, and its vicinity, that he intends performing a Concert of Instrumental Music this Evening at the Assembly Room.

"Mr. Garnet having been ever studious in his endeavors for the improvement of those gentlemen, who have honoured him with their tuition, is induced to hope their performance will give general satisfaction.

"He has selected a number of the most approved Marches, Minuets and Airs etc. (All of American composition) which he flatters himself will be most agreeable to the company.

"Knowing (from experience) that the polite inhabitants of this town, wish for the cultivation of the delightful science of music—as he will spare neither trouble or expense to make this Concert every way agreeable—he humbly solicits their patronage on this occasion.

"The performance to begin precisely at half past six o'clock. Tickets at 2s. each may be had of Mr. Garnet at Mr. Greenleaf's inn, and at this Printing-Office."

Garnet was a person of considerable artistic ability who contributed much to the musical life of Portsmouth. He seems, originally, to have made his appearance there during July of 1788 when he notified the public through the *Spy* of his intentions to teach instrumental music. The advertisement, which bears evidence of his versatility, reads: "Horatio Garnet, Humbly acquaints the public that having received his musical education in some of the principal cities in Europe, he proposes teaching the Violin, Bass-Viol, Hautboy, Clarionet, Flute etc. and also to give Lessons to Ladies on the Guittar. Those who wish to acquire a practical knowledge in the most delightful science, and will honor him with their commands, may depend on his most strenuous exertions for their instruction and improvement, on any or all the above mentioned instruments, on the most moderate terms, which may be known by applying to him at his lodgings with Mr. Samuel Place, of this town." [4]

Evidently Garnet's first eight months in Portsmouth proved rewarding, for in the March 20, 1789, *Spy* he "Returns his most sincere thanks to the Ladies and Gentlemen of this town, for the Encouragement he has hitherto met with—and begs leave to inform them that he proposes (should encouragement offer) to reside in Town during the ensuing Season, for the purpose of teaching instrumental Musick in its various branches viz. Violin, Violincello, Guittar, Germ. Flute, Clarionet & Hautboy, likewise the Harpsichord, Spinnet etc.

"Music copied in the most accurate manner. Also Key'd Instruments tuned on the shortest Notice. His terms (which are very moderate) may be known by applying to him at Greenleaf's inn."

A concert of vocal and instrumental music consisting of "new Federal Songs, Choruses etc" followed by a ball was given by Garnet on the evening of July 6, 1789. The affair, in the nature of an Independence Day observance, was thus announced in the *Spy*:

"The Fourth of July, Being on Saturday, on which will be celebrated the Anniversary of American Independence, and as the Ladies cannot partake of the Amusements of the day: Therefore, Mr. Garnet intends performing a Concert of vocal and instrumental Music, on Monday Evening the 6th inst. at the Assembly-Room—consisting of some new Federal Songs, Choruses, etc. which he hopes will give satisfaction to those who shall honour him with their attendance.

"The Concert will begin precisely at half-past six o'clock, P.M. and at eight will be opened a Ball, which being by subscription, it is requested that the Room may be cleared immediately after the Concert; and to prevent confusion, the Drawing Rooms will be than opened for the reception of the Subscribers, in order to have the Assembly-Room swept.

"Tickets for the Concert, at 2s. each, may be had of Mr. Garnet, at Greenleaf's inn, etc.

"Strangers will be admitted to the Ball, if introduced by a Subscriber, upon paying one dollar." [5]

There is no critical review of Garnet's Independence Day concert in the newspaper, although the *Spy* reported that along with "a number of patriotic toasts—several excellent songs were sung, accompanied with instrumental music." [6]

It is possible that some of the works on this program, as well as the previous one, were Garnet's own compositions. In this connection we have already referred to Garnet performing his own *Clarinet Concerto*. He also wrote the "Ode for American Independence" which is extant, and probably many other compositions which are no longer available. The "Ode for American Independence, July 4th, 1789, By Daniel George" and set to music by Garnet appears in the *Massachusetts Magazine,* Boston, July, 1789, pages 452-453.[7] The verse is written in two parts, melody and bass, with accompanying text, followed by three part chorus. It is reproduced on an open score. The July 11, 1789, *New Hampshire Spy* contains the entire text of this ode which includes no less than seven verses, each succeeded by the chorus. Exalting patriotism and the spirit of liberty, the first verse tells of the Declaration of Independence and its signing by John Hancock. The following four verses retrace the events of the Revolution from Burgoyne's defeat to the capitulation of Cornwallis. The sixth and seventh verses laud Washington and peace:

> Now shall the useful arts of peace prevail,
> And commerce flourish, flavor'd by each gale,
> > Discord, forever cease
> > Let Liberty and Peace,
> > and Justice reign;
> For Washington protects the scientific train.

On September 24 of the same year (1789), Garnet announced another "Concert of Instrumental Musick" also to be followed by a ball if sufficient interest was displayed. The notice, which appeared in the *Gazette*, has nothing to say concerning the music to be performed:

"Concert. Mr. Garnet begs leave to inform the Ladies and Gentlemen of this Town and its Vicinity, that there will be a Concert of Instrumental Musick at the Assembly-Room on Monday evening next the 28th inst.

"Should sufficient number of Subscribers apply, there will be given a Ball immediately after the Concert, at one Dollar for each Gentleman.

"The Musick, Entertainment, etc. the same as at the Assemblies last Winter.

"Tickets at one shilling and six pense each, and nine pense for Children, may be had of Mr. Garnet and at this Office.

"Doors to be open at Six, and the performance to begin precisely at Seven O'clock." [8]

Although we have found but three advertisements of concerts given by Garnet, it is important to note that the allusion above —"the Music, Entertainment, etc. the same as at the Assemblies last Winter"—proves that Portsmouth had occasion to enjoy a number of other concerts during the winter of 1788-1789.

The last reference to Garnet's concert activities projects the accomplished musician-teacher in the role of organist. When the Grand Masonic Lodge of New Hampshire announced plans for the celebration of the "Festival of St. John the Baptist" in the *Spy*,[9] it also reported that "several pieces of musick will be performed upon the organ by Mr. Garnet, accompanied with vocal musick." Following the end of the theatrical season on August 1 of the same year, with which he had in the meantime been occupied, Horatio Garnet seems to vanish, as most of these eighteenth-century itinerants were wont to do. Although he may have conceivably lingered in Portsmouth for a brief time afterwards, we have no idea as to his whereabouts subsequent to this date.

When George Washington stopped at Boston during his

famous inaugural tour in 1789, "An Oratorio; or, Concert of Sacred Musick" prepared by the Independent Musical Society was presented in his honor. Initially the program had been planned as a benefit concert to "assist in finishing the Colonnade or Portico" of Stone Chapel. Sonneck conjectured that the managers, seeing an imposing opportunity to perform for the President, postponed the affair for a few days "in order to turn the benefit—into a publick ornament in honor of George Washington." [10] It is interesting to note that the entire program was printed in the October 17, 1789, *Spy*.

Part the First

1. Full Anthem—composed by Mr. Selby [11]
2. The favourite Air in the Messiah (composed by the celebrated Handel)
   'Comfort Ye my People'—by Mr. Rea
3. Organ Concerto—by Mr. Selby
4. The favourite Air in the Oratorio of Samson (composed by the celebrated Handel)
   'Let the bright Seraphim'—by Mr. Rea
5. Full Anthem—composed by Mr. Selby

Part the Second

"The oratorio of Jonah complete. The solos by Messrs. Rea, Fay, Brewer and Dr. Rogerson. The choruses by the Independent Musical Society: The instrumental parts by a Society of Gentlemen, with the Band of His Most Christian Majesty's Fleet.

"As the above Oratorio has been highly applauded by the best judges and has never been performed in America; [12] and as the best performers of this country will be joined by the excellent Band of His Most Christian Majesty's squadron; the Public will have every reason to expect a more finished and delightful Performance than ever was exhibited in the United States."

The admission fee to this rather grandiose affair was "half a dollar." The music was scheduled to begin at half past two.

This is the only instance of a Boston concert being advertised in a Portsmouth paper that we have come across, and it is reasonable to assume that the Boston music impresarios must have expected to draw a substantial number of patrons from out of town. Traveling between Portsmouth and Boston was not uncommon in those days. Family ties, commercial interests, and the attractions of a large city, then as now, stimulated a steady traffic between the two cities.

At any rate, here was a Boston "Concert of Sacred Musick" being advertised a distance of some sixty miles away. In all probability some of the wealthy "genteel ladies and gentlemen" of Portsmouth sat and listened with Washington to S. Feldsted's complete oratorio of *Jonah*.[13]

Concerts interspersed with readings and lectures in connection with the singing schools and societies were probably much more common at this time than the newspapers would lead one to believe. Such an exercise of "Music and Oratory" was performed at the Reverend Buckminster's meeting-house on December 21, 1791.[14] The program as reported by the *Spy* of the same day was conducted in the following order:
1. Music,
2. An Oration.
3. Music,
4. Address on Charity.
"Then, a collection, for the purchase of books, slates, etc. for the poor children in the public schools—the money to be deposited in the hands of the school committees to be by them appropriated.
5. Music.
6. A sacred eclogue.
7. Music.
"The music to be performed by singers from all the societies in town, accompanied with instruments. The Oratory by Mr. A. [Abraham] Bishop."

An invitation was extended to "His Excellency the President of the State, to the officers and members of the hon. Legislature, to the inhabitants of Portsmouth and to strangers." From the *Spy* [15] we learn that "many members of the Hon. Legislature—

and a very large number of respectable inhabitants—, were most agreeable entertained ... by an oration, address on charity ... and pieces of instrumental and vocal music performed at the intervals by J. M. Sewall Esq. and other patrons and lovers of that pleasing art. ... The highest gratitude was expressed by the public, the poor in particular, to the stranger and musicions [sic] for the favor of the entertainment, and to the company for the acceptable bounty collected for the poor children."

What the choristers sang that evening, who directed the music, what instruments were employed for accompaniment unfortunately are not revealed in the newspaper.

The Reverend Buckminster, at whose meeting house the program of music and oratory took place, was keenly interested in promoting church music. "His voice was strong and musical, and possessed the peculiarity that its lowest tones were singularly clear, and could be distinctly heard in the remotest corner of the vast meeting-house, with its two galleries." It could always be distinguished in the full choir, by its "purity and bell-like, silver sound"; [16] he delighted, in the absence of the ladies of the choir, "to take the contralto part." [17]

Buckminster's fondness for music was passed on to his son, Joseph Stevens, who learned to play the flute before he went to Exeter Academy at the age of eleven. Fearing for his son's health, however, the father discouraged Joseph Stevens from continuing. Afterwards the boy took some lessons on the violin and violincello, but relinquished them, "as creating a too passionate love that interfered with his other studies." Later he began to study the organ when he found that "he could unite his favorite pursuit with the improvement of church music." [18]

The presence in Boston of the youthful and capable blind musician, John L. Berkenhead, was first noted in 1795, when on January 6 of that year, according to the *Columbian Centinel*, a concert of sacred music was performed at the Universal Meeting House for his benefit. [19] Sonneck provides a substantial résumé of his concert activities but makes no mention of his teaching, which was a necessary part of his musical life. In 1796, according to Brooks, Berkenhead became organist of Trinity Church, Newport, Rhode Island, and continued in that position for eight years.[20] It was here, also, that Oliver Shaw, the American psalmodist, studied organ with Berkenhead.[21]

It is of some historical interest to note that Berkenhead resided in Portsmouth, where he taught the "keyed instruments" and gave some concerts, for over a year before he introduced himself to Boston musical circles, a fact unknown to Sonneck.

An advertisement in the *Oracle*, which appeared no less than seven times, duly notified the inhabitants of Portsmouth in November, 1793, that

"John L. Berkenhead, Lately From Europe, Having from a very early period received his tuition under the most accomplished masters and performers of Music in Great-Britain, particularly the Great Doctor Wainwright [22] and the celebrated Bomgarton,[23] of London; respectfully informs the public, that on the most reasonable terms he gives Lessons on the Organ, Harpsichord, Piano-Forte, and other keyed instruments—Tunes and Repairs them—and punctually attends the commands of all those who are pleased to honour him with any.

"He takes this opportunity most gratefully to acknowledge the many favors he has already received from some of the most respectable characters in this town, in his professional line, which he begs leave to assure them, he shall, by the most strenuous exertions, endeavour to deserve.

"His terms may be known by applying to him at his lodgings, at Mr. John Davenport's near Mr. William Sheafe's Store." [24]

It is evident that Berkenhead had been in Portsmouth for some time before this notification appeared in the *Oracle*. Little is known of his teaching and concert activities during his residence in the town. A reference to a projected concert appears in the May 10, 1794, *Oracle* in the form of an apology "for not performing his Concert on Friday evening, according to his engagement—Delicacy and a tender regard to those who were the means of preventing it, forbid him to unfold the cause of the disappointment." Doctor Berkenhead, however, assured the public that the concert would be performed at the Assembly Room on Monday evening next "Agreeably to the hand-bill already given out." [25]

Regrettably we have no handbill which would provide us with the musical fare for this occasion, but a glance at several concert programs held in Boston during the ensuing year, in which Berkenhead participated, affords an inkling of what might have constituted his Portsmouth offerings. Among other things, there was an "Overture" by Vanhall, an unidentified Grand Concerto on the Piano-Forte," a "Symphony on the Grand Piano-Forte" by Clementi, a "Grand Lesson" by Hook, and a military piece of his own composition entitled "The Demolition of the Bastille on the Harpsichord or Piano-Forte." [26]

Berkenhead's *Bastille* reflects the rage in both Europe and America for programmatic military music. In this country, the popularity of the idiom was heightened by obvious appeals to patriotism, by a harkening back to the Revolution. James Hewitt's "Battle of Trenton," a sonata for pianoforte dedicated to George Washington, is perhaps the best known American example. But Franz Kotzwara's insipid "Battle of Prague" (on the pianoforte with accompaniments), the "rage on both sides of the Atlantic as late as 1850," led the field.[27] In similar vein, Dr. Berkenhead composed his "Demolition of the Bastille" which he "admirably played" on the harpsichord or pianoforte to audiences in Boston,[28] Salem,[29] and most likely in Portsmouth.

At this juncture of the Berkenhead story we are confronted with a puzzling situation. In the May 9, 1795, *Oracle* an announcement appears under the name of Thomas Berkenhead. The notice, which is similar in content to the one in the November 23, 1793, *Oracle*, suggests a probable error on the part of the printer and the conclusion is that Thomas Berkenhead is still none other than John L. Berkenhead. The entire advertisement will allow the reader to judge for himself:

"Thomas Berkenhead returns his sincere thanks for the liberal encouragement he has experienced from the inhabitants of Portsmouth in general, for the liberal encouragement he has experienced from them; he at the same time begs leave to solicit a continuance of their patronage and favour, and likewise to inform them that he teaches the Organ, Harpsichord, and Piano-Forte, in their various stiles [sic] etc.—Also that he Tunes and Repairs Instruments in the best manner in town and country.

"Mr. Berkenhead flatters himself that he possesses Abilities, Politeness and Patience, which are so very necessary for a good Teacher.

"His terms may be known by application to him, who will wait on either Ladies or Gentlemen at their houses."

The first part of this notice suggests that Dr. Berkenhead was probably referring to other activity beside teaching which, in our opinion, implies concertizing. This conclusion is largely based on the extensive amount of performing he had been doing in Boston about this time. This thesis, however, is largely a matter of conjecture; the newspapers are unrewarding.

The advertisement above, which was also published in the May 12, 16, and 23 issues of the *Oracle*, is the last reference we have to Berkenhead's Portsmouth residence. How long he remained in town after this is not known to us. As has been mentioned, early in the next year he assumed the duties of organist at Trinity Church in Newport, where he remained for eight years.[30]

Meanwhile in October of 1795 the *Oracle* [31] announced a benefit "Concert of Sacred Music, Vocal and Instrumental" for one Mr. Winthrop Bennet "as an acknowledgement of his assiduity in promoting the practice of Psalmody" in Portsmouth. The advertisement disclosed that the concert was to be held at the Universalist Meeting House at three o'clock. The occasion also called for a discourse by the Reverend George Richards and a collection for the purpose above mentioned.

There is no suggestion in the newspaper of the selections performed on this program, but it is likely that several psalm and hymn tunes and perhaps the customary "Grand Hallelujah Chorus" from Handel's *Messiah* were included. Most of the concert, according to current practices, was probably accompanied by instrumental music.

Mr. Bennet seems to have made his initial appearance in Portsmouth in December of 1789 when he advertised in the *Spy* [32] that he "Proposes opening his Singing-School on Thursday Evening next, at Mr. Davenport's House." Subsequent allusions to Bennet in the press attest to the continuance of his singing schools. Consequently, it is safe to assume that between 1789 and 1795 he was responsible for presenting other such concerts in the town.

Several weeks before a small theatrical company from Boston launched a series of subscription plays and operas in Portsmouth in the fall of 1796; its leader and one of its most brilliant members, Mrs. Arnold, whom we have already met in the foregoing chapter, placed her vocal talents at the disposal of the musical citizens of the town by performing two concerts. Mrs. Arnold, a former member of the Theatre Royal, Covent Garden, London, who had arrived from England the previous January, was currently associated with the Boston Theatre.

Fortunately Mrs. Arnold has left the contents of both programs for posterity. The announcement of her initial concert is found in the July 23, 1796, *Gazette* and reads:

"Concert; Mrs. Arnold Most respectfully informs the Ladies and Gentlemen of Portsmouth, she intends having a Concert at the Assembly Room, on Wednesday, August 3*d*; assures them she will use her every exertion to render the intertainment of the evening worthy of their patronage. The following is a part of the selection for the occasion.

Song	The Bonny Bold Soldier	Mrs. Arnold
Song	The Market Lass	Mrs. Arnold
Song	Ellen, or the Richmond primrose girl, as sung by Mrs. Arnold repeatedly at the Boston theatre, with universal applause, accompanied on the Forte Piano	Mrs. Arnold
Voluntary Pieces.		
Song	Henry's Cottage Maid	Mrs. Arnold
Song	By Moonlight on the Green	Mrs. Arnold
Song	The heaving of the Lead	Mrs. Arnold

| Song O listen, listen to the voice of Love | Mrs. Arnold |
| Song Mary's Dream, or Sandy's Ghost, by particular desire, accompanied on the Forte Piano | Mrs. Arnold |

This concert and the succeeding one were set up on a sub-scription basis. The announcement stated that the subscription fee was "one dollar each Gentlemen" admitting one lady, while the fee for an additional lady was half a dollar. Music was to be provided for those ladies and gentlemen who wished to dance after the concert. "Subscription papers to be left at Capt. Furniss's and at Mr. Daniel Symes's Daniel Street," added the *Gazette*.[33]

The second concert was presented two weeks later on August 18. In the newspaper Mrs. Arnold proclaimed to the inhabitants of Portsmouth that "she flatters herself they will find it worthy their further patronage. The selection of Songs," she continues, "are varied, and every other exertion will be used . . . to render the entertainments of the evening adequate to their wishes." [34]

This program somewhat duplicates the earlier one, and gives some idea of current popular tastes:

Song 1st The Bonny Bold Soldier	Mrs. Arnold
Voluntary Piece	
Song 2nd The favorite Air of Somebody	Miss Arnold
Song 3rd Ellen, or the Richmond Primrose Girl, as performed at the Boston Theatre with unbounded applause, accompanied on Forte Piano	Mrs. Arnold
Song 4th The favorite and popular Air of the Rosary	Mrs. Arnold
Song 5th The Pretty Lad	Mrs. Arnold
Song 6th Market Lass	Miss Arnold
Song 7th By desire, The Heaving of the Lead	Mrs. Arnold
Voluntary Piece	
Song 8th The Moon Light on the Greens	Mrs. Arnold
Voluntary piece on Forte Piano	
Song 9th Fair Rosalie.	

The Miss Arnold who appears on this program was Mrs. Arnold's nine-year-old daughter Elizabeth Arnold, already alluded to in the last chapter.

As has been mentioned, following these two concerts, the inhabitants of Portsmouth were treated to several months of theatrical entertainments in which Mrs. Arnold and her daughter played a prominent part. We note no further references to concerts for the remainder of the year and the first half of the next year in the newspaper files.

In June of 1797,[35] however, the *Gazette* carries a notice of a miscellaneous entertainment which is called, "Just in time. Such things have been; such things may be; such things are." The newspaper gives a lengthy and engaging description of the whole:

This evening At the Assembly-Room

"Mess'rs Chalmers, Williamson and Barrett,[36] from the Theatres in Boston, most respectfully inform the ladies and gentlemen of the town of Portsmouth that they intend to amuse them with.

"Their Evening's Lounge, being an antidote for the Spleen. Or just in time. Such things have been; such things may be; such things are. Mirth, Song & Sentiment, Consisting of Readings, Lectures, Recitations, and Songs, as performed at Dibdin's Vauxhall, and the theatres in Europe. Being a Comic, Satiric, Whimsical, Humorous, Moral illustrative Dissertation and display of Heads, Hearts, Passions, Humors, Whims, Oddities and Characters.—To 'Catch the living manners as they rise.' Has ever been held not only allowable, but meritorious; so it is hoped the same wish to please and entertain, will in the present case, be viewed at least with candour. The amusements will be divided into three acts.

"For further particulars see the bills of the day."

Chalmers and Williamson alone presented a similar amusement to the inhabitants of Annapolis, Maryland, in December of the same year (1797), referred to as "the TABLET, or just in time, consisting of readings, recitations and songs." [37]

Sonneck points out that "besides songs these entertainments contained sonatas and overtures played on the pianoforte." [38]

Following the performance of this *potpourri*, no further mention is made of a concert, in either the *Gazette* or the *Oracle*, for a period of three years. The cause for this is not readily explained. Sonneck asserts that during the last years of the century, "for reasons not wholly on the surface," concert life in Boston, Philadelphia, and New York was at a "very low ebb." He suggests an examination of the newspapers for partial proof.[39] It is, nevertheless, well to bear in mind that the singing schools and music societies, which were currently flourishing, provided numerous sacred concerts of vocal and instrumental music for an interested public.

On June 3, 1800, through the medium of the *Gazette* and the *Oracle* the "principal Musicians from Boston" duly notified the Portsmouth public that a "Concert of Vocal and Instrumental Music" to be followed by a ball, was to be held that same evening at the New Hampshire Hotel Tavern. The leader of this apparently very fine group was Gottlieb Graupner,[40] one of Boston's outstanding musical figures and founder of the Philharmonic Society. The remainder of the entourage included several other well-known performers of Boston, such as Jacobus Pick, Fredrick Granger, Mr. and Mrs. Peter Albrecht Van Hagen, and Graupner's wife.

Both the *Gazette* and the *Oracle* provide us with a complete program of their offering, which also includes most of the names of the performers and an occasional reference to the composer.

Part First

Overture	Composed by Van Hall
Concerto on the French Horn	Mr. Pick
Song, 'Did not tyrant custom'	Mrs. Graupner
Concerto on the Clarinet	Mr. Granger
Song, 'How do ye do,' (Echo)	Mrs. Graupner
Accompanied on the Hautboy by	Mr. Graupner
Concerto on the Forte Piano by	Mrs. Von Hagen

Part Second

Concerto on the Violin	Mr. Von Hagen [41]
Song 'The Little Sailor boy'	Mrs. Graupner
Concerto on the Hautboy	Mr. Graupner
	Mrs. Graupner
Trio Song	Mrs. Von Hagen
	Mr. Pick
Finale	Composed by Hayden [sic]

"The Concert will commence at half past seven O'clock. Tickets to admit a Lady and Gentleman, one dollar; a single ticket 75 cents, to be had at Mr. Waldron's Hotel Tavern."

A suggestion of the prevalence of the polite arts in the life of Portsmouth society during the year 1800 is conveyed in the June 3 issue of the *Gazette*, which contained advertisements of a concert of secular music, a concert of sacred music, a play, *Bunker Hill*, which was billed with a farce, and a theatrical critique of *Bunker Hill*, which had been performed the previous evening.[42]

Two days later (June 5), at four o'clock in the afternoon, Graupner and his musicians presented a "Concert of Sacred Music" at St. John's Chapel for the poor of the town. Handel's music was the main attraction:

"The celebrated Grand Oratorio of the Messiah, composed by Handel, will be part of the performance.

"A variety of hymns and Psalms will be executed by vocal performers.

"Particulars of the whole Concert will be explained in the hand-bill previous to the performance.

"Tickets at 1s 6 may be had at the Hotel, or at the store occupied by Mr. J. L. Shannon.

"N.B. One quarter of the neat [sic] proceeds of the money collected from the sales of Tickets the performers will deliver to the Ministers of the different societies preaching the gospel in this town, to be distributed by them to such of the poor of their congregations as they shall think proper. The performance no doubt will meet the approbation of a generous public, as it

will be performed with the solemnity of a Sacred Musical performance—and the proceeds appropriated to the relief of the
distressed." [43]

The disposal of the remaining three-quarters of the net
proceeds is not mentioned, although it is safe to assume that it
was used to pay for the services of the professional musicians.

Graupner's competent group, having obviously gained the
approval of the public, announced a second concert of sacred
music in the *Oracle* [44] four days later, on June 9, which in
content appears to be somewhat similar to the one performed
earlier:

"Concert By particular desire of the Ladies and Gentlemen
of this town, the principal Musicians from Boston Will for the
Last Time Perform on Monday next, the 9th inst. at St. John's
Chapel at 4 o'clock in the afternoon a Concert of Sacred Music,
With a variety of Songs out of Handel, etc.—Particulars of the
Concert will be explained in the Hand-Bills.

"Tickets at 1s 6, may be had at the Columbian Bookstore,
Museum & Hotel."

Following Graupner's June 9 appearance, no other reference
to a concert in Portsmouth is found in either the *Oracle* or the
Gazette for the remainder of the year.

Elsewhere in the state music development took on an entirely
different aspect. Unfortunately, no town outside of Portsmouth
enjoyed the fine traveling theatrical companies as well as its
own local thespians, concert groups, and ostensibly skilled
foreign musicians to assist with the musical progress of the community. Portsmouth and its immediate environs were settled
fully a hundred years earlier than the remainder of the state;
its people were different in thought and interests. Its advan-
tageous position as a seacoast town, carrying on a lively trade
with many countries of Europe, was a compelling factor in its
retention of the Old World concepts and way of life. Thus,
Portsmouth's unique cultural as well as musical development
was largely affected by its close European ties.

The musical leadership in such villages as Concord, Walpole,
Charlestown, Amherst, and Hanover was drawn mainly from

native talent; musicians who had been schooled, often not too well, in the indigenous idiom of psalmody. Consequently, a definite musical awakening did not take place here until well into the nineteenth century, at which time a new crop of skilled foreign musicians reached our shores. Many of them, eager to display their wares, traveled the dirt roads on the back-woods circuit performing on the violin and pianoforte (when available), and singing many tunes from the popular European operas of the day.

Meanwhile, following the Revolutionary War, many singing schools were established in these communities for the expressed purpose of improving the music of divine worship. Out of these singing schools emerged the singing society, which carried musical development beyond the limited scope of church psalmody. It also made provisions for the performing of frequent public concerts of "sacred music, vocal and instrumental." This institution was a sincere, enthusiastic exponent of the musical art, "fully aware of its importance as a factor of civilization." [45] It played a vital part in the development of religious and secular music, concert life, and music education in America. A glimpse of the beginnings of the Concord Musical Society will afford the reader with an insight into this institution's role in the community as a vehicle for social and religious musical development.

In August of 1792 the Selectmen of Concord inserted an article in the town-meeting warrant "To see what encouragement the Town will give to hire a singing master." [46] Five months later Asa McFarland,[47] afterwards pastor of the First Congregational Church, came down from Dartmouth and established a singing school.

This new singing school was heralded in the January 21, 1793, *Mirrour:* "Singing School. To the Lovers of Harmony. Whereas a great Number of Inhabitants, desirous to promote the Art and Practice of Sacred Music in this Town, have subscribed to pay an able Teacher of Psalmody, (Mr. MacFarland) —Therefore, all Persons willing to improve the Advantage of Free Singing School, are requested to leave their Names, before the first of February next, with either persons of the following Committee, *viz.* Capt. Jonathan Eastman, Capt. Timothy Chandler, Lieut. David Davis, Lieutenant Amos Abbott, junior, and Mr. Levi Abbott."

The subscribers were requested to meet on February 19 in order to "receive a Constitution for their Regulation and Government" according to the *Mirrour* (February 18, 1793). At the same time it was announced:

"Those who wish to acquire a knowledge of Music, are informed that a Free Singing School is kept in this Town; and their attendance is requested—We have been at considerable Cost in procuring a Master—and 'tis a Pity we should not now have a respectable School; the only Way to effect this, is, a particular Attention of those who are desirous of the Reputation of the Town, and who will contribute to the Harmony and Respectability of the Performance of Singing: and a tender Regard for the Feelings of our worthy and generous Pastor,[48] ought to urge them to an attendance on the School, that they may perform on the Sabbath with Order, Beauty, Harmony and Concord.

"Spectators will be admitted in the Singing School on Thursday Evenings—and No other."

On November 7, 1796, it was "voted that the Singing Society may make use of the town House to Sing in when the House is not in use by the town, they to Leave the House in as good Repair as it is when they go into sd House." [49]

The success of the singing society was assured when, in January, 1797, it announced in the *Courier* that "for the purpose of improving in Psalmody the Singers in Concord are desired to give their attendance at the Town House, every Friday evening at 6 o'clock—for the public performing of Sacred Music, vocal and instrumental." This practice provided not only the means for "improving in psalmody" but also a vehicle for presenting public concerts which were no doubt a welcome diversion for the inhabitants. The notice concludes: "And as there is now an opportunity of receiving the instructions of an experienced Teacher, free of expense to the Scholars, it is wished as many would attend from the different parts of the town as can possibly make it convenient." [50]

The Concord Musical Society, having evolved into a singing group of considerable membership and influence, was legally incorporated by an act of the State Legislature on June 15, 1799. It was duly organized on September 10, 1799, at a meeting in the town hall with Timothy Walker, Esq., as president, Jacob Abbot, Jr., first chorister,[51] and Thomas Stickney, Jr., assistant chorister. The introduction to the sixteen articles of the constitution reads: "Whereas Psalmody is justly esteemed and essential part of divine worship and having obtained an Incorporation for the better enabling us to encourage the Knowledge and Practice of Sacred Music [we] do adopt the following rules and regulations as By-Laws for the Government of the Concord Musical Society." [52]

The "rules and regulations" of this self-governing group generally deal with the mechanical functions of the organization and are therefore not necessary to quote. Five of the articles, however, can be more appropriately assigned to the category of music instruction; these we reproduce in full from the original manuscript:

"*Article 6.* The Librarian shall receive all music books belonging to the Society—shall keep a record of them and lend them to persons for the benefit of the Society to be returned Quarter Yearly rec[k]oning from the annual meeting they paying for the abuse of said Books. . . .

"*Article 8.* All officers of said Society shall be Chosen by ballot Except the Chorister's Assistant who may be Nominated by the Chorister. . . .

"*Article 12.* The Librarian shall Keep a record of the Number and Kinds of Musicall [*sic*] Instruments and take charge of them at all times when not call'd for by the Chorister by Order of the President & Director.

"*Article 13.* The Chorister with Consent of the President & directors may loan the Musicall Instruments belonging to the Society to such persons as will most conduce to the Im-

provement of the Music, they being answerable for the Damage
should the Instrument be abused. . . .

"*Article 15.* The Librarian shall make a return of all Books
and Musical Instruments belonging to this Society to the President and Directors at the Annual Meeting." [53]

In April of 1801 Deacon Joseph Hall demonstrated more than
a casual interest in the welfare of the society by contributing
the sum of five hundred dollars as a permanent fund, "from a
desire to encourage and promote the practice of sacred music
in the town of Concord." The ideal and the idea are contained
in the document, which reads thus:

"Whereas I, Joseph Hall of Concord, in the County of
Rockingham and State of New-Hampshire, Gentleman, from a
desire to Encourage and Promote the Practice of Sacred music
in said Town of Concord have thought proper to make a
Donation to the 'Concord Musical Society' of the sum of five
hundred Dollars in the funded debt of the United States, bear-
ing at this time an interest of six per cent. per annum—Now, to
the intent that a full understanding of my will in respect to the
said donation may be known to the members of the said Society
and all others whom it may concern, I do hereby voluntarily
enter the same on the record of the said society.

"1st. The sum of five Hundred Dollars shall always be kept
on interest, entire and undiminished—Therefore, the payments
which Government may from time to time make of the Principal
of the aforesaid stock, shall, by the trustees of said society
for the time being, immediately upon receipt thereof be again
put to interest upon Good Security; so that Lawful interest upon
the said sum of five hundred Dollars, may annually and forever
accrue to the said society—

"2nd. The interest which shall arise upon the aforesaid
donation, shall always be subject to the Disposal of the society
in that way which they shall judge will best promote and
Encourage the use and Practice of sacred Music in said Town.

"In witness whereof I have hereunto set my hand & seal, this
thirtieth day of April Anno Domini one Thousand Eight
Hundred and one.   Joseph Hall

"Signed and sealed in presence of—Obadiah Carrigain, Philip Carrigain Jun.[54]

The fund was safely and judiciously invested,[55] we learn; moreover, it proved "highly conducive to the proposed end." [56] Not only did religious music gain from this continued support but secular music also. The Concord Musical Society prospered until 1865. The far-sightedness and enthusiasm of Asa McFarland, Jacob Abbot, Timothy Chandler, Joseph Hall, and a host of other Concordians established a tradition of community music still alive and flourishing in Concord. Here was music education in America in its embryonic stage, crude perhaps, but forceful, providing any interested persons, children as well as adults, with the opportunity, without charge, to learn to sing and play vocal and instrumental music.

The current genuine interest in, and understanding of, the place of music in the lives of the people on the part of a substantial number of the citizens of Concord can, in some measure, be attributed to the vision of the founders of the Concord Musical Society. The same can be said with respect to musical development in other towns and cities throughout New England. In other words, the musical society became a potent instrument for the general dispensing of musical knowledge.

In conclusion, a rather lengthy but worthwhile account from the publication, *The New Star*, September, 1797, in connection with the Concord Musical Society provides us with a vivid description of the organization's musical activities:

MUSICAL SOCIETY

"Tuesday last was the anniversary meeting of CONCORD MUSICAL SOCIETY—at 11 o'clock, the Members of the Society met at the Town House; and at three o'clock they moved in procession to the Meeting House, preceded by a number of musical performers belonging to the Society, playing on instruments, and accompanied by a numerous crowd of Spectators belonging to this and the adjacent towns. The Rev. Mr. PARKER, of Canterbury, introduced the exercises of the day, by a most ingenious, excellent & sublime prayer, perfectly adapted to the occasion, addressed to the throne of the Great Author of 'Harmony Divine'—Several pieces of music, vocal and instrumental, were performed—A really classical Oration on Music, neat in composition, ingenious in design, was delivered by PHILIP CARRIGAIN, Jr. A.M. In which he gave a brief but enlightening view of Music in general, from the earliest ages to the present day; stated the general principles of the nature of the art; delightfully describing its pleasing captivating charms; tracing its astonishing and beneficial influence over the mind, and its various socializing effects upon the heart of man, both in his natively ferocious and more civilized state—justly ascribing to the powers and influence of music, not a little of the glory of the triumphs of our veteran armies over the minions of tyrants, in our late contest for liberty with Great-britain, in which Americans were made Freemen, and led to glory and honor by a WASHINGTON—& attributing to it much of the unprecendented courage and bravery of the numerous legions of BUONAPARTE, whom he has conducted to immortal fame, rendered invulnerable by the extatic inspirations of this heavenly science, every nerve beating time to the music of 'Marseilles Hymn', and other popular songs.—In the style and delivery of this Oration, we observed with pleasure, those traits of genius, and gesticulations characteristic of the refined orator, which truly deserve and must ever command respect; and which gained Mr. CARRIGAIN the liveliest testimonials of public applause from a most brilliant, respectable and very numerous and learned audience. He closed with a moral apostrophe, addressed to the auditory, in which (after a next comparison of the human frame to a musical instrument) he enchantingly invited all, so to attune their hearts and lives, that they might meet in unison in the Great Musical Society above.—This is but an inadequate comment on the work of this Oration: we hope to see it soon in print, when it will gain from the lovers of the belleslettres the eulogiums it merits.

"Perhaps there were never seen so many people together in this town, where all appeared so well satisfied; and where such unanimous applause was given the performances—the tribute was warm, general and hearty—Great thanks are due Mr. FLAGG, for his attention, and the complaisant Mr. MAURICE, & the obliging messrs. LONGS, for their assistance, in the Musical exercises:—All was harmony; and a brilliant Ball graced the evening of the festive day." [57]

If Walpole, the active, industrious village with a population of 1,500 on the Connecticut River in the southwestern part of the state, where Joseph Dennie, the American essayist, and his small coterie of *literati* held forth between 1795 and 1799, had any concert life previous to 1798, it was not revealed in the columns of the *Farmer's Weekly Museum*. In August of that year, however, we learn of the presentation by John Hubbard of the comic opera *Lionel and Clarissa* and the musical entertainment of *Cymon*,[58] previously mentioned in the chapter on opera. Although this is the only allusion we can find in the news files, it is reasonable to assume that it was probably not the first or last of the exhibitions in Walpole. Frequent references to music in the *Weekly Museum* editorials [59] and "for sale" items suggest that other musical fare was occasionally provided for the local inhabitants.

Meanwhile, in the autumn of 1796, a few miles up the river in the small, attractive village of Charlestown, with a population of about 1,200, the parents of those children who attended the local seminary had every reason to be satisfied with themselves for having acquired the capable services of Mr. Abner Cheney [60] as preceptor of the Charlestown Academy. His plan of education was "pleasant and salutary combining useful studies with the ornamental." It was generally understood that he proposed to direct the taste of his pupils to music, reports the *Farmer's Weekly Museum*, "and from his powers of vocal execution and his accurate theory we anticipate the rapid improvement of his scholars." [61] The inference here to Mr. Cheney's vocal powers strongly suggests that Mr. Cheney had entertained the inhabitants of Charlestown and surrounding communities with an occasional recital of vocal music.

Although the year 1800 has been chosen, for practical reasons, as a terminal point for this study, this date does not imply the conclusion of a musical era. Actually, the last decade of the eighteenth century was the beginning of a new, exciting chapter in the history of American music, which witnessed the establishment of theaters along the Atlantic seaboard from Charleston, South Carolina, to Portland, Maine, largely occupied by traveling English troupes of "actor-singers," and aided, in certain instances, by local "gentlemen performers." The concert hall was host to a parade of such artists as William Selby, Mrs. Arnold, Dr. John L. Berkenhead, Horatio Garnet, the Graupners, and the talented Von Hagens, to name only a few associated with New England, who performed the works of Haydn, Handel, Gluck, Gretry, and Arne, as well as their own compositions. The singing school emerged as a welcome vehicle for social diversion, and the musical society grew to a position of importance guided by American psalmodists like James Lyon, Josiah Flagg, William Billings, Samuel Holyoke, Timothy Swan, Oliver Holden, Daniel Read, Andrew Law, and a host of others.

This same decade witnessed the beginnings of small but significant private enterprises in instrument making and music publishing, bringing instruments and music within the budgetary limits of family incomes. The importation of both music and musical instruments also figures largely in this aspect of our musical growth. In this period of newly acquired leisure, the itinerant teacher, European and native, helped to create an awareness of the growing need for diversified music instruction on all social levels. Ultimately this led to a further expansion of the concert hall, the opera house, and the musical society, and to the establishment of music education in the public and private schools and, to some extent, in the colleges of the nation.

ix. Teachers

MUSIC education in America during the latter half of the eighteenth century remained largely in the hands of a few itinerant native teachers, a number of ostensibly well-trained English musicians, and an occasional German or Italian, who came to the New World to make the teaching of music a full-time occupation. Still others from France who had crossed the ocean in Lafayette's entourage to fight in the war of independence, subsequently tarrying in the States, earned their livelihood teaching the "polite arts" of dancing, the violin, or the French language.

Information on music instruction in New Hampshire during the first hundred years of the settlement is meager, yet there is enough to establish that such instruction was by no means entirely neglected. This instruction, of course, was in connection with church music. For instance, the Hampton town meeting of 1650 considered a proposal "To see if the parish will vote that those persons that Come nighest the approved Rule of Singing may have the Previlidge of Being Seated to Gether in the Second Long Seat in the men's Galery, for the Benefit of helping Each other in said Rule; and that they may be Seated to gather, to prevent Disorder they Desire to be Seated in Said Seat, or Elsewhere, to Gather in said meeting house."

An affirmative vote was given on the proposal "that those persons that Can Sing by Rule Shall Set to Gather in the meeting house in the front Short Seats in the men's Gallery." [1]

Choir directors were known as early as 1661 in Portsmouth, according to the regulations of the town. The duties of the school teacher as prescribed by these regulations included leading the choir on Sundays as well as acting as "a court messenger, to serve summonses . . ., to ring the bell for public worship, to dig the graves, to take charge of the school and to perform other occasional duties." [2]

The music of the worship service received early and special attention. The Reverend Thomas Symmes, who graduated from Harvard in 1698, states in his discourse on *The Reasonableness of Regular Singing; or, Singing by Note* (1720) that music "was studied, known and approved of in our College [Harvard], for many years after its first founding. This is evident from the Musical theses, which were formerly printed; and from some writings containing some tunes, with directions for singing by note, as they are now sung: and these are yet in being though of more than sixty years standing." [3]

"The first settlers sang by note," Symmes continues: "There are many persons of credit now living, children and grandchildren of the first settlers of New England who can very well remember that their ancestors sung by note, and they learned so to sing of them; and they have more than their bare words to prove that they speak the truth; for many of them can sing tunes exactly by note, which they learned of their Fore-fathers, and they say that they sung all the tunes after the same manner and these people now sing those tunes most agreeable to note, which have been least practiced in the congregation." [4]

In the same tract, Symnes points out that singing schools existed in the early days of the colonies and asserts that singing declined because "singing schools and singing books being laid aside, there was no way to learn." [5] Another reason for the decline of singing may have been the lack of printed tunes in the *Bay Psalm Book*, which, previous to the 1698 edition, did not include any music. At any rate, it is probably true that a certain amount of crude and frequently haphazard music instruction persisted during this period chiefly intended for the improvement of church psalmody.

The earliest and undeniably best sources for tracing the beginnings of music education in America are the news files, where may be found numerous advertisements of the itinerant music instructor of the latter half of the eighteenth century. It was general practice to advertise one's intention to give lessons in the "exact Rules of Vocal Musick," on the violin, flute, harpsichord, organ, and other instruments, and in the polite art of dancing. One of the first such advertisements appeared in the *Boston Evening Post* in 1743, when "Mr. Peter Pelham Jun." informed the public that he was prepared to "give lessons on the harpsichord and in the Rudiments of Psalmody, Hymns, Anthems, etc." [6] The first such advertisement in New Hampshire is in the March 15, 1765, *Gazette*. The advertiser, John Williams, of Portsmouth, a writing and ciphering instructor, announces the opening of his singing school: "This is to inform the Public, that John Williams Has opened a School opposite Mr. John Gardner's, Taylor, for teaching young Gentlemen and Ladies to Sing by the exact Rules of Vocal Musick. Young Gentlemen on Thursday and Saturday Afternoons at Six Pound per Quarter, and on Monday and Thursday Evenings at Ditto per Quarter. The Ladies on Tuesday and Friday Evenings at the same Price. Likewise Teaches Young Ladies to Write and Cipher every day from Seven to Eight and from Twelve to One in the Morning at Six Pound per Quarter."

The Portsmouth newspapers from 1765 through 1800 abound in similar advertisements. These quaint notices convey vividly an idea of the variety of instruction offered during the period. We submit the following excerpts chronologically arranged. (The complete text and sources of all material utilized in this directory as well as in the remainder of the chapter, unless otherwise indicated, appear in Appendix A.) [7]

Directory of Teachers of Music

1765. "John Williams, 'Has opened a School-for Teaching young Gentlemen and Ladies to Sing by the exact Rules of Vocal Musick'; Opposite Mr. John Gardner's Taylor; 'Likewise Teaches Young Ladies to Write and Cipher.'"

1767. "Peter Curtis, Dancing and Violin 'in a convenient Room under the Printing Office'; [1769] 'at the House lately improved by Capt. Bunbury, in the new pav'd Street, opposite the printing office.'"

1769. "Edward Hackett, 'From Europe' dancing 'in the politest manner' 'at the new Assembly-House.' Hackett, 'has taught Dancing in many of the Principal Towns in England, Ireland and America. He will only be in town on Thursdays and Fridays, the remainder of his Time taken up at Newbury, etc. [1774] 'at the Assembly House' also keeps school at Newburyport and Haverhill."

1772. "William S. Morgan, Musico Theorico 'Harpsichord, Violin etc., etc.' 'He is to be spoke with at Mr. Stavers.' [1773] 'Opened his Academy for Musick and Dancing at the Assembly House.'"

1773. "St. George de Viart, Minuets, French Jiggs, Horn-Pipes, Rigadoons, and English Country Dances of all kinds. 'Academy at his Lodgings in a House belonging to the Hon. Daniel Warner, Esq.; near the long wharf.' Teaches the French language 'in the easiest manner . . . and several other Arts and Sciences.' [1774] Dancing, Fencing and the French language, 'at the Assembly-Room.' Monsieur De Viart 'has resided for three years last at Salem and taught-there⋅ at Marblehead and Glocester.' [1775] 'He shall endeavour to follow exactly the Rule of Horace concerning the Education of Youth. Maxima debetur pueris reverentia.'"

1773. "William Crosbey, Music, Theorical [*sic*] Rudimental and Practical. 'At Capt. Tilton's in King Street.' Crosbey proposes teaching Psalmody in its various Branches, and has for Authors Handel, Purcell, Green, Knapp, and Williams &. from which he collects the best Tunes, Hymns and Athems: he has likewise a choice Collection of Canons, Fuges, Chorus's, an excellent Oratorio set by the celebrated Bull,[8] an Ode on Friendship, and several Manuscript Pieces by the famous Mr. Lyon.[9] He likewise . . . teaches all sorts of Dramatic Music, such as Songs, Airs, Solos, Duett's, Dialogues etc. And expects from London by the First Opportunity, a choice Collection of

Vocal Music, and set by the celebrated Arne, Boyce and Handel consisting of the newest and best Songs, as they are now sung at the Mary-Bone, Vaux-Hall and Covent Gardens.' He proposes to teach the 'Young Gentlemen of the Town who are disposed to join together in a singing society and learn Psalmody. . . . He sits for and teaches the scale of the Violin, Flute, Harpsichord and Organ.' His 'School of Music' will open at the Assembly-Room."

1781. "Benjamin Dearborn,[10] Evening School 'Rules of Vocal Music (as far as may be learned without singing)' also exercises in 'Grammar, Reading, Writing, Spelling and Arithmetic.' At his house 'in pav'd Street.' His 'Writing and Singing-Schools which have been kept thro' the Summer, will be continu'd during the Winter.' [1783] Singing-School; 'at his house.' [1785] Singing-School. [1791] 'Portsmouth Academy. Is now open for the reception of Boarders and Scholars for instruction in Spelling, Reading, Writing, Arithmetic, Accounts, English Grammar, Geography, Chronology, History Composition, Embroidery, plain Needle-Work, Vocal Music, Instrumental Music, Dancing, Drawing, French Language, etc.' "

1785. "Francis Drew of 'Newmarket, Newfields . . . will teach Drummers and Fifers . . . in the easiest and best manner.' "

1785. John White, Dancing-Master; 'Minuet dancing etc.' will open at the Assembly-Room.' [1786] 'Proposes . . . to open every Monday Evening, for the ensuing season, a Ball at the Assembly-Room.' "

1785. Winthrop Bennet, Singing School, 'at his house near the Rope Walks.' [1789] 'At Mr. Davenport's House in this Town.' [1791] 'At the House of Capt. M'Hard . . . His Evening-School is continued as usual.' 'At the house of Mrs. Gregory, opposite the dwelling house of Dr. John Jackson.' [1793] Singing School 'at Captain Smith's House, in Washington-Street, opposite Dr. Hall Jackson's.' "

1788. "Horatio Garnet, from Europe. Lodges with Mr. Samuel Place. Violin, Violincello, Guittar, Germ. Flute, Clarionet & Hautboy, likewise the Harpsichord, Spinnet etc. 'Music copied in the most accurate manner.—Also, Key'd Instruments

tuned on the shortest Notice.' [1789] Apply to him at Greenleaf's Inn. [Garnet remained in Portsmouth until 1792 but he
evidently did no further advertising.]"

1788. "Mr. Samuel H. Flagg,[11] Dancing Master, Returns his
'greatful acknowledgements' for the 'encouragement' he has
received since his residence here. Intends 'opening an Evening
School' the ensuing season and to hold 'a Scholar's Ball on
Thursday the 6th. . . . Particular care will be taken to have
good music.' [1789] 'Will teach the mode of the English
Minuets, Cotillions, and the newest Contra-Dances . . . Harpsichord, and Spinnet.' Apply to him at Capt. Robert Furniss's.'"

1789. "John Reed, Singing School 'at the House of Mr.
Nathaniel Shannon.' [1791] 'At the house lately occupied by
Mr. J. Marshall in Pleasant Street near Capt. John Pickering's
Mills.' [1792] 'In the house lately occupied by Capt. S. Nichols,
near the fourth Meeting-house.' [1793] 'At the house of Capt.
Samuel Storer opposite Mr. Samuel Hill's store.'"

1792. "Mr. Civil, July, will open a dancing school at the
Assembly-room; also teaches the French language. 'Miniature
Painting-Done in the most elegant manner at Seven Dollars
each." November, the dancing school was moved to the 'late
Portsmouth Academy.' [1792] Dancing-School will be held at
the Assembly-Room; French and Drawing at the Bow-Street
theatre."

1792. "School for females, Mrs. Spillard. 'A music, drawing
and writing master, will also attend.'"

1793. "Mr. Allen, Dancing-School at Capt. Whidden's Assembly Room."

1793. "John L. Berkenhead, Lately from Europe, teaches the
Organ, Harpsichord, Piano-Forte, and other keyed instruments,
and tunes and repairs them. Apply to him 'at his lodgings, at
Mr. John Davenport's near Mr. William Sheafe's store.' [1795]
No address given."

1794. "Mr. Duport,[12] Dancing Master from Paris and at the
Southward. 'A Subscription Paper is lodged at Capt. Whidden's
Assembly Room.' In a later advertisement Duport announced
that 'Forty Scholars are expected.'"

1794. "Mr. St. Amand, opened dancing school at Assembly-House."

1794. "Alexander Outin,[13] teaches dancing, violin and French language. Inquire of the Printer, or of Anthony Chapouil."

1795. "Francis Maurice,[14] 'Master of the French Language, Dancing and Music at Medford Academy, and Harvard University.' Leave names 'at Mr. Peirce's bookstore in Court-Street.' [1796] 'The subscription paper is lodged at Mr. Melcher's Printing-Office.' [1797] 'If encouragement offers,' will teach piano-forte and violin. Apply to Mr. Maurice, 'at Mr. Jotham Rindge's foot of Daniel Street.' [1799] Professor of the French Language, Music, Dancing and Fencing. 'Proposes to teach those beautiful and useful arts—.' Apply to him 'at the Hotel.' "

1795. "Isaac Lane,[15] Music 'as it is sung in congregations' or for 'own private amusement.' At Mr. Whidden's large hall 'Where there may be accomodations for two hundred scholars.' "

1795. "Joseph Akerman, Jr. and Job Harris, Singing School at Mr. Diman's Hall. Instruction in the 'sacred employment.' [1797] Apply to the Clergymen in town, who hold subscription papers."

1796. "Mr. Johnson, the 'science and practice of Instrumental Music' and the 'more useful accomplishment of vocal harmony.' At Mr. Davenport's. Apply to him 'at his lodging at the Ark.' "

Ichabod Johnson was a fifer in the Revolutionary Army and "was rather celebrated as a teacher of vocal and instrumental music." He did not have much of a voice, but he did possess a "wonderful faculty" for stimulating the interest of the young and old. Thus with the assistance of his violin, his "forced voice" and the voluntary services of old singers, "he scarcely ever failed in advancing a school rapidly." The music that Johnson taught "was not of the most inferior kind." He also achieved success in the teaching of wind and stringed instruments "in many towns in New England," and became "celebrated" as a teacher and conductor of bands of martial music.[16]

In 1805 or 1806 Johnson kept "large" singing school in New Ipswich, New Hampshire, where he introduced a "lighter kind of music." He was "popular" and for the most part "gave impulse" to music generally "when he was sober" though at times he rather "detracted from the devotional spirit."

Johnson's school was the first that was granted a "permanent station in the gallery, as a choir." [17] A military band founded in the town in 1804 or 1805, "principally by the exertions" of Nathaniel D. Gould, a resident and also author of *History of Church Music in America*, was next instructed by Ichabod Johnson, "with the addition of other performers, and was really well drilled and performed wonderously." [18]

In 1795 he was listed in the catalogue of Phillip's Academy in Andover, Massachusetts, thus: "Ichabod Johnson Instructor in Music 1795 Son of Jonathan Johnson and Sarah Wilson; born Woburn (now Burlington) [Massachusetts], Sept. 6, 1764; had been fifer in the Revolutionary army, died Quincy, Aug. 5, 1807. On his tombstone at Quincy: 'Master Ichabod Johnson, celebrated teacher of Musick.' " [19]

1797. "Messrs Renard and Barbot, Country-Dances, Cotillions, Minuet, Allemand, and Horn Pipe. Apply 'to the printer hereof, who has lodged with him a subscription paper.' [1798] Dancing-School at the Assembly-House."

1798. "J. H. Smith, Organist and Professor of Music, Piano-Forte, Harpsichord, Spinnet, Singing, the Violin, Tenor, Bass Viol, and Flute. Also 'tunes instruments.' Apply 'at Mr. Melchers printing office or at Capt. Smith's, Water Street near the hotel.' "

This directory indicates the presence in New Hampshire from 1765 to 1800 of a number of itinerant musicians who taught music. Some were English, some French, and some were native born. Apart from vocal music (private and group), lessons were available on a variety of string instruments (the guitar included), and on woodwind, brass, percussion, and keyboard instruments. Some theory was taught. Dancing was cultivated as a social grace.

The teachers evidently observed no sharp distinction between instruction in religious and in secular music, although some taught vocal music exclusively, while others restricted themselves to the instrumental field. As for the dancing masters, most taught the violin and the harpsichord as well. Instruction was offered both for the young and the old. Apparently few made a successful living solely from teaching music; a few taught other subjects and most were engaged in a variety of employments outside the area of music and teaching. The training and background of the teachers ranged all the way from the self-taught Yankee psalm tune peddler to the European conservatory-trained musician. The latter, aware of his advantage, often advertised the superiority of his training. It would be futile at this late date to inquire into the validity of his credentials. We tend to look askance at the formalities of eighteenth-century self-appreciation, and to regard the self-supplied superlatives in the advertisements of music teachers much as we now read real estate notices in the daily newspapers. With all due regard to the nature of advertising, however, the formalities of the age, and the obvious snobbishness with which the European-trained musician called attention to his foreign refinements, there is no reason not to suppose that a few, at least, were musicians of considerable skill.

The fees levied by the teachers present an interesting picture of the economics of the period and the professional pride or personal needs of the individual instructors. To evaluate these charges is futile, inasmuch as the monetary medium of exchange from 1765 when the first advertisement appears) to 1800 was in a state of perpetual flux and resists any attempt at comparison.

Prior to the Confederation in 1778 as many systems of money existed as there were distinct colonies. Since most of the inhabitants were of British descent and trading was carried on mainly with the mother country, the monetary units were in some measure similar. Coins in use in New Hampshire were generally computed in pounds, shillings, and pence, but in actual transactions other currencies, chiefly the Spanish dollar and its subdivisions, constituted the medium of exchange. Beside the British pieces, other gold coins in use were the French guinea and pistole, the Portugese moidore and johannes or "joe," and the Spanish doubloon and pistole.

In an effort to find an equivalence between the money of "account" and that of "exchange," the practice of reckoning the dollar at so many shillings obtained. In New Hampshire the dollar was divided into six shillings and a shillling included twelve pence.

The fees for music instruction were generally stated in shillings and pence or dollars in the advertisements. Occasionally, however, the pound, the pistole, and even the guinea constituted the medium of exchange. To ascertain the relationship, for instance, between the daily compensation of a carpenter and the remuneration of a music teacher who taught by the quarter, by the month (both of which customarily implied groups), or by the lesson, we have discovered that there exist variables *ad infinitum* which render the task impossible.[20]

It is, nevertheless, possible to convey an approximate idea of the expense for instruction. Over a period of thirty-five years, there appears to be very little consistency; the terms varied according to each teacher. The examination of a few advertisements will serve to illustrate the point.

John Williams, for instance, notified the public in 1765 that he would teach "psalmody" on Thursday and Saturday afternoons at "six pounds per quarter," while Peter Curtis, two years later (1767) advertised lessons in dancing three times a week at four dollars per quarter and lessons on the violin "at a certain price." When William S. Morgan began his teaching activities in Portsmouth during the same period, he distinguished between the rate of instruction in "Musick" and that of instruction in dancing. On the basis of two meetings each week, the former cost "a pistole [21] a month," while the latter cost "Four Dollars the Quarter."

From the *Gazette* of August 27, 1773, we quote the rates fixed by William Crosbey: "Mr. Crosbey—To morrow opens his School of Music at the Assembly Room, there to continue to teach by the Month, or Quarter, on Mondays, Thursdays and Saturdays, 3 Hours each day, beginning at 3 o'clock P.M. Those who attend accordingly will be instructed at 3 Dollars per Quarter. Those who take Lessons once a Day are waited on at their own Lodging, after the Rate of 3 Dollars the Month. One third of the Money for each Condition to be paid at Entrance."

Mr. Crosbey also stipulated that "those whose affairs detain them in the day time" could receive instruction for an hour and a half on the evenings of Monday and Thursday "at one Dollar per Quarter."

Monsieur St. George de Viart, "Professor of the polite Arts," who seems to have been in Portsmouth during the years of 1773-1775, taught dancing, fencing, and the French language. He charged four dollars per quarter for three instruction periods per week, Mondays, Thursdays, and Saturdays, "from Two to Six o'clock P.M."

Although Benjamin Dearborn first advertised his intention to teach vocal music in 1781, we have no inkling of his instruction rates until 1785 when he announced the opening of a singing school. It was to be kept on Tuesdays and Fridays "from 7 to 9 o'clock, P.M." the tuition being eight shillings per quarter.

Horatio Garnet, a musician by trade, who appeared in Portsmouth in 1788 as a teacher of the "violin, Violincello, Guittar, Germ. Flute, Clarionet & Hautboy, likewise the Harpsichord, Spinnet, etc.," did not advertise his lesson rates. He simply announced that he would teach "any or all the above mentioned instruments, on the most moderate terms.' It is entirely conceivable that Garnet asked for and received a slightly higher fee than any of his competitors; he was undeniably the finest musician in Portsmouth during his four years of residence.

In 1788, Mr. Flagg, who taught dancing and gave lessons on the harpsichord and spinnet "at a very low rate," announced that "wood and candles" were acceptable instead of money. John Reed opened a singing school in the town in 1789 and advertised that he was "ready to receive Scholars at Five Shillings per quarter... the school will be attended two evenings every week, from six to nine o'clock." Two years later, he raised his price to six shillings per quarter, but retained the same number of hours for instruction.

Mr. Winthrop Bennett, whose first intentions of teaching the "pleasing art" of singing appeared in the October 21, 1785, *Gazette*, announced in 1791 that "those who have made any proficiency in singing, will by taught two evenings each week, by themselves, at 6 s [shillings] per Quarter; those who have not received any instruction before, will be taught likewise by themselves, two evenings each week at 7 s per Quarter.' Mr. Bennett requested that one half of the fee be paid at entrance, the remainder at the expiration of the quarter. The advance deposit expected by most of the teachers gives evidence of their seriousness of purpose. It also provided some pecuniary guarantee.

John Latham Berkenhead, like Garnet before him, did not reveal fees in his advertisements, but simply stated in the November 23, 1795, *Oracle* that lessons on the "Organ Harpsichord Piano-Forte, and other keyed instruments" would be given on the "most reasonable terms." The absence of specific charges in the press leads one to believe that there may have existed some relationship between a teacher's competence and the necessity for publishing his fees. It is plausible that those teachers who resorted to the greatest amount of advertising were the ones most in need of pupils, while then, as now, a number of the better instructors carried on a lively practice without recourse to the newspapers.[22]

During the year 1795 Isaac Lane proposed the opening of a "School for Sacred Vocal Music" which would be "kept 12 weeks; every other evening from half past five, to eight o'clock." His terms were "6 shillings a scholar." The school was at the Assembly-Room where there were "accommodations for two hundred scholars." Mr. Lane requested that "as many as conveniently can" attend on the first evening "(if not, on either of the two succeeding evenings)" as he wished to determine whether there was any prospect of having a school "so as to make it an object for him to tarry ... otherwise he must be

under the painful necessity of leaving this town immediately."
Mr. Lane opened his school several days later. We do not know
how many pupils he enrolled, but it was probably considerably
less than two hundred!

Francis Maurice, who advertised himself as a master of the
French Language, Dancing, and Music at Medford Academy
and Harvard University, taught the "very polite accomplishment of dancing," the violin and the pianoforte in Portsmouth
during the last five years of the century. He also held school in
the towns of Exeter, Concord, and Hopkinton. His terms for
dancing lessons, as they in the March 18, 1797 *Gazette*, read:

"1st. For the first quarter six dollars, and for the second, and
of those that have before attended his school one guinea [23]
each per quarter.

"2nd. Two dollars of which to be paid at entrance.

"3rd. The school to commence on the first Saturday of April
next, at the Assembly-Room, at three o'clock in the afternoon,
and to be continued Thursdays and Saturdays, from three
o'clock to sunset."

In the advertisement, the mention of lessons on the piano-
forte was directed to the ladies: "Mr. Maurice informs the
Ladies that he intends, if encouragement offers, to open a
Music-School, will teach them the Fortpienno at their houses,
or at his Music-School where he will furnish those who wish
with a Fortepienno to learn on; the school will be kept from six
to twelve o'clock in the morning, two days in each week. . . .
He informs those young gentlemen who wish to be instructed
on the violin, that he will if encouragement offers, teach them
two evenings in each week at his Music-School, which will be
open as soon as twelve scholars apply."

In 1798 J. H. Smith, Organist and Professor of Music, announced his object to teach the pianoforte, harpsichord,
spinnet, singing, the violin, tenor, bass violin, and flute in
Portsmouth. The readers of the *Gazette* were told that when
parents sent their daughters to boarding schools in Boston or
New York, "they pay 4 dollars entrance, and 4 shillings a
lesson," but Smith's terms, however, were considerably less:

"two dollars entrance, and 2s6 a lesson." The professor also tuned instruments for two dollars.

Judicious use of advertising, in an attempt to capture the fancy of the prospective client, was part of the teacher's stock-in-trade. His appeal to vanity, his patronizing approach and his "humble solicitations," although undeniably directed toward earning a livelihood, also produced worthwhile results in terms of an awakening music consciousness. Quite often, however, the immediate appeal was not so much to the value of music for itself, but as an amenity which would help one cut a more graceful figure in the social world. A music teacher like Peter Curtis, for example, assured parents that his teaching was done "in the most polite Manner" and that he would instil into the minds of their children "the principles of Good Manners and Genteel Deportment." A dancing master was, perhaps, prone to make even more of this point than just a music teacher. Monsieur de Viart's advertisement,[24] for example, emphasizes the importance of dancing as a vehicle for acquiring the proper social graces. It is his claim that "It is not everyone who pretends to teach this delicate Art, who will take the Pains to instruct their Scholars in those Rules of Decorum and Politeness which are absolutely necessary to be known before young Persons can step abroad into the World with Elegance and Ease.—And it often happens that Scholars, through the Ignorance of their Masters, are guilty of great Rudeness and commit gross Blunders on their first going into Company."

The "Charms, Beauties and Advantages of Music are so universally known, that it is quite unnecessary to say any Thing for recommending it," asserted William Crosbey in the *Gazette* for August 20, 1773. "But it is observed . . . that it looses most of its Beauties when not performed under the proper Restrictions of Rule and Judgement." The study of music in particular, "is rendered much more engaging, and the Practice vastly more pleasing, when regulated by Tune, Time and Concord."

Benjamin Dearborn proposed a new system of teaching vocal

music "entirely by Letters" which he had found by experience to be "much more expeditious than that heretofore used" and so easy as to scarcely "perplex the youngest child who can read." Horatio Garnet, on the other hand, addressed himself to those who were desirous of acquiring a "practical knowledge in the most delightful science" of music through the study of instruments.

To teach such music "as it is sung in congregations" was Isaac Lane's design. He was eager to instruct not only those who joined the choirs in public worship but others who wished to cultivate music for their own private amusement. Neither was youth's musical education neglected during the period, for, according to Lane, those who favored him with the attendance and care of their children, "may depend that every suitable attention will be paid them by their humble servant."

Mr. Johnson, in 1796, having already opened a school for the instruction of gentlemen in the "science and practice" of instrumental music, sought further patronage in Portsmouth by proposing the opening of another school for the "initiation of the youth of both sexes in the still more useful accomplishment of vocal harmony."

In August of 1774 an editorial "On Dancing. . . . On Music" appeared, curiously enough, on the front page of the *Gazette*, a spot commonly reserved for the more important political events of the day. Its location is the more remarkable when it is remembered that at this time the rebellious attitude of the people, caused mainly by the unfair stamp tax, was about to precipitate the Revolutionary War. The author of the editorial, whose name is not disclosed, extols the virtues of these arts, notes their place in the sacred and secular circumstances of society, and points out the advantages in their study. The editorial deals with dancing as a religious expression, as an "innocent Mirth," and as a polite accomplishment. Regarding music, its therapeutic values, its biblical origins, etymology, and its place in divine worship are evaluated. The entire document follows:

"On Dancing. Dancing is the Art of making regular Steps,

and keeping the Body in an agreeable Position according to
the Sound of Music, etc. civilized, on an Occasion of a happy
Deliverance from Slaughter, the more painful Idea of Servitude:
the Daughters of Liberty came forth out of the Cities of Israel
Singing and Dancing, to meet King Saul, with Tabrets, with
Joy and with Instruments of Music: etc. vide 1st Samuel XVIII
Chap., 6v Judges XXI Chap. 21 verse.

"And as it is an innocent Mirth in itself, it was once attempted
by a favourite Prince of Israel, and is a lively Expression of
Innocence and Joy; vide VI. Chap. 2. Samuel, 14 verse.

"Country Dances are very simple and agreeable and possess
the Mind of Youth with pleasing and sprightly Ideas. The
advantage of Dancing add to every Motion of the Body a
certain attractive Grace which never can be sufficiently admir'd
gives a free and open Air in the Gait; a happy Address in
Company and adds the finishing Embellishments in the sexes,
to every species of polite Education.

"On Musick. Musick is the Science which teaches to make
some Sounds agreeable to the Ear, and rules the Harmony: it
refreshes agreeably the Mind, and gives it a new Strength, so
that one can apply with more Satisfaction to his Labours; It
serves also to soften the troubles of the Human Mind, particularly those troubles that proceed from Melancoly. See an
example of it in Saul, 1st. Sam. XVI. Chap. 23 ver. 'And it came
to pass when the evil Spirit from God was upon Saul, that
David took an Harp and played with his Hand: So Saul was
refreshed and was well, and the evil Spirit departed from him.'

"The first invention of Musick was attributed to Appolo;
some attribute it to Mercury, but this seems to be very un-
certain, what appears more probable is that the holy Scripture
learns us that Jubal; Son of Lemech was Inventor of the Violin
and Organ: vide Gen. IV Chap. 21 Verse.

"Its Etymology is derived from the Muses, which the Pagans
looked upon as the Goddesses of Sciences; they knew of them,
it has receiv'd its perfection from the Hebrews, but now it is
practiced with more Eclat & Invention; in fine, Musick has
been universally esteem'd by all Nations, principally that,

which is made use of in the Divine Service, because it excites us to Virtue, and animates our Zeal and Devotion: Tho' imperfect, yet it gives us a delightful Idea of those happy Concerts that are form'd in Heaven."

Another aspect of the advertisements deals with the recommendations offered by the itinerant music teacher with respect to his special talents, ambitions, and qualifications for such employment. Emphasis was placed on background, training, and experience. In other words, how did he refer to himself in the newspaper? John White, for example, who taught "Minuet Dancing and a variety of other Dances etc. in the genteelest Manner," notified the public through the April 29, 1785, *Gazette* that "If a knowledge of the Art, after the most approved French Taste, is a recommendation, he flatters himself he shall give general satisfaction."

As was often the case, John L. Berkenhead called attention to his training, which from a very early period had been received "under the most accomplished masters and performers of Music in Great-Britain, particularly the great Doctor Wainwright, and the celebrated Bamgarton, of London." His announcement also noted that he "punctually attends the commands of those who are pleased to honor him," and he "flatters himself that he possesses Abilities, Politeness and Patience, which are so necesssary for a good Teacher."

Mr. Isaac Lane advertised in Portsmouth that he "is willing, besides producing credentials both as to moral character, and with regard to his abilities as a Musician, to submit to a strict examination as to his theoretical knowledge, from any person in this town: as to his skill as a performer, or his abilities as a teacher, time will determine, should he be so fortunate as to meet with the confidence of the people of this place."

Mr. Duport, dancing-master and composer originally from Paris and more recently from Charleston, South Carolina,[25] appeared in Portsmouth in 1794 and proposed giving private tuition in the "polite accomplishment" of dancing. According to the March 8, 1794, *Gazette*, Duport "engages in three months to perfect those . . . who shall please to honor him with their attendance. Several of the first Families at the Southward, he has perfected in this accomplishment . . . from whom he has letters of Recommendation."

In 1791 John Reed opened a singing school for children and an evening school for "young people of both sexes." The Portsmouth public was informed that "As he is lame, and can do no other business to obtain a livelihood for himself and family he hopes the hearts of all feeling parents will expand to commiserate his present situation, and thereby patronize his assiduous undertaking."

In a later advertisement Mr. Reed appealed to the compassionate: "He flatters himself, the humane and benevolent, will be excited to commisserate his situation, as he can do little else for a livelihood—so shall the blessing of the indigent come upon them, and the soul ready to perish to pray for their prosperity."

Mr. Johnson, advertising in the May 12, 1796, *Oracle*, let it be known that "his ability and long experience" as a teacher of instrumental and vocal music, will be "sufficiently vouched" for by persons acquainted with his work. "All the respectable musical characters in town will attest to his abilities . . . and he hopes to merit the patronage of the public by his assiduity.'"

Finally, J. H. Smith announced in the *Gazette* for November 21, 1798, that he had instructed in the "first families and young ladies' boarding schools in the United States and Europe" and that he "will punctually attend to any line or message left at Mr. Melchers."

In summary, it would seem that music instruction on a modest scale existed in New Hampshire during the seventeenth and early eighteenth century. An obvious expansion of the field, in variety of instruction offered, in numbers of instructors, and in motivations to study, took place during the latter half of the eighteenth century. Instrumental music began to receive increasing attention, and a point was reached where instrumental instruction was more widely featured in advertisements than the teaching of voice. Interestingly enough (and this may provide much of the explanation), instruction was no longer exclusively or even primarily recommended as necessary for improving the condition of church music, but more often than not, the stress was upon music as a social grace, an essential accomplishment in a person of culture. In particular, the European-trained music teacher was apt to stress this point, and it would appear that the market was already there for an appeal of this sort. Related to this development is the gradual disappearance of the itinerant music teacher offering instruction either at the pupil's home or in temporary rented quarters. More regular instruction, and perhaps more disciplined instruction, became the norm, much of it still private, but much of it also offered in schools of music.

x. Music in the Academies

FOLLOWING the Revolutionary War, the academy movement came into being in American education. Its ideals embodied the democratic concept of public education—that is, education for all youth. Heretofore, in the so-called Latin schools, all instruction was given in Latin. The academies, on the other hand, adopted English as the medium of learning, although Latin and Greek were still to be studied.[1]

With the rise of the academies in New Hampshire, prior to 1800, music was given a place in the curriculum, not as a polite art but as a vital branch of general education. When Phillips Exeter Academy, the first of its kind in the state, was established in 1781, music was mentioned in its Act of Incorporation: "for the education of Youth in the English, Latin and Greek Languages; in Writing, Arithmetic, Musick & the Art of Speaking; Practical Geometry, Logic, and Geography."[2]

At the dedication of the new building for the use of the Academy, the May 10, 1783, *Gazette* reported that the ceremony opened and closed with singing. The Reverend Bentley, who visited there in September 1801, wrote in his diary that "the young Masters were in the same house at a Dancing School under Mr. Turner of the Boston family so well known in that employment."[3]

Five other academies, New Ipswich founded in 1789, Atkinson and Charlestown in 1791, Haverhill in 1794, and Salisbury in 1795, likewise included music in their Acts of Incorporation. Three others, Chesterfield, established in 1790,

Amherst (Aurean Academy) in 1791, and Gilmanton in 1794, do not mention music specifically in their Acts of Incorporation,[4] but from the data at hand it may be safely said that some attention was given to music. For instance, a "public exhibition" presented by the students of the Aurean Academy of Amherst is notable for the six "pieces of music performed by voices and instruments," according to the May 30, 1792, *Spy*.

Additional insight into the musical activities of the academies prior to 1800 may be gained by considering in some detail the history of Atkinson Academy of Atkinson, New Hampshire. This coeducational institution was founded in 1787 and finally incorporated in 1791 for the purpose of "promoting piety and virtue and for the instruction of youth in the english, latin and greek languages in writing, arithmetic, music and the art of speaking: in geography, logic and geometry as opportunity may permit and the trustees hereinafter provided shall direct." [5]

Singing, says Mrs. Harriet Marr, was popular at Atkinson.[6] The Reverend Stephen Peabody, one of the founders of the Academy and a man whose musical powers were deemed "extraordinary," makes frequent references to singing in his diary. For instance, "The scholars were in here to sing," or "Our young craft went to-night to a singing meeting." Concerning a local performance, he records that "the music was pretty good, there were some terrible flats in it." [7]

Dancing classes, outside of school hours, were held for the academy pupils.[8] In 1792, the diary tells of a dance at James Dow's. The cost of dancing instruction at that time was eleven shillings, about two dollars. In 1801, a ball was held at Bassetts. The parson must have been disturbed with his student boarders, for he writes, "They staid like fools as usual almost all night. They were noisy when they came home. I called to them and they were stiller." [9] Dancing fees were increased to three dollars a term in 1804 and four dollars a term in 1809.

The exhibitions, which were a regular part of academy activities, inevitably involved vocal and instrumental music. It is safe to conclude that this music was closely allied to academy instruction.

During the first year of its existence (1787) Atkinson Academy staged an exhibition at the meeting house. The performance included "a number of diverting scenes with singing interspersed," and "the scene was closed with the 'Mock Doctor' and singing." [10] In 1793 the pupils "erected a stage in the meeting house" in preparation for another exhibition. "The musick," noted Parson Peabody, "which they had was good." [11] With respect to an exhibition held at the Academy on August 15, 1803, Peabody wrote that the "Musicians performed very well." In the evening following the entertainment "they had a ball in the academy." [12]

The leader of the group who established Atkinson Academy was Stephen Peabody (1740-1819), a native of Andover, Massachusetts. He was twenty-nine at the time of his graduation from Harvard (1769), where he had studied divinity. He became the first minister of the Congregational Church in Atkinson, and except for a short tour of duty as a chaplain during the Revolution, he spent his entire life as a clergyman there. He maintained a lively interest in the affairs of the community and frequently distinguished himself in local political matters. He was also a keen observer of national and foreign developments.[13] His efforts for the welfare of the Academy were evident. He was secretary and treasurer of the Board of Trustees and even with his own impecunious circumstances tried to assume "a large part of the debt of the institution." [14] When the academy opened many students lived at the parsonage.

"Parson Peabody," as he was affectionately known, appears to have possessed considerable skill as a musician. Although we lack information regarding his musical education, we know that he played the violin and bass viol. He was a stanch member of the church choir and loved to sing when at work. In his diary the entry "went to singing meeting" occurs repeatedly. Almost annually Peabody attended Commencement at Harvard and, on one of these occasions, he was asked by the president to "lead in singing." [15]

Samuel Gilman, a former pupil at Atkinson by virtue of the Parson's munificence, paid tribute to Peabody's musical activities in his volume of reminiscences: "His musical powers and habits were extraordinary, and he almost revelled through life in an atmosphere of sweet sounds of his own creating. On rainy days, when unlikely to be disturbed by captious or narrow-minded visitors, he would take out his golden-toned violin from a little closet, and draw from its strings the richest and most bewitching notes, a sweet and serene half-smile all the time playing over his lip, and cheek, and eye. His voice was of vast compass, and exquisitely flexible. He was at home in every part in music. When there was no choir in the meeting-house he led the singing himself; and when there was one, he supplied the deficient parts, rolling out a mellow and deep-toned bass, or warbling with his treble or counter over the whole concert, like an animated mocking-bird. He sang on week-days at his work, and sometimes talked aloud to himself most agreeably. He would sing on his rides about the town, or when travelling in his chaise, alone or accompanied, by night or by day; and all the solitudes and echoes of that region have many a time rung with his melodious voice. He was most fond of sacred music, but did not disdain a scrap now and then of secular. He would sing you, in perfect taste, with graceful gesture and a happy look, either sitting or standing, various extracts from the delightful old anthems of Arne or Purcell, or from the oratorios of Handel. Coming home from public worship, if a favorite tune had just been sung there, he would repeat it over and over as he entered the house stopping you in a companionable way, looking you smilingly in the face, and asking if it was not beautiful. He would, except on Sunday morning, awaken the whole household of sleepers at sunrise, or as soon as he made the fires, by singing up and down stairs, 'The bright, rosy morning peeps over the hills,' 'The hounds are all out,' or some other hunting-song equally stirring.—On some warm summer afternoon, when all the windows of the house were open, and one of his young boarders, far up in the garret at his studies, should happen, for variety's sake, to burst out in some cherished tune or strain, for instance, as old St. Anne's, his venerable friend, in the lower story below, awakening from his transitory nap, would fall in with his mellifluous bass, and so would they sing for a long time to-gether, until, looking out of their respective windows, they would smile upon each other, as who should say,—Were there ever two better friends than we." [16]

It is reasonable to assume that Parson Peabody's intense interest in and fondness for music were potent factors in the progress and development of this subject at the Academy.

Music instruction, as we have seen, became a regular part of the academy curriculum in New Hampshire in 1781. Music was cultivated as a means of spiritual expression and as a diversion. Both vocal and instrumental music received attention as well as the ever popular art of dancing.

xi. John Hubbard

JOHN HUBBARD (1759-1810), now remembered in the annals of American psalmody for his frequently quoted *Essay on Music* [1] in which he leveled a blast against the banalities of current church music, was during his lifetime a farmer, a minister, a teacher of various subjects (including music), a preceptor (principal), a probate judge, an apothecary, a postmaster, town treasurer, and professor of mathematics and natural philosophy at Dartmouth College. His musical activities included teaching, conducting, composing, lecturing, and playing the violincello.

From Gould we learn that Hubbard was "a man of superior talent, knowledge and taste, in the science of music." During his lifetime he had at his disposal "more means for acquiring a musical education than any other man in America," [2] in the form of English publications and treatises on music, which at one time in the library of the Handel Society at Dartmouth College. Unfortunately, since the decline of the society, the whole has vanished; nobody seems to know how. [3] He spent most of his productive life in the State of New Hampshire.

Hubbard, descended from George Hubbard of Guilford, Connecticut, and son of John and Mary (Ball) Hubbard of Townsend, Massachusetts, was born (a posthumous child) in Townsend on August 8, 1759. Little is known of his early life except that most of the time was employed in the labors of agriculture. At the age of twenty-one, he began his formal studies and the next year entered Dartmouth College. There Hubbard gave indications of his approaching eminence. Because of a tenacious memory, his progress in the languages was remarkably rapid. He was charmed with the classic beauty of the Greek and Roman authors, and his memory was stored with numerous favorite passages. Following his graduation from Dartmouth in 1785, his love of knowledge, his delight in religious inquiries, and his devout regard for the best interests of man quite naturally led him to the study and practice of theology.[4] A vocal weakness, however, ultimately forced him to abandon any idea of a ministerial career.

In 1787 Hubbard became a teacher in the town of New Ipswich, New Hampshire, and upon the incorporation of New Ipswich Academy was chosen its first preceptor at a yearly salary of sixty pounds. Under his capable guidance the Academy achieved distinction and was held in high esteem by the public. He was not only an excellent instructor but an exemplary Christian and public-spirited citizen. The town of New Ipswich was "much indebted" to him for raising musical standards there: "No individual . . . had so great an influence in forming the taste for classical music, and in elevating the style of performance as Mr. Hubbard, who was about this time teacher of the grammar school and subsequently preceptor of the Academy. He had made music a study, and was quite in advance of his age." [5]

About five years after his passing New Ipswich established the Hubbard Society (1815) in his honor. Its membership included persons of "cultivated taste" from many of the neighboring towns, whose object was to meet for the performance of anthems, and to select and publish, as well as perform, psalmody of higher style than was to be found in any American music books then in use.[6] For several years the organization was conducted by Nathaniel Gould, author of *Church Music in America,* and was considered an excellent society. Its performances were in advance of the day and, with the exception of the firmly established Handel and Haydn Society of Boston, "no other musical society in the country surpassed it." [7]

During his last year at New Ipswich, Hubbard was elected to fill the post of town clerk. In 1796 he moved to Walpole, where he continued to teach for a while. Two years later (1798) he was appointed Judge of Probate for Cheshire County and the following year became postmaster in Walpole. During most of his residence there Hubbard was also an apothecary. In this respect he was successful in developing a vegetable pill which in female complaints "operates like a charm," in consumptive complaints "is the best remedy yet known," while "fainting, indigestion, and hypochondriac affections, vapours, or lowness of spirits, are carried off by the use of a single box." [8] Regarding this recently compounded "atonic" pill the *Farmer's Museum* had this to say: "The Vegetable Pill deserves credit as an American invention, and may be used by even timid patients, as an efficacious remedy. We are not in the habit of writing quack advertisements, and have little disposition to circulate a mountebank's bill. It is our constant duty to notice useful discoveries, to promote the extension of science, and to give the Genius of our country its merited praise." [9]

The 1799 Fourth of July observance in Walpole included "an excellent and chaste oration of the historical class" from the pen of John Hubbard, Esquire, which was delivered by the Reverend Thomas Fessenden, according to the *Farmer's Museum*,[10] and the day began with a procession of soldiers and citizens led by an "excellent band." At intervals several favorite marches were played, and the "pleasing sorcery of music produced all its enchantment on the mind." An ode composed by "certain of our own poets" was performed to the well-known tune of "Hail Columbia" to which was added, "When first the sun o'er ocean glow'd" a popular patriotic song by Mr. Thomas Paine.

In the evening a "large and brilliant party" danced away the merry hours at the inn of Mr. S. Grant. "The language of each dancer was that of Comus," said the *Farmer's Museum*, borrowing from John Milton:

> Ere the tell tale sun descry
> Our conceal'd solemnity,
> Come, knit hands and beat the ground
> In a light fantastic round.

While at Walpole, Hubbard presented the "comic opera" of

Lionel and Clarissa and the "musical entertainment" *Cymon*. This is significant because it shows that he was apparently interested in secular as well as religious music. According to Nathan Appleton, a former student at New Ipswich Academy, Hubbard "gave exhibitions in very superior style." [11]

In the year of 1802, after finding the several political posts "not congenial with his love of study and his delight in the instruction of youth," [12] Hubbard accordingly accepted the position of preceptor at Deerfield (Massachusetts) Academy. While there he published in 1803 his *Rudiments of Geography* and a year later *The American Reader,* which ran into four or more editions. The introduction to the latter is a discourse on how to teach reading by applying the techniques of teaching music. Hubbard, who recognizes no pedagogical dichotomy between the two subjects, states his case thus: "Reading, like music, is more easily taught by example than precept. Those soft flowing modulations and cadences of the voice, indispensably necessary for reading with elegance, can never be acquired by any particular rule. The reader and musician must either form their tones and the modulations of the voice, by their own ears, or learn them from others. The organs of speech, like the hands, feet and other organs of the body, require much exercise and practice, before they can perform their office with elegance and propriety. All voices are not equally soft and flexible; but almost every voice may be rendered in some measure agreeable by applications. Instructors are generally too negligent in teaching their pupils by example. They seldom attempt any thing more in reading, than correct pronunciation, and wholly neglect the modulations and cadences of the voice. Should any person attempt to teach music, and never give his pupils any other examples or specimens of sound than the eight notes, would not he be thought a very deficient instructor? Is not the person who attempts to teach reading without giving examples equally deficient?" [13]

In 1805 Hubbard returned to Dartmouth College as a professor of mathematics and natural philosophy. He retained this post until his death in 1810.[14]

The *Essay on Music*, mentioned at the beginning of this chapter, was read before the Middlesex Musical Society of Dunstable, Massachusetts, in 1807. It was a harsh criticism of American religious composition and particularly a rejection of the currently popular fuging style. In the oration Hubbard lauds the mode of European sacred music as represented by such sublime examples as Handel's "Grand Hallelujah" from the *Messiah*, "Return, O God of hosts, return" from *Samson*, "In Sweetest harmony they liv'd" from *Saul*, Giardini's "Cambridge," and Pergolesi's "Eja, Mater, fons amoris" from the *Stabat Mater*, and castigates the "bombastic" American style with its "laboured notes and strains, disconnected from any exalted ideas." Hubbard crystallizes his sentiments in these words: "In this style, our unfortunate country has been peculiarly fruitful. Almost every pedant, after learning his eight notes, has commenced author. With a genius sterile as the deserts of Arabia, he has attempted to rival the great masters of music. On the leaden wings of dullness, he has attempted to soar into those regions of science, never penetrated but by real genius. From such distempered imaginations, no regular productions can be expected. The unhappy writers after torturing every note in the octave, have fallen into oblivion, and have generally outlived their insignificant works. To the great injury of true religion, this kind of music has been introduced into our places of public worship. Devotion, appalled by its destructive presence, has fled from the unhallowed sound." [15]

It is difficult to question the sincerity of Hubbard's convictions, although we are inclined to think that he was somewhat premature in his denunciations. American psalmody, admittedly crude, was actually never given an opportunity to develop. Hubbard's reaction, later exploited by Lowell Mason and his contemporaries, succeeded in completely stifling the youthful and energetic impulses which might have matured into a truly indigenous art deeply rooted in folk sources.

Continuing his criticism, Hubbard states that the "common fuge" is one of the most prominent faults of this so-called "bombastic" style. He writes: "As the intention of vocal music is to communicate ideas, whatever renders these ideas indistinct or obscure, must be a perversion. Let us now examine music of the style last mentioned. We shall here find four parts, in harmonic order, each, at the same time, pronouncing different words. As a striking instance of this impropriety, we will mention a fuge in a piece of music called 'Montague.' Beginning at the Bass, and proceeding up to the treble, the bar, in the four parts, pronounced at the same time, will read thus; 'of brilliant light'; 'those spacious fields'; 'Let the high heav'ns; and 'your songs invite.' The four emphasis will fall on the words, 'brilliant,' 'spacious,' 'the,' 'songs.' To catch an idea uttered from such chaos of words, uttered at the same time, a hearer must be furnished with ear as numerous as the eyes of Argus. . . . Such music can never be of more consequence than an oration well pronounced in an unknown language." [16]

Obviously confusing the English "fuging tune" with the more intricate classical fugue, Hubbard points out that "The fuge may be considered as very difficult to manage with propriety. Handel, Purcell, Croft, Dr. Arnold, and others have introduced it advantageously. They have generally practiced the method of suspending one or more parts on long notes, while the others were jointly pronounced short notes. Perfect specimens of the fuge may be seen in Handel's Grand Hallelujah, in Purcell's anthem, Blessed is he, and in Dr. Arnold's Upton." [17]

Hubbard focuses attention upon another weakness of current church music—that which concerned the origin of many of the tunes: "From the midnight revel, from the staggering bachanal, from the profane altar of Comus they have stolen and prostituted air, and, with sacrilegious hands, have offered it in the temple of Jehovah. Such profanation must wound every feeling heart. Devotion ever assumes a dignity. It cannot delight in the tinkling bustle of unmeaning sounds. The air of a catch, a glee, a dance, a march, or a common ballard, is very improper for the worship of the Most High." [18]

He observes that any one who examines the songs in the *Beggar's Opera* will find "from what sources many of our modern tunes are derived." To those arbiters who insist that sound is only a vehicle to convey ideas and that one tune is as good as another, Hubbard asks if the theater is as proper for public worship as any place. In spite of his uncompromising stand, however, he concedes that several American composers have written music in an "agreeable and appropriate style," while a few have been fortunate enough to "reach the sublime." [19]

During his professorship at Dartmouth, Hubbard, with the assistance of Francis Brown, a tutor at the college, and several members of the "old musical choir," was instrumental in establishing, on July 25, 1807, the well-known Handel Society of Dartmouth College. Hubbard became the first president of the society, its objective being "to improve and cultivate the taste and promote true and genuine music and discountenance trifling unfinished pieces."

The history of this distinguished musical group goes back to the initial commencement, when it was recorded that "there were performed several anthems, one of which was composed and set to music by the young gentlemen candidates for a degree." The poet was Levi Frisbie and the musical composer, Sylvanus Ripley. Commencement programs and newspapers make frequent references to "the choir" or the "musical society." In 1785 "some pieces of vocal and instrumental music closed the exercises," while in 1787 "an agreeable concert of music was then exhibited," before the degrees were conferred.[20] In 1791 the observance included a "concert of musick, vocal and instrumental" and the "Ode to commencement" set to music by John Hubbard, A.M. (perhaps written when he was a student there). The succeeding year (1792) on August 20 we note that "the Musical Society convened in the chapel where was delivered an excellent and well composed oration by George K. Kirkland, on music and the fine arts; likewise were performed several pieces of music." Kirkland, a member of the graduating class, received from the Trustees a "special testimonial of his musical talents and proficiency." [21] President Dwight of Yale, who in the course of his travels attended divine services at Dartmouth in October, 1803, declared that "never, unless in a few instances at Wethersfield, many years since, had he heard music which exhibited so much taste, and skill, as were displayed here." [22]

Like other college societies, the newly organized Handel Society was nominally secret, but in order to insure a firm foundation it was necessary for the group to solicit the patronage and protection of Dartmouth College. All members were required to provide themselves with a "blank book" and to transcribe, or procure a copy of, every tune that was ordered to be sung at a future meeting.[23] Regular meetings of the society were held every Friday evening at the Academy Hall, and later in Alden's Hall, but more frequently "in a social way" at the homes of Professor Hubbard, Esquire Woodward, and other citizens. In 1809 it began to admit members of the college who were essentially instrumentalists. An orchestra, in time, became an important feature of the organization.[24]

Ritter, customarily so caustic in his evaluation of our early musical activities, has an uncharacteristically kind word to say of the Dartmouth organization: "Among those musical societies which at the early part of this century were formed throughout New England, I consider the above-mentioned Handel Society of Dartmouth College—next to the Boston Handel and Haydn Society—the one that was in many respects most beneficial in its influence." [25]

The Society began to decline around the middle of the century and was finally supplanted by the Dartmouth Glee Club during the decade of the seventies. Its last recorded meeting was held June 19, 1888.[26] In 1926 a community organization resumed the name of the Handel Society, and today it is listed in the college catalogue as the Handel Society Orchestra and Chorus.

As has been pointed out, Hubbard's influence did not terminate with his death. In 1816, the year following the organization of the world-famous Handel and Haydn Society of Boston, Orford and Piermont, two towns bordering the Connecticut river immediately above Hanover, established the Orford and Piermont Hubbard Musical Society. The preamble to its constitution projects the musical ideals of the man who was its inspiration: "We the Subscribers, conceiving the performance of *Good Music* to be important, not only as it tends to refine and exalt the mind, but also as constituting one of the most essential exercises in our houses of worship—that exercise, which, of all others, renders the feelings most devotional and solemn, and best adapted to the adoration of the Supreme Being, and being fully aware that many of the compositions now in use are altogether unfit for that purpose, do voluntarily enter into an association by the name of the Orford & Piermont Hubbard Musical Society. Our object being the promotion and encouragement of *Correct Grammatical Music* and our own improvement therein;—to this end, we agree to use our utmost endeavors, so far as may consist with prudence, to counter-act and discourage the efforts of unskilful [sic] teachers, in propagating the weak, imperfect productions of ignorant authors." [27]

Meetings were held twice a month, no person to be considered a qualified member "who cannot with facility read the common music of those authors from which the society think proper to select." The organization admitted "skillful musicians" [28] as honorary members, and its repertoire was chosen "from Handel, Arne, Madan, Croft, Lockhart, Giardini, Worgan, Purcell, Burney, Arnold, Busby, Williams, Clark, Cobb, Miller, Millgrove, Calcott, Bononcini, Playell, Thorley, Haydn and others who have in the estimation of good performers, written finished and correct Music." [29]

The services of this musical group were in large demand in the vicinity and on special occasions it performed "to the great edification of its audience," as far as Hanover and Windsor (Vermont). The society was incorporated by the legislature on December 7, 1816, and its records show an uninterrupted existence for sixteen years.

Apparently the spirit of John Hubbard also succeeded in reaching into the small community of Amherst, New Hampshire. A notice in the September 25, 1810, *New Hampshire Patriot* of Concord announcing the officers of the "Handellian [30] Musical Society" (incorporated in 1805), let it be known that

its views were "in consonance with the growing correct taste."
On September 19, 1810, a concert of "Sacred Music" was
scheduled to be performed by the combined forces of the
Middlesex (Massachusetts) Musical Society and the Handel
Society of Dartmouth, in Concord (New Hampshire) under
Hubbard's direction. An address by the Reverend Samuel
Worcester,[31] author of the *Christian Psalmody*, was to be part
of the program. Hubbard wrote to Worcester a number of
weeks before the appointed meeting, saying: "I trust nothing
will prevent your being present—the meeting I have long
desired: the object of it is most dear to my heart, as it must be
to yours; and I anticipate the day as one of the happiest of my
life." [32]

Sadly enough, Hubbard died about five weeks before the
concert. Owing to this turn of events, the *Patriot* pessimisti-
cally declared that "On account of the death of Professor
Hubbard, who was President of the Handel Society, our
prospects respecting the public performances are clouded and
diminished: still the lovers of devotional Music may expect to
hear a few pieces of that character." [33]

The Reverend Worcester, also lamenting his absence, concluded his address in panegyric fashion: "Hubbard, the amiable, the excellent Hubbard, the lover of sacred song, the friend
of man, the friend of God, is not in his expected place. That
countenance, which was life and joy, and would have imparted
animation and delight to all our hearts, we do not see;—that
voice which was music itself, and would have led our united
voices to emulate the symphonies of angels, we do not hear!
Come, brothers, let us join in the funereal dirge—let us conse-
crate the urn with our tears; for he, whom we all loved—our
friend, our Musical Chief—is dead." [34]

A review of the concert appeared in the September 25, 1810,
Patriot. Because it projects, among other things, Hubbard's
musical concepts with respect to standards as expressed in his
Essay, it is worth quoting in full. The newspaper also recorded part of the program:

Musical Exhibition

"On Wednesday last the united Societies of Handel at Dartmouth College and Middlesex of Massachusetts, met at this place and exhibited one of the most splendid musical performances probably ever witnessed in New England. The tunes performed were, Old Hundred, Giardini's Cambridge, Anthem, 'Arise Shine O Zion' by Williams, the Chorus from Handel's Grand Hallelujah, etc. In pointing out the various excellence of the choir, we cannot omit to mention with approbation the voices of the Miss Woodwards on the treble, and that of Mr. Curtis on the counter. Perhaps it was invidious, however, to give the preference to any of the performers, as they all excelled everything we have before heard. An Address, replete with correct sentiments on the intrinsical value of music in which the chaff was effectually sifted from the wheat—in which true harmony and melody were distinguished from the spurious—was pronounced by the Rev. Samuel Worcester, of Salem. When the orator touched, at the conclusion, upon the exit of Hubbard, 'the patron of music' and the 'friend of man' the audience were intuitively drawn into tears. Notwithstanding the day was stormy, a large concourse of people was collected.

"We are pleased to see a correct Musical taste growing out of the jargon which has too long been prevalent in our churches. We are glad to see the performances of Williams, of Handel, of Giardini preferred to the 'unmeaning and frivolous airs' of American authors who present nothing like 'concert of sweet sound'—nothing of the spirit of true devotion."

The concert in Concord had even attracted some attention in nearby Boston. A communication from a Boston paper [35] to the *Patriot*,[36] in advance of the affair, expressed approval of the efforts of the Handel and Middlesex Societies to encourage the performance of "correct psalmody" by Handel and others who had composed in a similar style. In part, the message reads:

"The depraved musical taste that has long pervaded a majority of our churches has ever been a source of affliction to many. Frivolous, unmeaning rhapsody has for a long period supplanted the composition of approved masters; and light unfinished music has been adopted to the exclusion of that which is genuine and solemn, and alone suitable for the worship of God. A reformation is most devoutly to be wished by every true friend to pure and correct psalmody: This truely laudable work has already been begun. Societies have been formed whose avowed object is the attainment of this desirable end. Among these we notice with pleasure the exertions and influence of the Handel society of Dartmouth College and the Middlesex society of Massachusetts. Those societies profess to adopt and encourage compositions of the great master, whose name the former of them bears, and of the authors who have written in a similar style. To render this kind of music an object of public attention, the above mentioned Societies propose meeting at Concord, N.H. . . . for the purpose of performing some pieces selected for the occasion. . . . We hail this as an occasion auspicious to the prevalence of correct musical taste; and we joyfully anticipate the time when our ears shall no longer be stunned by the Babel confusion of voices, and the solemn impressions of religious truths put to flight, by airy rhapsody of the present day."

Four years after Hubbard's death his wife, Rebecca H. Hubbard, secured a copyright for a collection of anthems which he had prepared in manuscript. The title page of this work, a copy of which is in the New Hampshire Historical Society, is reproduced here: "A Volume of Sacred Music containing Thirty Anthems selected from the Works of Handel, Purcell, Croft, and Other Eminent European Authors. By the Late Hon. John Hubbard, Prof. Math. & Nat. Phil. in the University of Dartmouth. Newburyport: Published by E. Little & Co. and sold at their Respective Bookstores in Newburyport & Portland. Sold also by R. P. & C. Williams, Boston 1814. C. Norris & Co. Printer."

During the period, Hubbard's book was deemed the "best in the country" and was in wide use by the singing societies throughout New England. The collection includes thirty anthems. One of them, "Thy mercy, O Lord, is in the Heav'ns," was composed by Hubbard himself. The music and words of this composition, declares Gould, "speak the man breathing the spirit of devotion." It seems to be the only music written by Hubbard ever printed,[37] but, according to Gould, it was not all he wrote. However, "his was not of a character to be received at that time, even if it had been presented to the public, differing from the popular music of the day." [38]

Gould, who knew Hubbard, has more to say concerning his creative activities: "We well remember when, about the commencement of the present century, he used to ask two boys, with soprano voices, who had acquired the art of reading notes, to meet him in the study, and request us to sing music in manuscript. We wondered at the time why he should write such tunes, being unlike the music we had been accustomed to sing; but, notwithstanding, it gave a peculiar sensation which will never be forgotten; and the more so, as it seemed to delight and gratify him so much; for, as he used to lead us with his voice and violincello, singing one part, and we, two others, when we mounted the high notes, well do we remember how he shook his sides with laughter, so as, many times, to prevent his singing. Some passages and tunes sound in memory's ears still, distant, but sweetly. How gladly would we sing the same tunes again, with grum [sic] voice of age, had we the opportunity!" [39]

John Hubbard died on August 14, 1810; his obituary appeared in the August 20, 1810, *Farmer's Museum:*

Died

"In Hanover, on Tuesday last, the Hon. John Hubbard, aged 50, Professor of Mathematicks and Natural Philosophy in Dartmouth College; formerly of this town. Not only the College and his family, but the publick at large have sustained a heavy loss by the Death of Mr. Hubbard, a Christian, a Scholar and a gentleman. Amiable and engaging in his manners, pure and uncorrupt in his life, able and assiduous in his profession, he has left imprinted on the hearts of many friends the remembrance of his worth. With him is lost to the world a fund of science, which he was imparting to others, and thereby multiplying the stock of literature."

His premature death left his family in precarious circumstances. The junior class at Dartmouth presented a mourning suit to the widow, which was received with "uncontrollable emotion." Hubbard was buried in the village cemetery at Hanover, where a marble slab with many Latin inscriptions still marks his grave.[40]

John Hubbard's accomplishments were manifold, but music "ruled his affections" to the end. However mistaken, in our opinion, he may have been in his attack upon our native musical tradition, and however misguided his attempt to foist European concepts of correct composition upon our own composers, his influence in refining musical taste and in elevating performance standards was without doubt as beneficial as it was important.

XII. Benjamin Dearborn

ONE of the most "ingenious and enterprising men of his time" [1]
was Benjamin Dearborn (1754-1838), a native of Portsmouth.
The early years of his life were spent in the town of his birth.
His numerous advertisements, inserted in the *Gazette* from
1778 to 1792, reveal him as author, schoolmaster, auctioneer,
shopkeeper, printer, publisher, inventor, and singing master.
After 1792 he moved to Boston where he remained until his
death.

While still in his twenties, Dearborn manifested a lively
interest in music and especially music instruction, according
to several of his press notices for a projected singing school.
The earliest of these appeared in the September 29, 1781,
Gazette:

"An Evening School for young People of both Sexes,, If
Suitable Encouragement is given, will be opened by Benjamin
Dearborn, at his house in pav'd Street. On Tuesday the 9th of
October: To be attended three Evenings in the Week, from
half after 6 till 9 o'clock. The exercises proposed will be in
Grammar, Reading, Writing, Spelling, Arithmetic and the
Rules of Vocal Music (as far as may be learned without singing).
Any of the exercises will be omitted if desired.

"His Writing and Singing-Schools which have been kept
thro' the Summer, will be continued during the Winter, if the
present Encouragement continues."

The reference in the quotation to teaching the "Rules of
Vocal Music . . . without singing" is curious and invites specu-

lation. Whether this was common practice, we do not know; it does, however, reflect some interest in the teaching of theory as such.

In the *Gazette* for March 29, 1783,[2] Dearborn again notified the public of his intention to open a singing school, "if Suitable Encouragement offers . . . on Mondays, Tuesdays and Wednesdays, from Five to Six o'Clock" in the afternoon. Simultaneously he was running a shop and advertised for sale "singing books"[3] and several copies of Andrew Law's tune books and *Rudiments of Music*.[4]

Apparently it was during this period of preoccupation with the singing school that Dearborn evolved and put into practice his unique plan for facilitating the teaching of music. In April of 1785 the *Gazette*[5] announced that it was being published:

". . . Said Dearborn has now in the press, Rules for teaching Vocal Music entirely by Letters, and for bringing all its characters within the compass of common fount of printing types. The mode of instruction he has found by experience, to be much more expeditious than that heretofore used; and so simple as scarcely to perplex the youngest child who can read.

"To make these rules more extensively useful, he proposes to open a Singing School on Tuesdays and Fridays, from 7 to 9 o'clock P.M."

The title page of Dearborn's small music book reads as follows: "A Scheme for reducing the Science of Music to a more simple state and to bring all its characters within the compass of a common fount of printing-types; especially calculated for the convenience of learners. By Benjamin Dearborn. Portsmouth, New Hampshire 1785."

The book is eight and a half by sixteen and a quarter centimeters in size, and consists of sixteen pages (including the title page), which are held together by a single stitch. According to Margaret E. Lippencott,[6] Dearborn's *opus* "is probably the earliest known attempt by an American to change the system of music notation." The only copy located is in the Library of the New York Historical Society.[7]

The preface of the "Scheme" which follows the title page

explains that "The author's design in this invention, was to remove the principal difficulties in printing, and in teaching music: having by experiment fully gratified his expectations, he submits it to the public eye; If errors be discovered in the execution, he will thank any candid observer to point them out."

The preface is succeeded by four pages of rules which are presented in a succinct manner. The music book contains the following six tunes printed with their texts: "Bridgewater," "All Saints," "Buckland," "Norwich," the "136th Psalm," and "Colchester." Dearborn did not utilize a staff, and what similarities to music notation exist lie in the designation of the time at the beginning of each tune, and the horizontal writing of parts. Instead of notes, he employed letters on a line, while numbers indicated the length of time for each letter. Sharps, flats, marks of expression, clefs, and the end of the tune are indicated by various common type characters. To illustrate, we quote four measures from his "All Saints":

```
:3: G § c 1 e 'dc' 1 b c 1   g g 1 g b l
:2: G   2  1 4'  1 2   1 2  1 2  1 2

                g      g                    g
:3: G † e l g Λf l g e 1   d d 1 e g l
:2: G   2  1  2 1 2   1 2  1 2

:3: G ‡ c 1 'cb' a l g c 1 'dc' b l c d l
:2: G   2       1 2         1 2

          2   1 2  1 2           1
:3: G * c l c  d  l e c l g  g l c g l
:2: G              1  2    2
```

When transcribed to modern notation, they would look like this:

The remarkable man who originated this novel way of teaching music was the only son of Dr. Benjamin Dearborn (1725-1755), a physician in his native town of Portsmouth, New Hampshire. The exact date of young Benjamin's birth is not known, although a record of his baptism was entered by the Reverend Samuel Langdon on April 28, 1754 [8] in the files of the North Church in the town.[9] When he was twenty-two years old he began publishing, in May of 1775, *The Freeman's Journal; or, New Hampshire Gazette,* having been taught the art of printing by Daniel Fowle who had published the same paper under the title of *The New Hampshire Gazette.* While engaged in the printer's trade, Dearborn kept a shop in Queen Street where he sold "West India and New England Rum;—Sugar; Cotton; Coffee, etc." [10] A short time later he relinquished the newspaper business and turned to other pursuits for a livelihood. An advertisement in the January 25, 1783, *Gazette* throws light on his interest in auctioneering: "To be sold, at public Vendue next Thursday Afternoon, at Dearborn's Auction-Room; A great Variety of Articles, consisting chiefly of English and European Goods, and a valuable Hadley's Quadrant."

In the *Gazette* of August 2, 1783, Dearborn advertised "a quantity of China & Glass Ware for sale," while in the issue of October 28, 1785, he announced the opening of his "Intelligence Office" for the purpose of acting as an agent for "estates, houses, vessels, horses, cattle, servants (except slaves)." He simultaneously engaged in the hiring of, and procuring employment for, "well-recommended" people.

Dearborn's concern for education was evident as early as 1779, when in April of that year he opened a school to "instruct young misses in Writing, Cyphering, etc. from 9 to 12 o'clock A.M.; and from 3 to 6 P.M." at his house opposite the Printing Office.[11] By June, Dearborn had added "reading and spelling" to the curriculum.[12] Two years later (1781) music became a regular study. Simultaneously, he began to hold classes for boys but at different times, and a school in the evening for those who were prevented from attending during the day.[13].

During this period Dearborn became interested in teaching music, and produced his *Scheme.* Several other text books, which he wrote for his classes, also made their appearance at this time. The first of these was printed in 1782: *The Pupils Guide: Being a Collection of the Most Useful Rules in Arithmetic, Calculated for the Benefit of Schools.*[14] *The Pupils Guide, or Assistant in Writing, Etc.*[15] was published in 1792, and the *Columbian Grammar* [16] printed in Boston in 1795.

In 1791 Dearborn, influenced by the success of his labor in the cause of education, initiated plans for the establishment of an academy for young ladies.[17] A "Master" was to be engaged to teach dancing and the French language, and a "Mistress" to instruct in the useful and ornamental branches of needlework, "both of whom must be well recommended as completely qualified for their respective departments," and must, if convenient, board in the house, assisting in "superintending the Manners and Morals" of the students.

The curriculum of the Academy, which suggests a modern comprehensive public school, strongly belies the often confused notion of early New England educational institutions where learning was presumably confined to the proverbial three R's. Dearborn's expanded educational ideas displayed both breadth and variety in his choice of subjects which included "Spelling, Reading, Writing, Arithmetic, Accounts, English Grammar, Geography, Chronology, History, Composition, Embroidery, plain Needle-Work, Vocal Music, Instrumental Music, Dancing, Drawing, French Language, etc." Moreover, conscious of individual needs, Dearborn explained in the advertisement that "any of the above branches will be taught separately to those who may chuse it."

Portsmouth Academy was opened on April 30, 1791.[18] Earlier, the *Spy* [19] had approved the undertaking: Mr. Dearborn's Academy will be opened in April next. His exertions in the education of youth entitle him to the patronage of the public, and the esteem of mankind."

The elaborate ceremony attending the opening was originally scheduled to be held at the Academy, but had to be adjourned to Mr. Buckminster's meeting house because the audience overflowed the Academy hall. The whole proceedings are appropriately described in the April 30, 1791, *Gazette*: "The performance was opened by the Rev. Mr. Buckminster's addressing the throne of Grace; after which the Rev. Mr. Ogden delivered an excellent discourse, pointing out the many advantages arising from an early education, as helping the cause of religion, morality and virtue. At the conclusion the following ode, written by the Rev. Dr. Haven, and set to musick by Mr. Garnet, musick-master to the Academy, was performed in a most masterly manner, and met the hearty approbation of a crouded audience."

Garnet's music seems to be nonexistent, nevertheless the entire ode is reproduced here as it appeared in the newspaper:

Recitative

Come gentle youth, Virtue's fair Daughters come,
The Muse salutes you with a Virgin's blush,
Dares to forestall the pleasures of this happy Dome,
Where use and graceful ornament unite their Charms,
And call forth ardent emulation to excel
In Female Worth and Elegance.

Air

Happy the Spot, where many a virtuous maid
Shall date her high improvements in the
Way to Fame.

Chorus

Ten thousand blessings to these youths be giv'n
To swell the founder's Breast, and all conduct
to Heav'n.

Air

Thrice happy School, where elegance and art,
Add beauty to the cheek, and mend the heart.

Chorus

Ten thousand blessings to these youths be giv'n
To swell the founder's Breast, and all conduct
to Heav'n.

In his address, the Reverend Ogden emphasized the values of improving the music of the worship service: "Music, and particularly the vocal, deservedly demands cultivation; principally as it relates to praise—that sublime part of public worship, in which every one ought to share; from which pride or any wrong sentiment ought not to lead us to withdraw. Both men and women of the greatest respectability in our country have, and their children do, every Sunday perform a part in choirs and singing seats. Much discouragement arises on this head from an ungracious reluctance; an affected cough or cold: This often disgusts and offends—affords an opportunity to deny that pleasure which enlivens company and cheers the sad. Good singers are often the most disobliging persons we meet with." [20]

Dancing, he continued, also "forms a part of education as it begets that easy deportment which makes us appear less aukward and restrained in company. It is an innocent recreation and relaxation for the sedentary. It promotes health and cheerfulness. It is part of the amusement of social hours among friends and strangers—among persons of various pursuits and principles. It wears away the rust of prejudice. Seeing each other in their best dress and most pleasant face, the blood being set into circulation by motion and music, spleen flies—harmony reigns, and imperceptibly diffuses its pleasing effects. But all these, under the strictest rules of decorum and good order." [21]

The Portsmouth Academy evidently proved unsuccessful, for in the *Gazette* of October 20, 1791, Dearborn notified the public that "on account of support being withdrawn from some of the branches of instruction . . . and given to a rival institution," he was obliged to discontinue the Academy on the thirtieth of September. He subsequently moved to Boston, where he established another academy for the boarding and the instruction of young ladies "in all the branches of useful and polite education."

In the Boston directory for 1798 Dearborn is listed as a schoolmaster and auctioneer, but following this period he was more closely associated with his inventions and manufactures which are adequately covered in Miss Lippencott's article.[22]

Concerning inventions, the reader is referred to Chapter V which mentions Dearborn's "new invented Printing-Press" employed in striking off songs during the procession for the celebration of the Federal Constitution ratification.

In February, 1797, Dearborn, obviously still interested in the problem of music instruction, obtained a copyright for his "The Vocal Instructor, published in numbers. No. 1 containing the rules of vocal music, by principle, in questions and answers; and hints for recovering its respectability. A morning and evening hymn, composed and set to music, for this work; and a sliding music scale, never before published; in which a more able index points out the names and distances of the notes in all variations. The other numbers of the work will contain sacred, moral or sentimental psalms, hymns, songs, and adapted to particular and general occasions, for the improvement and pleasure of youth. By Benjamin Dearborn. Boston: 1797. 113th Massachusetts District Copyright, issued to Benjamin Dearborn as Author, 28 February, 1797." [23]

The music in this work was apparently original. In his *History of Church Music in America*,[24] Gould includes this publication in a list of thirty-one works by American authors who were writing and publishing music of the same character as that of William Billings, but which Gould considered "inferior to his merit." This is all the data we have concerning Dearborn's *Vocal Instructor*, and it is likewise the last bit of information regarding his musical activities that has come to our attention.

Benjamin Dearborn died in Boston on February 22, 1838, and was buried in the family tomb in the Central Burying Ground. His interest in the cause of music instruction, especially directed toward youth, his labors as a teacher of singing, his foresight in attempting to evolve a system for making music reading easier, and his pioneering endeavors resulting in two publications to that end justifiably earned him a modest place in the development of music education in America.

XIII. Samuel Holyoke

SAMUEL HOLYOKE (1762-1820), composer, compiler, and teacher of sacred and secular vocal and instrumental music, has received fair treatment at the hands of American biographers, but his story is by no means complete. The object of this chapter is to shed further light on his personal life as well as upon his musical achievements. We shall concentrate chiefly, but not exclusively, upon his career in New Hampshire, where he spent his last months teaching and where most of his music seems to have been printed.

Holyoke was born in Boxford, Massachusetts, on October 15, 1762. In 1783, at the age of twenty, he entered Phillips Andover Academy and was graduated from Harvard in 1789.[1] In 1791 Dartmouth College conferred upon him the degree of Master of Arts, seemingly an honorary one.[2]

He taught singing schools and conducted numerous concerts of vocal and instrumental music in and around Salem, Massachusetts.[3] Although his voice was never "melodious," his talent for teaching was "rather popular." During his last years he used the clarinet while teaching singing, and "the tone of his instrument was as harsh as his voice."[4] The year of 1809-1810 he joined the staff of Phillips Andover as a teacher of sacred music. He is listed in the *Biographical Catalogue* thus: "1809 Samuel Holyoke Instructor in Sacred Music 1810 Son of Rev. Elizur Holyoke and Hannah Peabody; born Boxford, Oct. 25,[5] 1762; Phillips Academy, 1783-85. Famous teacher and composer of music; compiler of Columbian Repository of Sacred Harmony and other works. Died, Concord, N.H., Feb. 7, 1820."[6]

As a composer, Holyoke remained aloof from the "fuging music" of his contemporaries, preferring to write in the slower and more stately homophonic style. In the preface of his initial publication, *Harmonia Americana,* he expressed his opposition in the following words: "Perhaps some may be disappointed that fuguing pieces are in general omitted. But the principal reason why few were inserted was the trifling effect produced by that sort of music; for the parts falling in, one after another, each conveying a different idea, confound the sense, and render the performance a mere jargon of words." [7]

Holyoke's music, which demonstrates a certain academic learnedness, seems to lack the originality and the soul of a Billings, a Law, or a Kimball. The only tune that has survived to this day is "Arnheim," his first composition, written when he was sixteen. In his *Encyclopedia of Music,* John Weeks Moore asserts that it was the last piece Holyoke ever sang. At a social gathering of his musical friends in the house of Jacob B. Moore, in Concord, Holyoke requested the group present to sing "Arnheim," remarking that perhaps he would "never meet with a choir on earth so well calculated to do justice to his first composition." The tune was performed twice and Holyoke "was effected to tears." Five days later, at Lang's Tavern, in East Concord, he died of an attack of lung fever. Holyoke had been teaching at Concord during the winter. He never married. [8]

His obituary recorded in the *New Hampshire Patriot & State Gazette* for February 29, 1820, of Concord is disappointingly brief: "Died. . . . In this town, of lung fever, Mr. Samuel Holyoke, of Boston,[9] Aged 57 celebrated as a teacher and composer of Sacred Music.

As a compiler, composer, and author of several music books, Holyoke made some invaluable contributions to early American music education. Such works as his *Harmonia Americana* (1791), *Massachusetts Compiler* (1795), *Columbian Repository* (1799), *Instrumental Assistant* Vol. 1 (1800), Vol. 2 (1807)— all with concise instructions—were widely used throughout the state.

When the *Columbian Repository* was about to be released, an editorial comment appeared in the November 23, 1799, *Courier* praising Holyoke's newest work. The writer of the critique simultaneously expounded upon the unfortunate state of music in the divine worship, hoping that the book would soon be procured as a remedy. It is important to note that the editorial also serves to establish a date (1799) for this publication, which heretofore has been in question.[10] It is reproduced in full: "Mr. Holyoke, a celebrated Musician in Massachusetts engaged in collecting and composing a variety of Tunes 'adapted for the use of schools and worshipping assemblies,' the airs of which are to be suited to the different subjects of the psalms and hymns in Watt's version and others; each tune to be set with the psalm or hymn in which it is to be sung; the whole to be published in one volume quarto containing 500 pages, price 3 dollars—It is hoped that these books will soon be in use in our several churches. They may teach some of our wiseacres wisdom and convince them of their accountable stupidity and folly. Not to mention the incapacity of some of our would-be-thought adepts in music, to comprehend sounds and modulate the voice—Their uniform apathy and statue-like gesture; not even hint at those qualifications, so necessarily essential to their conceited rashness—They not only transgress against every musical propriety, but most outrageously affront even common sense. What more absurd than for penitence, sorrow and prayer, to assume the airs of gladness; or for cheerfulness, thanksgiving and joy, to wear the garment of lamentation?—Yet do some of our modest choristers so charming couple such opposses [opposites] that they make Joy to sigh, and Praise to utter groans—and penitence, sorrow and prayer, break out in sallies of pleasantry and loud peals of laughter." [11]

The *Columbian Repository* (undated), a copy of which is in the New Hampshire Historical Society, includes four hundred and ninety-five pages printed on oblong quarto paper. These are its various divisions:

Title page	
Dedication and Advertisement	1 page
Music Instruction	22 pages
Body (Music)	464 pages
Errata	1 page
Index to 'Psalm' and 'Hymn tunes	6 pages
List of Subscribers	1 page

The title page reads: "The Columbian Repository of Sacred Harmony Selected From European and American Authors, With Many New Tunes Not Before Published. Including the whole of Dr. Watts' Psalms and Hymns, to each of which a Tune is adapted, and some additional Tunes suited to the particular Metres in Tate and Brady's and Dr. Belknap's Collection of Psalms and Hymns. With an Introduction of Practical Principles. The Whole Designed For The Use of Schools, Musical Societies, And Worshipping Assemblies. By Samuel Holyoke, A.M. Published According To Act of Congress. From the Music-Press of Henry Ranlet, Exeter, New Hampshire."

The advertisement states that "It is presumed that there has no work of the kind yet appeared in the United States in which there is a greater variety of Style to be found, than in the present; and should the encouragement be equivalent to the time and labor bestowed upon it, the design will be answered."

The first volume of Holyoke's *Instrumental Assistant,* printed in Exeter, New Hampshire by Ranlet, made its appearance in 1800.[12] Holyoke describes his new work and dwells upon its relative merits for improving music instruction in a lengthy advertisement from the *Oracle* for November 29, 1800. The notice, which follows in full, also reflects some vicissitudes of current teaching practices:

"Just Published And To Be Sold By Henry Ranlet, Exeter A new Musical Work, entitled, The Instrumental Assistant, Containing Instructions for the Violin, German Flute, Clarionett, Bass-Viol and Hautboy;—Compiled from late European publications.—progressively arranged and adapted for the use of Learners. By Samuel Holyoke, A.M.

"In this Work the Compiler has attempted to give some assistance to beginners upon Musical Instruments.—As a book of this kind has been much wanted, he hopes that the design will meet approbation.

Learners, when attempting to perform in concert, have been continually embarrased by the disagreement of their copies, errors in transcribing their pieces, and the want of seconds & basses etc. Those inconveniences, should the work meet acceptance, will be remedied, as most of the music is in three parts; and which is intended to conduct the beginner, gradually, from simple, to more difficult execution.

"The difficulty, in many instances, of procuring copies of the music, and the labor of transcribing may be hereby avoided, from which instructors may anticipate some abridgement of their talks.

"The instructions for different instruments, which are inserted in this volume when sold separately, amount to 22 s 6, and the music which commonly accompanies those instructions, though chiefly of one part, seldom agrees.

"The variety, comprised in this book, renders it the cheapest for instrumental performers, that can be purchased.
"Exeter, Nov. 28, 1800."

The original issue seems not to be extant, but we have for our examination a copy of "Vol. I," undated, bound with Volume II, 1807.[13] From the data available it may be assumed that this Volume I is essentially identical with the original issue. Sonneck records that the original was copyrighted in Massachusetts, August 30, 1800.[14]

In order to establish securely the identity of the first volume with the original issue, as described in the *Oracle of the Day* advertisement, we quote the title page of the former, which the reader may compare with the above-quoted advertisement: "The Instrumental Assistant. Containing instructions for the Violin, German Flute, Clarionett, Bass-Viol, and Hautboy. Compiled from late European publications. Also A Selection of favorite Airs, Marches, etc. Progressively Arranged and adapted for the use of Learners. By Samuel Holyoke, A.M.

Published according to Act of Congress Vol. I. Printed at Exeter, New Hampshire, By H. Ranlet, and sold at his Book-Store—Sold also by most of the booksellers in the United States. Price 1 doll. 25 cents by the 100, 1 doll. 50 cents by the dozen, 1 doll. 75 cents single, sewed in blue."

The eighty pages which make up this work include: the title page; dictionary of musical terms; "fifteen pages of clear and concise instructions for the various instruments"; five pages of general rules of music; three pages of "Introductory Lessons" (eight lessons written as duets and trios); fifty-five pages of instrumental selections arranged as trios on open scores; and an index. The instrumental instructions, carefully illustrated with fingering charts, treat the following:

"Instruction for the Violin . . . Plain Scale for the Violin . . . Scale for Tuning the Strings . . . Scale of Flats, Sharps, and Shifts . . . Of Bowing . . . Lessons of Intervals for the Bow . . .

"Instruction for the German Flute . . . Plain Scale . . . Scale of Flats and Sharps . . . Scale on the pitch of D with two sharps . . . Scale of Shakes for the Plain Notes . . . Scale of Shakes for the Flats and Sharps . . . Of Double Tonguing . . . Graces as applied to the Flute . . .

"Instructions for the Clarionett . . . Plain Scale for the Clario-nett . . . Scale of the Flatted and Sharped Letters . . .

"Instructions for the Bass Viol [cello] . . . First Scale for the Finger Board . . . Scale for Tuning the Bass Viol . . . Scale of Notes . . . Scale of Flats and Sharps . . . Of Bowing . . .

"Instructions for the Hautboy . . . Plain Scale . . . Scale of Flats and Sharps . . . Scale of Shakes . . .

The contents of this book afford an idea of the repertory of the instrumentalist and also provide a sample of current taste:

Air	Boston March
Air in Rosina	Boston Quick Step
Baron Stuben's March	British Muse
Beauties of Fancy	Canada Farewell
Belleisle March	Capt. Mackintosh's March
Black Cockade	Col. Orne's March

Count Brown's March
Dog and Gun
Dorsetshire March
Duettino
Duke of Holstein's March
Duke of York's March
Durham March
Echo
Essex March
Favorite Air
Felton's Gavot
Foot's Minuet
For there's no luck about the house
Free Mason's March
Garner's Air
Gen. Green's March
Gen. Knox's March
Gen. Washington's March
Gen. Wayne's March
God Save America
Grano's March
Handel's Clarionett
Handel's Gavot
Handel's Water Piece
Handyside's March
Heathen Mythology

La Contille Cotillion
Lesson by Morelli
London March
Love's March
Malbrouk
March alla Millitaire
March in the God of Love
March in the Water Music
March to Boston
Marquis of Granby's March
New German March
O Dear what can the Matter be
Philadelphia March
President's March
Prince Eugene's March
Quick March
Quick March in Cymon
Rakes of London
Serenade
Sonata
Stamitz Air
Straffordshire March
Suffolk March
Swiss Guard's March
When First I saw
Yankee Doodle

Volume II of Holyoke's *Instrumental Assistant*, published in 1807, was copyrighted in New Hampshire under the proprietorship of Ranlet and Norris, the printers. It contained instructions for the French horn and bassoon, and one who possessed both volumes would "have a complete set of Scales for the instruments, which are at present used in this Country."

"The faded blue cover and title page are identical: The Instrumental Assistant; Volume II. Containing a selection of Minuets, Airs, Duettos, Rondos and Marches: with Instructions for the French-Horn and Bassoon. Compiled by Samuel Holyoke, A.M. Exeter, New Hampshire Printed and sold by Ranlet and Norris, by the hundred, dozen, or single—sold also, by Thomas and Andrews, David and John West, William Andrews, Ethridge and Bliss, F. and J. Larkin, Caleb Bingham, Manning and Loring, Boston Cushing and Appleton, B.B. Macanulty, Salem—Ebenezer Stedman, Thomas and Whipple, Newburyport—Thomas and Tappan, Charles Peirce, Portsmouth—Isaac Adams, Thomas Clark, T.B. Wait and Co. Portland—Price, 175 cents Single. 1807."

It includes one hundred and four pages: imprint, title page, copyright, six pages of instruction, ninety-five pages of music arranged on open scores as instrumental duets, trios, quartets, quintets, sextets and septets, and finally the index.

A copy of an original anthem in four parts by Holyoke, published separately in oblong quarto size and numbering seven pages, is also in the New Hampshire Historical Society. The title page follows: "Exeter: for Thanksgiving By Samuel Holyoke A.B. Exeter: Printed by Henry Ranlet, M,DCC,XCVIII."

Holyoke, a versatile musician interested in both vocal and instrumental music, preferred the musical traditions of Europe to those of America, like his contemporary, Hubbard. He was a prolific composer and compiler of hymn tunes and anthems. To improve and promote music education, he wrote a number of carefully developed instruction manuals. His music has long since been forgotten, but he may be remembered as one of America's earliest professional music teachers.

XIV. The Village Harmony

THE reform in singing in America was chiefly instigated, early in the eighteenth century, by a small group of discerning clergymen who could no longer condone the appalling conditions which prevailed in the music of the church. The controversy between "singing by rote" and "singing by note," precipitated by this attempt at reform, was in the end resolved in favor of the latter. The events of this musical upheaval led to the opening of singing schools and to the appearance of itinerant singing teachers.

At the outset, the movement was centered in New England, and it eventually made its way to New York and Pennsylvania and ultimately to the West and South.

During the Revolution, with its birth of national feelings, the movement was identified with secular singing of the patriotic type. Anthem and odes were added to the repertory of tunes. It was likewise closely linked with the appearance, soon after 1760, of numerous tune books which usually included a section devoted music instruction. In spite of the fact that these early music books were manifestly imperfect and littered with typographical errors, they did much to spread skill in singing, to awaken popular interest in music, and to prepare the way for more artistic enterprises.[1]

One such tune book of the period was *The Village Harmony*. This work, "designed principally for the use of schools and singing societies," was originally compiled and printed by Henry Ranlet and his successors at Exeter. Our data show that over a period of twenty-six years, from 1795 [2] to 1821, it ran into seventeen editions with two additional printings.[3] The book saw widespread use throughout New England. The preface to the seventh edition notes that "in the course of nine years" this music book had sold "about twenty-seven thousand copies."

The initial edition of *The Village Harmony* made its appearance in the year 1795. It was announced for sale by the *Oracle* for November 21, 1795: "New Singing-Book. Just Published, and to be sold by the quantity or single, at C. Peirce's Book-Store, In Court-Street, Portsmouth, The Village Harmony, or Youth's Assistant to Sacred Music,—Containing a Concise Introduction to the Grounds of Music, with such a collection of the most approved Psalm Tunes, Anthems, and other Pieces, in three and four parts, as are most suitable for divine worship. Designed for the use of Schools & Singing Societies."

The first edition is listed in Evans's *American Bibliography,* which, in addition to the information already given, notes that the tune book was "Printed at Exeter, by H. Ranlet, and sold at his Book-store. 1795 pp. 150." [4]

The second edition came off the press a year later, according to an advertisement in the *New Hampshire Diary or Almanack* (Ranlet, 1797). This edition "To which is added Eighty Pages of the best Music current" was enlarged to one hundred and ninety pages. "Price 10 dolls. per dozen, 1 dollar single." [5]

The third edition was published by Henry Ranlet in 1797, the title page being similar to that of the previous edition.[6] The fourth edition, "corrected and improved," printed in 1798, was advertised thus in *Ranlet's New Hampshire and Massachusetts Almanack for . . . 1799:* "Just Published, and ready for sale the Fourth Edition of the Village Harmony. Price . . . 9 dolls. per dozen by the hundred . . . 10 dolls. single dozen and 1 dollar single. Exeter Nov. 1798." [7] This issue had grown to two hundred and three pages and was printed in oblong octavo.

The fifth edition received two printings, the first probably in 1799, the second in 1800. Although we do not have access to a commercial copy of the original imprint, in the New Hampshire Historical Society may be found, curiously enough, a manuscript replica of this volume, bound in calfskin. The meticulous task was accomplished by one James Baker of Holderness, New Hampshire, in February, 1799.[8] The title page, which excludes all publication data, reads:

"The Village Harmony or Youths Assistant to Sacred Musick containing A concise Introduction to the Grounds of Musick, with such a collection of the most approved Psalm Tunes, Anthems, and other Pieces suitable for Divine Worship. Designed for the Use of Schools and Singing Societies.

> Music to rapture swells the list'ning mind,
> Sooths the sad heart with melting strains refin'd,
> Controls the passions, checks impure desires,
> And the soul kindles with Devotion's fires.

Fifth Edition, Corrected and Improved. By James Baker of New-Holderness N.H. February 1799."

This book is made up of one hundred and eighty-eight pages. It does not include an advertisement or an index, while the "Grounds of Music" appear to be compressed into three pages. It contains one hundred and ninety-nine tunes with no composers given.

The second printing of the fifth edition, a copy of which is in the New Hampshire Historical Society, made its appearance a year later (1800). Some idea of the nature, character, and general organization of previous issues may be gained by quoting extensively from this revision. We begin with the title page:

"The Village Harmony or Youth's Assistant to Sacred Music. Containing A concise Introduction to the Grounds of Music, with such a collection of the most approved Psalm Tunes, Anthems, and other Pieces, as are most suitable for Divine Worship. Designed Principally for the use of Schools and Singing Societies.

> Music to rapture swells the list'ning mind,
> Sooths the sad heart with melting strains refin'd,
> Controuls the passions, checks impure desires,
> And the soul kindles with Devotion's fires.

"Fifth Edition, Corrected and Improved. Published agreeably to Act of Congress. Printed at Exeter, New-Hampshire, by Henry Ranlet, And sold at his Book-Store, by the Hundred, Dozen or Single; Sold also by Thomas & Andrews, David and John West, and Caleb Bingham, Boston; Thomas C. Cushing, Salem; Edmund M. Blunt, Newburyport; Stephen Patten, Port-land; David Howe, Haverhill; William A. Kent, Concord, and Charles Peirce, Portsmouth.—Price 10 dolls. per dozen, and 1 doll. single. 1800." [9]

The advertisement which follows the title page conveys some interesting facts concerning the compiler's intent, current variances in taste, and the merit of the book as an instruction manual:

"The Proprietor of the Village Harmony has taken great pains to improve this fifth edition. In some instances he has left out pieces, and compressed others, to insert in their room such Music as is best calculated to please the taste of those who possess the delicate tone and the nicest ear.

"It is not an easy matter to please everybody. His principal design is to please as many as possible and leave others to please themselves.

"The Village Harmony is so well known, and so generally used, that it needs no comment to recommend it to the public. It contains as good an assortment, and as rich a variety of Music, as any book in the United States. Its Rules are plain, concise, and easy for beginners. The greater part of the Music, is easy and animating, and will be found to be extremely well calcu-lated for Divine Worship.

"In so great a variety of Music, there can be found a sufficient number of Tunes, of different Metres, which will be pleasing to almost every class of Singer. However,

"It is not uncommon for the best Theoretical as well as Practical Singer to differ in their taste for Music—for which reason I have been induced to insert some tunes merely to please all. But should I miss of my aim, I shall freely ac-knowledge I have committed a very common fault. Henri Ranlet."

Henry Ranlet, referred to above, was known in New Hampshire and throughout most of New England as a "skillful printer." The list of his publications was "remarkable in number and variety." He was one of the earliest printers to procure musical type for his establishment, and during his years in Exeter, from 1785 to 1807, he produced an undetermined number of musical publications, which included both vocal and instrumental music.[10] The Reverend William Bentley, who visited Exeter in 1801, remarks in his diary that "much music printed by types has been spread in New England from Ranlet's press." [11]

Ranlet not only compiled and printed the first seven editions of *The Village Harmony*, but was also responsible for publishing other tune books such as Jacob Kimball's *Essex Harmony* (1800); Jeremiah Ingalls's *Christian Harmony* (1805); Amos Blanchard's[12] *Newburyport Collection of Sacred Musick* (1807); and many works of Samuel Holyoke already mentioned in the previous chapter.

Ranlet's interest in music seems to have been more than purely commercial. From the various personal comments in the advertisements with respect to revisions and enlargements, it is fair to guess that he possessed some musical knowledge and a certain degree of discerment.

When Ranlet died in 1807, the proprietorship of the firm was assumed by Charles Norris, a business associate, who continued publishing *The Village Harmony* and other music books.

Ranlet's fifth edition of *The Village Harmony* devotes ten pages to "A concise Introduction to the Grounds of Music; with Rules for Learners." It deals with, first: "Of the General Scale of Music, or the Gamus ... Rules to Find the Mi ... Table of Transposition ... The Names of Notes used in Music and their Rests ... Musical Characters with their Explanation and Uses ... Of Syncopation or Driving notes ... Of the Keys used in Music ... Of Time ... Of Soft Singing ... Of Semitones ... Of the several Concord and Discords both Perfect and Imperfect ... Of Sounding the Eight Notes ... Lessons for

Tuning the Voice . . . General Observations . . . Scale Showing the Proportion of the Notes."

It comprises two hundred and five pages, two more than the fourth edition. It is notable that the tunes selected for this volume are predominantly works of American composers. The fuging tune is in great evidence. It may be assumed that the preponderance of American music in this edition holds true for the first four also.

The following is a list of the tunes and authors (when given) contained in the fifth edition of *The Village Harmony:*

Adieu	Allen	Buckingham	Williams
Africa	Billings	Burlington	
All Saints New	Hall	Buxton	
Alpha	Holden	Calvary	Reed
Amherst	Billings	Canterbury	
Amity	Reed	New	Smith
Andover	Wood	Charlestown	Reed
Annapolis	Reed [13]	Cheshunt	Lock Hospital
Anthem for			Coll.
Easter	Billings	Chester	Billings
Archdale		Christmas	
Arnheim	Holyoke	Hymn	
Ascension	Wood	Colchester	
Ashburnham	Kimball	New	
Ashby	Kimball	Complaint	Parmenter
Aylsbury	Williams	Conquest	Billings
Balloon	Swan	Corinth	Blanchard
Baltimore	Ingalls	Crucifixion	Reed
Bethesda		Danbury	Reed
Bolsover	Holyoke	Deanfield	
Bradford	Kimball	Dedicatory	
Brandywine	Rogerson	Poem	
Bridgewater	Edson	Denmark	Madan
Bristol	Madan	Devotion	Reed
Bristol	Swan	Dover	Williams' Coll.
Brookfield	Billings	Dunstam	Madan

Durham	Kimball	Keene	Dr. Arnold
Edom		Kingsbridge	Williams
Enfield	Chandler	Lebanon	Billings
Epsom	Smith	Lena	Belknap
Evening Hymn	Williams	Lenox	Edson
	Smith	Leverett	
Falmouth	Madan	Street	Lane
Fairford	Kimball	Lift up your	
Fairlee	Holden	heads	
Farmington	Gillet	Lisbon	Reed
Funeral		Lisbon	Swan
Anthem	Kimball	Little	
Funeral Dirge	Holyoke	Marlboro	Williams
Funeral Hymn	Holden	Loudon	Holyoke
Funeral		Lynnfield	Holden
Thought	Is. Smith	Majesty	Billings
Georgia		Malden	Kimball
Gethsemane	Wood	Maryland	Billings
Gloucester	Kimball	Mear	
Golgotha		Mentz	Holyoke
Greenfield	Edson	Middlesex	Holden
Greenwich	Reed	Middletown	Ball
Groton		Milford	Stephenson
Habakkuk	Madan	Mile's Lane	Shrubsole
Hadley		Montgomery	Morgan
Hampton	Milgrove	Montague	Swan
Harlem	Kimball	Mount	
Hebron		Ephraim	Milgrove
Hiding Place	Smith	Namure	
Hinsdale	Holyoke	New Canaan	Holden
Hollis	Holden	New	
Hotham	Madan	Jerusalem	Ingalls
Irish	Williams	New Market	Holyoke
Italy	Sacchini	New Salem	Holden
Jordan	Billings	New York	
Jubilee	Brownson	Northfield	
Judgement	Reed	Norwich	Brownson

Ocean	Swan	Stoneham	Kimball
Old Hundred	Luther	Stratfield	Goff
Omega	Holden	Sturbridge	Holyoke
Palmis		Suffield	King
Paris	Billings	Sunday	
Pembroke	Smith	Sutton	Williams
Pennsylvania	Ingalls	Sutton New	Goff
Plymouth		The Pilgrim	
Psalm, ed.	Stephenson	Topsfield	Kimball
Psalm, 24th.	Williams	Truro	Williams' Collection
Psalm, 25th.	Gillet		
Psalm, 34th.	Stephenson	Tunbridge	Kimball
Psalm, 46th.	Chandler	Vermont	Kimball
Psalm, 118th.	Smith	Victory	Reed
Psalm, 119th.	Smith	Virginia	Brownson
Psalm, 136th.	Deolph	Waterford	Kimball
Russia	Reed	Wells	Williams
Salem	Kimball	Westford	Holyoke
Sherburne	Reed	Windham	Reed
Solitude		Windsor	Kirby
Sophronia	King	Winter	Reed
Spring	Smith	Woburn	Kimball
Springwater		Woodrow	Holyoke
Stafford	Reed	Worcester	Wood
St. Anns		Worcester New	Mann
St. Ann's		Yarmouth	Kimball
St. Helens	Williams	Zion	Holden
St. Martin's	Tansur		

Most of the pieces are written for four parts; twenty-eight appear for three:

Alpha	Funeral thought	Dover	Hotham
Ascension	Gethsemane	Dunstan	Italy
Burlington	Habakkuk	Falmouth	Malden
Cheshunt	Hampton	Middlesex	Salem
Denmark	Harlem	Mount Ephraim	Spring

New		Omega	Truro
Jerusalem	Sturbridge	Psalm 24th.	Westford
New York	The Pilgrim		

The four-part settings are written for treble, counter, tenor, and bass with the air invariably occurring in the tenor. The three-part settings are written for treble, tenor, and bass. In twenty of the three-part pieces the air is in the tenor, while in the following eight the air appears in the soprano:

Alpha	Denmark	Harlem	Truro
Burlington	Falmouth	New York	Westford

Although a "Dictionary of Musical Terms" in the customary Italian does not appear until the eleventh edition, indications like "Slow," "Brisk," "Cheerful," "Loud," "Affectionately," "Increase," apparently in keeping with its American character, occur throughout the book. Not one Italian term is found in this entire edition. As has been already noted, the majority of the tunes are products of American composers. A few are by English composers, while there is only one instance of an Italian (Sacchini) and one of a German (Luther). Curiously enough, at a time when Handel was well known in this country, his music is omitted from this volume.

Following the turn of the century, however, *The Village Harmony*, in keeping with the trend, began to rid its pages of American music in favor of European. By the time it reached its seventeenth and final edition (1820), the American composer was noticeably missing. This changing attitude is summarized in the advertisement of the seventeenth edition: "Those alterations have been made which correspond to the progressive improvement of the publick taste in Sacred Musick. A few Classical European tunes have been substituted for some of a less perfect character, and the valuable foreign musick which is retained, and which the publick has not ceased to venerate and admire, is still preserved in this collection, secure from the touch of American innovation."

The following, which concludes this study of *The Village Harmony*, is a list of every edition, giving the name of printer, date of printing, and number of pages. All of the seventeen editions were printed in Exeter, New Hampshire.

Edition	Printer	Date	Pages
First	Henry Ranlet	1795	150 (plus)
Second	Henry Ranlet	1796	188
Third	Henry Ranlet	1797	?
Fourth	Henry Ranlet	1798	203
Fifth			
1st printing	Henry Ranlet	1800	206
2nd printing	Henry Ranlet	1800	205
Sixth	Henry Ranlet	1803	205
Seventh	Henry Ranlet	1806	223
Eighth	Charles Norris & John Sawyer	1807	230
Ninth	(no data)	1809?	?
Tenth	C. Norris & Co.	1811	283
Eleventh	C. Norris & Co.	1813	326
Twelfth	C. Norris & Co.	1815	332
Thirteenth	C. Norris & Co.	1816	334
Fourteenth	C. Norris	1817	350
Fifteenth	J. J. Williams	1818	350
Sixteenth	J. J. Williams	1819	350
Seventeenth			
1st printing	J. J. Williams	1820	350
2nd printing	J. J. Williams	1821	350

xv. Music Theory

THE knowledge of musical theory during the first half of the eighteenth century was extremely limited. The earliest American publications such as the *Bay Psalm Book* (beginning with the ninth edition which contained tunes), Tufts's *Introduction to the Art of Singing*, and Walter's *Grounds and Rules of Music* did include some theoretical material, but they afforded very little substance to the student of theory.

Soon after 1750 the works of William Tans'ur, an English composer, compiler, and theorist, began to apppear in our country. Through his *Royal Melody Compleat; or, New Harmony of Zion* (1756), *A New Musical Grammar and Dictionary* (1756), which evolved into the *Elements of Music Display'd; or, its Grammar or Ground Work Made Easy* (1772), Tans'ur "exercised a powerful influence over pre-revolutionary American psalmodists." [1]

A glance at the title of the third edition of the *New Musical Grammar* will convey some idea of the scope of musical theory during the period:

"A New Musical Grammar and Dictionary: or, a general Introduction to the whole Art of Musick. In four Books. Teaching

I. The Rudiments of Tones, Diatonick and Semitonick; according to the Gamut.—With Rules for Tuning the Voice and Beating the Time, the Nature of Keys and Transposition; and of all other characters used in Musick.

II. . . . Directions . . . for Tuning and Playing on the Organ, Harpsichord . . .

III. The Theory of Sound, from its Natural Causes . . .

IV. The Musicians historical and technical Dictionary.[2]

Other English composers who made a contribution to the development of music theory in colonial America were Aaron Williams, William Knapp, James Green, and James Evison. Tans'ur's and Williams's books were used in New Hampshire in 1769 and perhaps earlier, according to an advertisement in the *Gazette*: "Just imported from London by William Appleton and to be sold at his Store in Portsmouth . . . Tan'sur's Musical Grammar . . . Williams' Psalmody." [3]

The *Gazette* of March 17, 1775, reveals the presence in New Hampshire of *Salmon's Musical Grammar,* which we have traced to Thomas Salmon (1648-1706), an English writer on music.[4] The item, in the nature of a lost and found inquiry reads: "Whoever has in Possession a Book entitled Salmon's Musical Grammar, with Thomas Chadburne's Name in it, is desir'd to leave it at the Printing-Office."

Out of these English sources native psalmodists like Lyon, Flagg, Billings, Law, Holyoke, and others formulated their own theoretical basis for the teaching and writing of music. Thus evolved the introductory section on the "grounds of music" found in the majority of tune books of the period. By quoting several examples from the fifth edition of *The Village Harmony* and from Holyoke's *Instrumental Assistant,* we will gain an idea of the state of theoretical knowledge of music in America by the end of the eighteenth century.

"I. The general scale of music, or the gamut.

"Music is written on five lines, which, with the spaces with them included, are called a stave; but if it happens to ascend above or decend below those five lines, a line is added which is called a Ledger Line. . . .

"There are but seven distinct sounds in music, which are usually represented by the seven first letters of the Alphabet; five of these are whole tones, and two half tones, or semi-tones.

Above or below these seven notes or tones, the same order is repeated." [5]

The seven tones of the diatonic scale were represented by a set of four syllables in contrast to the seven used today. They were "faw sol law mi faw sol law mi." The "principal" or "leading note" was the second mi, which was pronounced "ma." [6]

"II. Musical characters and their explanation.

Staff		Five lines with their spaces whereon notes are written.
Brace	I or $\{$	Shows how many parts move together.
Ledger lines		Are added when notes ascend, or decend from the staff.
Cliffs		Are used to designate the parts.
F Cliff		Is so called from being placed on the letter F, and is used in the bass only, on the fourth line.
G Cliff		Is thus denominated from its place upon G the second line, and is always used in the parts above the bass.
C Cliff		Is some time used in instrumental music; it has its place commonly on C, though it is removeable to any other letter, in which case it removes the order of the other letters with it.
Sharp	♯	Set before a note raises it a semitone.
Flat	♭	Set before a note depresses it a semitone.
Natural	♮	Restores a note or letter to its original pitch.

Either a Flat or a Sharp set at the beginning of a Tune have influence through the Tune unless contradicted by a Natural.

Repeat		Shows what part of an air is to be played [or sung] over again.

Hold, Pause or Cadence	⌒	Is a mark of suspension, and shows that the time should be extended upon any note, over which it may be set.
Staccato Marks	❙ ❙ ❙ or ∴	Are either strokes or dots. The strokes should be performed distinctly, and the dots smoothly.
Slur	⌒	Over and under two or more notes, on the same line or space, unites them into one continued sound.
Figure	3	Placed over or under any three notes, implies that they must be performed in the time of the same kind, or three quavers to a crotchet.
Figure	6	Placed over notes reduces them to the time of four.
Direct	⚹	Set at the end of a staff shows the place of the first note in the next staff.
Appoggia-tura	♪♪	Are small notes placed before other notes, and their time deducted from them. When these small notes decend to their principals, they are called superior; when they ascend, inferior.
Single Bar	▤	Is a perpendicular stroke drawn across the staff, which serves to divide the notes into equal proportions.
Double Bar	▤	Serves to divide the first part of an air, from the second. They are often dotted on one or both sides, to signify a repeat. When dotted on one side, that part only is to be repeated; but when dotted on both sides, both parts, or strains must be played [or sung] twice over.
Close	▤	Signifies the conclusion of an air." [7]

"III. Syncopation.

"Notes of Syncopation or Driving Notes, are those which are forced out of order in the bar, or driven through the bar, and require the lifting or falling of the hand while the notes are sounding.[8]

"IV. Notes and corresponding rest values.

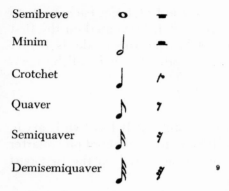

Semibreve	o	▬
Minim	♩	▬
Crotchet	♩	↱
Quaver	♪	𝄾
Semiquaver	♪	𝄿
Demisemiquaver	♫	𝅀

"V. Time and the manner of beating it."

Nine different Modes of Time were generally used, four of which were "Common," three "Triple," and two "Compound."

"Common Time

"First mode *Adagio* 𝄴

... denotes a flow movement, and has a Semibreve for its measure note, or notes or rests to that amount. It contains four beats in a bar, two of which are beat down, and two up. Each beat in this mode should contain the time of one second. The accents should be on the first and third parts of the bar. The manner of beating this mode is 1st let the ends of the fingers fall lightly,—2d, the heel of the hand,—3d, raise the hand a little, and partly shut it,—4th, raise it still higher, throwing it quite open at the same time, which completes the bar.

"Second mode *Largo* 𝄵

... likewise, has a semibreve for its measure note—has four beats in a bar, as in *Adagio,* and is beat in the same manner, only each beat is one quarter shorter. Accented the same as *Adagio.*

"Third mode *Allegro* 𝄴 or 𝄴

... also has a Semibreve for its measure note ... and only two beats in the bar, one down and one up. Each beat to the former character, contains one second of time; each beat, to the latter, is about one quarter shorter. Accented on the first part of the bar.—The manner of beating this mode, is 1st, let the hand fall lightly,—2d, raise it, and the bar will be completed.

"Fourth mode $\frac{2}{4}$

... has a minim for its measure note, ... It has two beats in a bar, one down and one up. It is performed about one quarter faster than the third mode, and is accented on the first part of the bar.

"Triple Time

"First mode $\frac{3}{2}$

... contains three minims in a bar, or other notes or rests to that amount. Each beat to be the length of one second in performing. In triple time the accent is commonly placed on the first part of the bar.—The manner of beating Triple Time, all the modes of which have three beats in a bar, is, 1st let the hand fall lightly,—2d, the heel of the hand,—3d, throw up the ends of the fingers which completes the bar.

"Second mode $\frac{3}{4}$

... contains three crotchets ... in each bar; it is performed in the same manner as the first mode, only about one quarter faster.

"Third mode $\frac{3}{8}$

... contains three quavers ... in each bar; it is performed in the same manner as the second mode, only about one quarter faster.

"Compound Time

"First mode $\frac{6}{4}$

... contains six crotchets, or other notes or rests to their amount, in each bar. There are two beats in a bar, each containing the time of one second.

"Second mode $\begin{smallmatrix}6\\8\end{smallmatrix}$

... contains six quavers ... in each bar, and beat in the same manner as the first mode, only one quarter faster. These modes of time are accented on the first and fourth parts of the bar.[10]

"VI. Keys. There are only two natural or primitive keys used in music, viz. the cheerful or lively, called the Major or Sharp Key, and the melancoly or mournful, called the Minor or Flat Key—C is the sharp, and A is the flat key. The last note in the Bass is always the key note, and is faw or law; if the key be sharp, it is faw, if flat, law. The key note is the foundation of the tune, and from it all the other parts are derived. In the sharp key, every 3d, 6th, and 7th, is half a tone higher than in the flat. When flats or sharps are placed at the beginning of a tune, they form what are called Artificial Keys, which have the same effect as the natural keys. The key note will not always be on C or A." [11]

The music most generally used in the churches consisted of three or four parts—namely treble, tenor, and bass; or, treble, counter, tenor, and bass. The distribution of the various vocal parts was a matter of grave concern and frequently precipitated strife and contention. It was the common practice to allot the air, or what is now the soprano, to the high male voices. "The part being prominent," says Gould, "all gentlemen who, by the greatest exertion, could reach a note that had any claim to be called high were sure to plead the right of being placed among the privileged ones." [12]

The ladies customarily sang the part written on the upper staff. The alto, or the "counter" as it was then known, was written on the second staff as at present, but an octave higher. This extraordinary aspect of the choir harked back to the "counter-tenor" parts in European music which were originally conceived for boys' voices. From this evolved the falsetto singing of the part by men; such was also the counter of New England. Alice Earle describes an instance of this rather distracting musical phenomenon as she recalled it: "It was my fortune to hear once in a country church an aged deacon sing counter. Reverence for the place and song and respect for the singer alike failed to control the irrepressible start of amazement and smile of amusement with which we greeted the weird and apparently demented shriek which rose high over the voices of the choir, but which did not at all disconcert their accustomed ears. Words, however chosen, would fail in attempting to describe the grotesque and uncanny sound.[13]

On rare occasions the counter, when attempted by women, "was usually sung at the top of their voices" exactly as written. But owing to the unpleasant effect when rendered with feminine voices, the lack of boys with sufficient skill to handle the part, and the absence of men who could fulfill the exceptional demands of the high *tessitura*, the counter was seldom sung. Those who could not be "pursuaded or forced to so high a point" as the tenor, contented themselves with the "humbler part of the bass" written on the lowest staff.[14]

Soon after the commencement of the third decade of the nineteenth century, the air or "leading part" of the tune was relegated to the females of the choir. "This was an interference with the rights of man," wrote Gould, "not readily acceded to, especially by those who had a tenor voice and had always sung the air." [15] Andrew Law, of Connecticut, a teacher, composer, and author of several tune books and instructional manuals, was one of the foremost leaders in the movement. Much was written on the subject. Some argued that it was "contrary to Scripture" and thus a "sin" [16] for women to assume the lead. In time, however, judicious musical discernment and common sense triumphed over vested interests and antediluvian complacency.

XVI. Conclusion

IT HAS been the purpose of this book to present an objective picture of musical life in New Hampshire prior to 1800. This work is essentially a source book; it is a vast accumulation of data, in the main new, which we hope will give a broader understanding of our country's cultural growth.

Musical life in New Hampshire before 1800 was closely related to that of Massachusetts, particularly Boston, and there was an exchange of musicians, teachers, concerts, and operas between these two areas. The conclusion that one might normally be expected to draw, that Boston was the musical center and New Hampshire merely a backwoods area where Boston musicians earned additional remuneration during the off-seasons, is not completely true. To be sure, the Van Hagens, Graupner, and Mrs. Arnold and her daughter Elizabeth were primarily Boston musicians who gave an occasional concert in New Hampshire, an "on tour" type of arrangement. But some musicians like Dr. Berkenhead came to Portsmouth first before going to Boston. Horatio Garnet, like others, made Portsmouth his residence for several years while in this country. One musician, William S. Morgan, who got into trouble in Boston, went to New Hampshire, returning to the former city when he thought the situation had cleared. Doubtless Boston had more to offer financially, culturally, and socially, although some musicians and impresarios came to New Hampshire from Boston simply because the atmosphere was more liberal, particularly in the matter of opera performances.

It is a curious fact that New Hampshire was enjoying opera, musical entertainments, and other theatricals at a time when nearby Boston was being restrained by the Massachusetts Antitheatre Law of 1750. As clearly related as New Hampshire's musical culture is to that of Massachusetts, there nevertheless was a spirit different from that of Massachusetts, and this difference is especially marked in the wider tolerance in New Hampshire for musical theater. This tolerance is rooted in the very origins of the settlement, for, unlike Massachusetts, New Hampshire was settled for commercial reasons, not religious. New Hampshire's healthy attitude toward the theater may have contributed valuable moral support to those in Massachusetts who finally brought about the revocation of the Antitheatre Law in 1797.

Records show that interest in theatrical entertainments was manifest as early as 1762. Prior to the Revolution, Portsmouth had the opportunity to hear and see "entertainments" consisting of songs, dances, instrumental selections, and pantomimes, interspersed with readings and recitations. During the final decade of the eighteenth century the currently popular operas were staged by traveling companies of professional English actor-singers, with local performers frequently participating. One such local performer, Charles Clapham of Dover, New Hampshire, evidently achieved professional status as an actor-singer on a par with his English counterpart, judging from the current press notices.

Much has been written concerning the absence of musical instruments in New England during the seventeenth century. This lack has been, more often than not, wrongfully attributed to the Puritans' "hatred for music," especially secular music. We have produced evidence, further dispelling this myth, that such instruments as the hautboy (oboe), recorder, treble viol, kit, trumpet, drum, virginal, and possibly the lute, existed during the period in New Hampshire. Moreover, the references to these instruments indicate a definite interest in secular music. The hautboys and recorders mentioned here, hitherto believed to have existed only in the homes of wealthy southern colonists, may be the first such allusions to these instruments with respect to seventeenth-century New England. It is highly probable that research in the other New England colonies of the period will bring to light additional references to the haut-boy and recorder.

Public secular concerts were given in the state soon after the Revolutionary War. These concerts usually included both vocal and instrumental music. Concerts by solo performers, as well as an occasional concerts by a military band, were also given. In New Hampshire, as in Boston and other New England towns, Mrs. Arnold entertained with numerous "favorite" songs; Berkenhead performed his patriotic "Bastille" on the pianoforte; and Graupner played his oboe as he had done under Haydn several years earlier in London. New Hampshire concerts compared favorably with those presented in other parts of New England.

Music also played an important role at public ceremonials and celebrations during the last four decades of the eighteenth century. A typical festive day in New Hampshire included: sacred music for the worship service, martial airs for the parade, songs to accompany the toasts at the banquet, a public concert preceding the ball, and finally the engaging lighter rhythms for the ball itself. The music which marked George Washington's visit to Portsmouth in 1789 was especially lavish, similar to that of other communities visited during his famous tour.

Sacred music was largely confined to congregational singing of psalms during the seventeenth and first half of the eighteenth century in the New England colonies, although our references indicate that the rendition of a psalm by a choir, or by a chosen group able to sing according to the "approved rule," was not unknown in New Hampshire before 1661. During the third decade of the following century New Hampshire joined in a country-wide movement to improve the music of the worship service (Sonneck, *Early Concert-Life in America,* p. 9) as initiated by Tufts and Walter. Out of this movement emerged the singing school and singing society, which ultimately led to the establishment of the church choir. By the turn of the century, musical instruments to support the singers had been introduced into the service. This innovation was opposed by some as "popish" and "sinful." Frequently it resulted in community strife and contention but was ultimately resolved.

The number of organs in the churches of New England before 1800 has been considered small. The first importation of an organ into this area (the Brattle organ) occurred in 1711. Although we have no date for the first organ imported into New Hampshire, our study shows that there must have been at least one in Portsmouth prior to 1765.

The efforts to improve church music quite naturally stimulated an interest in public sacred concerts. These concerts, however, were not so well received as the secular offerings of the day, possibly because the personal freedom and growing spirit of nationalism which resulted from the Revolution, the simultaneous loosening of clerical reins upon the lives of the people, the renewal of European trade as well as the further assimilation of European ideas and social customs, fostered a growing demand for the secular pleasures and adornments of life.

The need for diversified music instruction on all levels became apparent in the eighteenth century with the desire for better church music, the growing interest in public concerts, operas, and other musical entertainments, and the emphasis on music as a social refinement. Lessons in vocal and instrumental music as well as in the "polite art" of dancing were offered in New Hampshire before the Revolution. This teaching was carried on by a few skilled musicians from England and France and a number of capable native itinerant psalmodists, some of whom had achieved a certain facility as instrumentalists. It is notable that by the end of the century, according to newspaper advertisements, instrumental instruction was more widely featured than vocal. This important development, which Sonneck points up in the final chapter of his *Early Concert-Life in America,* was occurring throughout America at that time.

With the rise of the academies in New Hampshire during the

last two decades of the century, music became a regular part of their curricula, the teaching still largely in the hands of the itinerants.

The instruction manuals first used in the state, such as the works of Aaron Williams, William Tans'ur, William Knapp, and Thomas Salmon (Salmon's book has hitherto not been mentioned in other studies), were chiefly European. In time New Hampshire began to use American manuals from Boston, Newburyport, and Philadelphia, but it also developed a few of its own such as Benjamin Dearborn's *Scheme*, David Merrill's *Psalmodists' Companion*, and the very popular *Village Harmony*. Instruction manuals written by psalmodists from other states (as Holyoke and Kimball of Massachusetts), printed in New Hampshire, and the manuals of William Billings, Andrew Law, Oliver Holden, and Supply Belcher were likewise used here before 1800. The theoretical material in these American manuals, except for a few modifications, retained its basic European characteristics.

In the area of music publishing, Henry Ranlet of Exeter, New Hampshire, was one of the earliest printers in this country to own music type. Many tune books, issued from his "Music-Press," saw widespread use throughout New England. Among them was the *Village Harmony*, the first seven editions of which were compiled by Ranlet himself. This book, extending into seventeen editions, ran from 1795 to 1821.

New Hampshire had its own composers, some of whom wrote in the general style that characterized Billings, while others imitated the more polished manner of the European composer. Billings's influence can be seen in the preface to Richard Merrill's *Musical Practitioner*, although Merrill was a composer of definite musical personality. A few of his pieces ("Harvard" and "Easter") are comparable to the best produced anywhere in eighteenth-century America. David Merrill, Benjamin Dearborn, and John Hubbard also contributed to the musical literature of their day.

When Lowell Mason of Boston, in the late 1820s, rejected the cruder eighteenth-century indigenous music for the smooth harmonizations of tunes chosen from European sources, his preference for a more correct style in church music represented a point of view already well developed in New Hampshire some thirty years earlier by John Hubbard. Hubbard, who frowned upon the fuging tune and other native composition close to folk sources, may have had greater influence upon this drift away from the home-grown church music than has been hitherto suspected. The relationship between Mason and Hubbard may show that Boston was the focal point, but not necessarily the point of origin.

Another indication of this trend toward European style of composition is manifest in Boston's creation of a "Handel and Haydn Society" in 1815 instead of a "Billings Society" fifteen years after the latter's death. In New Hampshire this point of view notably emerged several years earlier, when the "Handellian Society" was formed in Amherst (N.H.) in 1805 and the "Handel Society of Dartmouth College" was founded in 1807. (John Hubbard was its first president.) So while Billings, who died in poverty, was never accorded the honor of having a musical society identified with his name, Hubbard was given this distinction twice. The Hubbard references suggest that similar finds may turn up in other areas of New England.

These, then, are the salient generalizations which can be drawn from the pages of this work. A more complete picture of New Hampshire's musical life before 1800, and its relation to the rest of the country and to Europe, will not be possible until numerous other area studies are carried out. Sonneck's plea, some forty years ago, for "a correct and abundant literature of city and state musical histories" (see page *iii*) echoes still. Actually, the task of compiling area studies has just begun, and with each new find the music historian becomes acutely aware of the need for further research. New England's musical development prior to 1800 cannot be safely written until state studies for the remaining five states, as well as a solid accumulation of city studies, become a reality.

APPENDIX A. Teachers' Advertisements

New Hampshire Gazette, March 15, 1765 [1]

"This is to inform the Public, that John Williams, Has opened a School opposite Mr. John Gardner's, Taylor, for Teaching young Gentlemen and Ladies to Sing by the exact Rules of Vocal Musick. Young Gentlemen on Thursday and Saturday Afternoons at Six Pound per Quarter, and on Monday and Thursday Evenings at Ditto per Quarter. The Ladies on Tuesday and Friday Evenings at the same Price. Likewise Teaches Young Ladies to Write and Cypher every day from Seven to Eight and from Twelve to One in the Morning at Six Pound per Quarter."

New Hampshire Gazette, December 18, 1767

"Peter Curtis Begs Leave to inform the Public that he will open a Dancing School next Monday in a convenient Room under the Printing Office, and will teach young Gentlemen and Ladies three Times a Week, viz. on Monday, Thursday, and Friday Afternoons and Evening, at the Rate of Five Dollars for the first Quarter, and Four Dollars per Quarter afterwards, two of which to be paid at Entrance. He will also teach any private Scholars at such Time as may best suit their Convenience. Any Gentlemen inclining to be instructed to play the Violin, shall be taught by the Lesson, either at their own Houses, or at Said Curtis's School, at a certain Price for every Lesson. Gentlemen who will please to put their Children under his Tuition may depend upon their being taught in the most polite Manner;—and that he will strive to instill into their Minds, the principles of Good Manners and Genteel Deportment."

New Hampshire Gazette, May 5, 1769

"Peter Curtis Begs leave to acquaint the Public, that he has again opened a School for teaching young Masters and Misses, Dancing and Good Manners, at the House lately improved by Capt. Bunbury, in the new pav'd Street, opposite the printing office in Portsmouth, New Hampshire. Any Gentlemen or Ladies who will be pleased to favour him with the Care of their Children may rely on his faithful Discharge of the Trust Committed to him: He will also attend any Gentleman or Lady who may chuse to be privately instructed."

New Hampshire Gazette, May 8, 1772

"Edward Hackett, From Europe Begs leave to acquaint the Gentlemen and Ladies, That at the Request of many of the Principal Inhabitants of the Town, he Shall on Thursday next open a Dancing School at the new Assembly-House, in Portsmouth, where he will Teach Dancing in the politest Manner, for the low Price of Four Dollars per Quarter, half to be paid at Entrance.— Those who send their Children may depend that great Care will be taken of their Education and good Order observed.—The times proposed for public Schools are Thursday in the Atfernoon, and Fridays in the Forenoon. He will wait on any Gentlemen or Ladies either at the assembly House, or their own Houses, at such hours, as may be agreed on.

"Said Hackett, has taught Dancing in many of the Principal Towns in England, Ireland and America. He will only be in Town on Thursdays and Fridays, the remainder of his Time being taken up at Newbury, etc. where he likewise keeps a School on Mondays and Wednesday."

New Hampshire Gazette, July 10, 1772

"Mr. Morgan, Musico Theorico. Having been particularly requested, purposes Instructing Ladies and Gentlemen on the Harpsichord, Violin, etc., etc. He is to be spoke with at Mr. Stavers."

New Hampshire Gazette, August 21, 1772

"Mr. Morgan Begs leave to inform his subscribers, and the Public in general, that the 2nd Week in September his Exhibition will begin with a Benefit Night for the Poor of the Town,—and the Subscribers Nights will commence the ensuing Evening."

New Hampshire Gazette, March 19, 1773

"Monsieur De Viart Begs Leave to inform those Gentlemen and Ladies, who design to favour him with the Instruction of their Children in the Art of Dancing, that he has always endeavoured to merit the Approbation of those who have hitherto favoured him with their Custom, by having at all Times Obliged himself to instruct his Pupils in those Principles which he received in that Profession himself.—It is not everyone who pretends to teach this delicate Art, who will take the Pains to instruct their Scholars in those Rules of Decorum and Politeness which are absolutely necessary to be known, before young Persons can step abroad into the World with Elegance and Ease.—And it often happens that Scholars, through the Ignorance of their Masters, are guilty of great Rudeness and commit gross Blunders on their first going into Company.

"He designs to open his Academy at his Lodgings in a House belonging to the Hon. Daniel Warner, Esq; near the long wharf, on the first Monday of April next, and to hold his School three Days in the Week, viz. Mondays, Thursdays and Saturdays, from Two to Six o'clock, P.M. Those Scholars who attended him in the summer past, are to pay only Two Dollars Per Quarter, and those that are new Comers, are to pay Two Dollars Entrance, and Two Dollars per Quarter.

"N.B. Said Viart teaches Minuets, French Jiggs, Horn-Pipes, Rigadoons, and English Country Dances of all Kinds.

"If any Gentlemen have a mind to be taught privately in the Evening, he will be ready to wait upon them at any time at their Leisure: and he likewise teaches the French Language in the easiest Method, so that Scholars may understand it in a very little Time; and several other Arts and Sciences which he is Master of; those Gentlemen and Ladies, who will honor him with their Custom may depend upon all the Satisfaction in the Power of their most humble and obedient Servant."

New Hampshire Gazette, Friday, August 6, 1773

"Mr. Morgan Takes this Method of informing the Public that on Tuesday last at three o'clock, P.M. he opened his Academy for

Musick and Dancing, at the Assembly House; and purposes attending three Tuesdays and Fridays. Those Ladies and Gentlemen who chuse to also honor him with the Care of their children may depend on the utmost Exertion of his Abilities in the Cultivation of their Education."

New Hampshire Gazette, Friday, August 20, 1773

"Mr. Morgan, Begs Leave to inform the Public, That he has opened his Academy for Music and Dancing, at the Assembly-House—Music at a Pistole a Month, and Dancing at Four Dollars the Quarter, two to be paid at Entrance, and purposes attending Tuesday and Friday Afternoon at present, and oftner as the School encreases.

"He likewise on Tuesday next shall open an Evening School, from seven o'Clock 'till Nine, for the Instruction of those whose Avocations prevent their attending in the Day-Time."

New Hampshire Gazette, August 20, 1773

"The Subscriber, Respectfully informs the Gentlemen and Ladies of this Town, and the Public in General, that he purposes to teach Music, Theorical, Rudimental and Practical.

"The Charms, Beauties and Advantages of Music are so universally known, that it is quite unnecessary to say any Thing for recommending it. But it is observed of this, (as of other Arts that Nature has any Share in) that it looses most of it's Beauties when not performed under the proper Restrictions of Rule and Judgement.—The Study of Music in particular, is rendered much more engaging, and the Practice vastly more pleasing, when regulated by Tune, Time and Concord.

"The Publisher purposes to teach Psalmody in it's various Branches, and has for Authors Handel, Purcel, Green, Knap and Williams, &. from which he collects the best Tunes, Hymns and Anthems; he has likewise a choice Collection of Canons, Fuges, Chorus's, an excellent Oratorio set by the celebrated Bull, an Ode on Friendship, and several Manuscript Pieces by the famous Mr. Lyon.

"He likewise advertizes the Ladies and Gentlemen that he teaches all sorts of Dramatic Music, such as Songs, Airs, Solo's, Duett's, Dialogues, etc.—And expects from London by the first Opportunity, a choice Collection of vocal Music, and set by the celebrated Arne, Boyce and Handel consisting of the newest and best Songs, as they are now sung at the Mary-Bone, Vaux-Hall and Covent Gardens.

"Those Gentlemen and Ladies who are inclined to gain a Knowledge in this entertaining, noble and pleasing Art, have now a Chance of practicing from the most easy Rules and approved Masters.

"For the Convenience of the Young Gentlemen in Town who are disposed to join together in a singing society and learn Psalmody the Publisher purposes to teach an hour and a Half in an Evening till they lengthen.

"The Ladies and Gentlemen who chuse to learn privately, and by themselves, are inform'd the Publisher will wait on them at his or their own Lodgings, as shall be most agreeable.

"N.B. He sits for, and teaches the Scale of the Violin, Flute, Harpsichord and Organ.—The Publisher and Subscriber may be spoke with by enquiring at Capt. Tilton's in King-Street, Portsmouth.   William Crosbey."

New Hampshire Gazette, August 27, 1773

"Mr. Crosbey, Further informs the Public, That, pursuant to his Advertisement of the 20th instant, he To-morrow opens his School of Music at the Assembly Room, there to continue to teach by the month, or Quarter, on Mondays, Thursdays and Saturdays, 3 Hours each day, beginning at 3 o'clock P.M. Those who attend accordingly will be instructed at 3 Dollars per Quarter. Those whose Affairs detain them in the Day Time, will be instructed Monday and Thursday Evening, an Hour and a half each Evening, at one Dollar per Quarter. Those who take Lessons once a Day are waited on at their own Lodgings, after the Rate of 3 Dollars the Month. One third of the Money for each Condition to be paid at Entrance.

"Mr. Crosbey desires that whatever Gentleman or Lady intends to Honor him with the Care of their Tuition, would attend at the Assembly Room, Tomorrow, three o'Clock, as he determines to open his School with a Dissertation on Music, in general, which will be beneficial to every young Beginner."

New Hampshire Gazette, September 10, 1773

"Six Pence O. T. Reward. Last Sunday Evening our Professor of

Music, Theorical, Rudimental and Practical, absconded; as the Damage the Public must sustain by his unexpected Retreat, will be very great, the above Reward of Six Pence O. T. is offered to any person who will apprehend W—— C..sbey Professor of Music, aforesaid, and convey him to this Town before the Fifth Day of November next.   The Sufferers.

"N.B. Said Professor had on when he went away, a green Coat, white Waistcoat and Breeches, and has a peculiar Mark, which Time will ne'er deface."

New Hampshire Gazette, February 25, 1774

"St. George de Viart, who has resided for three years last past at Salem, and taught Dancing, Fencing and the French Language, there, at Marblehead and Glocester, to general Approbation, having been favoured with encouragement to open Schools in this town for teaching the same polite and useful Accomplishments, begs leave to acquaint the Public, that he proposes to attend his Dancing-School every Monday, Wednesday and Saturday, from Two o'clock in the Afternoon, till Five, at the Assembly-Room; his Fencing-School on the Same Days, from Five o'clock in the Evening, till Eight, at the same Place; and French School from Six o'clock, till Eight in the Evening, at the same Place on Tuesday, Thursday and Fridays. He proposes also to Teach Dancing to any young Gentlemen whose Business will not permit them to attend in the Day, at the same Place on Tuesday, Thursday and Friday Evenings, from Eight o'clock till Ten.

"Mr. DeViart intends opening his Dancing School on the above-mentioned Days, in the First Week of March next; and his other Schools as soon as a sufficient Number of Scholars apply.

"Mr. DeViart's Terms may be known by applying to him, at his Lodgings, at Mrs. Gerrish's, in King-Street.   Portsmouth, 16th Feb. 1774.²"

New Hampshire Gazette, March 11, 1774

"Edward Hackett, Opens his Dancing School on the 24th of March Instant, at the Assembly House in Portsmouth, where he will instruct such Gentemen and Ladies as inclined to attend; and the utmost Pains and Cares will be taken with them—The Times for Attendance will be on Thursday in the Afternoon, and Friday's in the Forenoon. Said Hackett gives Notice also, that he keeps School at Newbury Port and Haverhill."

New Hampshire Gazette, April 22, 1774

"St. George de Viart, Professor of the polite Arts, Begs Leave to acquaint the Public that he opened his Academy for Dancing last Monday at the Assembly Room, where Ladies and Gentlemen who have not perfected themselves in that agreeable Accomplishment, may be taught in such a manner as to add Grace and Beauty to the Deportment of either Sex, in the Genteelest Characters in Life.

"Also said Viart teaches the French Language in the easiest Method, so that Scholars of the least Aptitude (in the Course of Six Months) may be sufficiently acquainted with the Rudiments of the Language; and pronounce and write it with Delicacy and Propriety.   Portsmouth April 15th, 1774."

New Hampshire Gazette, September 29, 1781

"An Evening School for young People of both Sexes. If suitable Encouragement is given, will be open'd by Benjamin Dearborn, at his House in pav'd Street. On Tuesday the 9th of October: To be attended three Evenings in the Week, from half after 6 'till 9 o'clock. The Exercises proposed will be, in Grammar, Reading, Writing, Spelling, Arithmetic and the Rules of Vocal Music (as far as may be learned without singing): Any of those Exercises will be omitted if desired.

"His Writing and Singing-Schools which have been kept thro' the Summer, will be continu'd during the Winter, if the present Encouragement continues.   Portsmouth 27th September, 1781."

New Hampshire Gazette, March 29, 1783

"If suitable Encouragement offers, a Singing-School will be open'd by Benjamin Dearborn. It will be attended at his house on Mondays, Tuesdays and Wednesdays, from Five to Six o'Clock, afternoon."

New Hampshire Mercury, March 29, 1785

"Francis Drew of Newmarket, Newfields, Hereby gives notice that he will teach Drummers and Fifers upon reasonable terms, and in the easiest and best manner.   Newmarket, March 24, 1785."

New Hampshire Gazette, April 1, 1785

"Misses from the Country, Taken to Board; and instructed in reading, writing, arithmetic, etc. by Benjamin Dearborn on Moderate Terms. Said Dearborn has now in the press, Rules for teaching Vocal Music entirely by Letters, and for bringing all its characters within the compass of common fount of printing types. This mode of instruction he has found by experience, to be much more expeditious than that heretofore used; and so simple as scarcely to perplex the youngest child who can read.

"To make these rules more extensively useful, he proposes to open a Singing School on Tuesday the 19th of April next, to be attended on Tuesdays and Fridays, from 7 to 9 o'clock, P.M.

"N.B. Scholars belonging to the writing-school the ensuing summer, whose parents desire they may attend the singing-school, shall have that privilege gratis. Those who are not of the writing-school will be recieved in the singing-school on reasonable terms.   Portsmouth, March 31, 1785."

New Hampshire Gazette, April 18, 1785

"John White, With respect, begs leave to offer his service to the Gentlemen and Ladies of this Town, to teach them at the Assembly Room, Minuet Dancing and a variety of other Dances, etc. in the genteelest Manner.—If a knowledge of the Art, after the most approved French Taste, is a recommendation, he flatters himself he shall give general Satisfaction. Wednesday and Thursdays are the Days proposed to teach on.—On Wednesday, 20th of April, he will open School. An Evening School will also be kept for an elder Class.—Should sufficient Encouragement be given, he will also teach the French and Spanish Languages.   Portsmouth, April 6, 1785."

New Hampshire Gazette, April, 29 1785

"John White, Dancing-Master, Would inform the respectable ladies and gentlemen, whom he proposed to teach the Minuet Dancing, etc. by means of the roads being yet impassable, has thought best to prolong. The time of opening his school, to the third day of May,—when he will open it at the Assembly-Room in this town."

New Hampshire Gazette, October 21, 1785

"Winthrop Bennet, Proposes to open a Singing-School on Wednesday Evening next, provided a suitable Number of Persons apply. Those who wish to be instructed in this noble Employment, are requested to call upon him at his house near the Rope-Walks, where they may be informed of the Terms.

"N.B. He desires that those who wish to be instructed would apply as soon as possible.   Portsmouth, October 13, 1785."

New Hampshire Gazette, April 1, 1786

"John White, Who had the honor of being an Instructor to many of the youths in this town, last spring, consequently his abilities are well known, again offers his service to the Ladies and Gentlemen that if sufficient encouragement presents, his School will be opened at the Assembly-Room, on the 1st of May next, where he will attend every Monday and Thursday afternoon, beginning at three o'Clock throughout the season.

"His price will only be Four Dollars per Quarter for his former Scholars, with the addition of Two Dollars at entrance for new ones.

"Mr. White intends likewise to keep an Evening-School at the above place.   Portsmouth, 27 March, 1786."

New Hampshire Gazette, April 29, 1786

"John White whose wish is to introduce polite and decent amusement in this town, proposes for that purpose to open every Monday Evening, for the ensuing season, a Ball at the Assembly Room from 8 to 11 o'clock, which hopes by his exactness in keeping up the dignity, decorum and good order requisite in such an undertaking, to merit the applause of the gentlemen and ladies.—No person will be admitted, whose education will not admit him into the polite company, and above the age of 17. A variety of new dances will be introduced by said White.

"Tickets may be had from 10 to 2 o'clock, at Mrs. Purcell's on said days, at a very reasonable price.   Portsmouth, June 29."

New Hampshire Spy, July 2, 1788

"Horatio Garnet, Humbly acquaints the public that having received his musical education in some of the principal cities in

Europe, he proposes teaching the Violin, Bass-viol, Hautboy, Clarionet, Flute, etc. and also to give Lessons to Ladies on the Guittar. Those who wish to acquire a practical knowledge in this most delightful science, and will honor him with their commands, may depend on his most strenuous exertions for their instruction and improvement, on any or all the above mentioned instruments, on the most moderate terms, which may be known by applying to him at his lodgings with Mr. Samuel Place, of this town. Portsmouth, June 23, 1788."

New Hampshire Gazette, October 30, 1788

"Scholar's Ball. Mr. Flagg Returns his most greatful acknowledgements to the Ladies and Gentlemen of this town, for the very polite attention and great encouragement he has received since his residence here, and begs leave most respectfully to inform them that he intends opening an Evening School for ladies and gentlemen during the ensuing season, on the same terms as in the season past (wood and candles excepted). He intends having a Scholar's Ball, on Thursday the 6th of November next, for the improvement, and hopes the proficiency they have already made under his tuition will meet the approbation of those who shall honor him with their company on the occasion. The scholars will dance from 6 'til 9 o'clock after which a Ball will commence for the company, who will be attended with the greatest politeness. Particular care will be taken to have good musick.—Scholar's tickets at 2s. and 3s. each may be had of Mr. Flagg, at Capt. Furnass's.

"Should ladies or gentlemen wish for private instruction, Mr. Flagg will be happy to wait on them at their houses.   Portsmouth, October 29."

New Hampshire Spy, March 20, 1789

"Mr. Garnet, Returns his most sincere thanks to the Ladies and Gentlemen of this town, for the Encouragement he has hitherto met with—and begs leave to inform them that he proposes (should encouragement offer to reside in Town during the ensuing Season, for the purpose of teaching instrumental Musick in its various branches viz.

"Violin, Violincello, Guittar, Germ. Flute, Clarionet & Hautboy, likewise the Harpsichord, Spinnet, etc.

"Music copied in the most accurate manner.—Also, Key'd Instruments tuned on the shortest Notice. His terms (which are very moderate) may be known by applying to him at Greenleaf's inn."

New Hampshire Spy, March 20, 1789

"Dancing-School. Mr. Flagg, Begs leave to inform those Ladies and Gentlemen who with their Children to acquire the knowledge of that polite Accomplishment—that he will again open a School, at the Assembly Room, on Wednesday the first of April next, and on the Saturday following, if a sufficient number of scholars offer. He will teach the mode of the English Minuets, Cotillions, and the newest Contra Dances.

"He proposes to teach the Harpsichord and Spinnet, at a very low Rate.

"The Terms may be known by applying to him at Capt. Robert Furniss's.   Portsmouth March 20, 1789."

New Hampshire Spy, December 4, 1789

"Mr. Bennet, Proposes opening his Singing-School on Thursday Evening next, at Mr. Davenport's House in this Town.   Portsmouth, November 30, 1789."

New Hampshire Spy, December 4, 1789

"John Reed, Respectfully informs the Public that he has opened a Singing-School, at the House of Mr. Nathaniel Shannon, in this town: and is ready to receive Scholars at Five Shillings per quarter; he finding room, fire and lights. The school will be attended two evenings every week, from six to nine o'clock.

"He flatters himself, the humane and benevolent, will be excited to commisserate his situation, as he can do little else for a livelihood—so shall the blessing of the indigent come upon them, and the soul ready to perish pray for their prosperity.   Portsmouth, November 20, 1789."

New Hampshire Spy, January 12, 1791

"Mr. Bennet, Proposes attending upon such Pupils as are desirous of being instructed in that pleasing Art, Singing, at the House of Capt. M'Hard, on Thursday and Saturday afternoons. His

Evening-School is continued as usual.   Portsmouth January 12, 1790."

New Hampshire Gazette, January 22, 1791

"The subscriber influenced by the success and encouragement of his labours in the cause of Education, is preparing accomodations for instituting an Academy for Young Ladies, connected with a Boarding House, for which purpose he wishes to engage a Master to teach the French Language and Dancing, and a Mistress, to instruct in the useful and ornamental branches of Needlework; both of whom must be well recommended as completely qualified for their respective departments, and must (if their convenience will permit) board in the house, giving their assistance in superintending the Manners and Morals of those who may be under their tuition.

"Any person willing to undertake either of the charges before mentioned is requested to make proposal to Benjamin Dearborn. Portsmo' N. Hampshire, January 1791."

New Hampshire Gazette, March 26, 1791

"John Reed respectfully informs the public, that he has opened a Singing-School for Children, on the afternoons of Thursday and Saturdays, from 3 to 6 o'clock, P.M. at six shillings per quarter, at the house lately occupied by Mr. J. Marshall, in Pleasant Street near Capt. John Pickering's Mills where he is ready to instruct scholars:—Likewise, an Evening-School for young people of both sexes, through the summer. As he is lame, and can do no other business to obtain a livelihood for himself and family he hopes the hearts of all feeling parents will expand to commiserate his present situation, and thereby patronize his assiduous undertaking.
Portsmouth, March 26, 1791."

New Hampshire Gazette, April 30, 1791

"Portsmouth Academy, Is now open for the reception of Boarders and Scholars for instruction in Spelling, Reading, Writing, Arithmetic, Accounts, English Grammar, Geography, Chronology, History, Composition, Embroidery, plain Needle-Work, Vocal Music, Instrumental Music, Dancing, Drawing, French Language, etc.

"Any of the above branches will be taught separately to those who may chuse it.   April 30, 1791."

New Hampshire Spy, July 27, 1791

"Mr. Civil Presents his respects to the Ladies and Gentlemen of Portsmouth and its vicinity, and begs leave to inform them that he will open a Dancing School at the assembly room on Saturday the 30th inst. which will be held the following Thursdays and Saturdays, at 3 o'clock in the afternoon, and should any young Gentleman wish for instruction in the evening, he will be happy in waiting on them, and any young ladies they may choose to introduce during the hours of instruction without any further expence.

"The French Language will be attended four mornings in the week, at 6 o'clock, and drawing every day from twelve to one.

"From the improvement of his pupils under his tuition in the above branches, during his residence at the Academy, Mr. Civil is induced to solicit their patronage on the present occasion, and hopes his future assiduities may merit their approbation.

"Each of the above mentioned branches at four dollars per quarter.

"N.B. Ladies and Gentlemen not wishing to attend the School, may be instructed at their houses, at the additional price of one dollar per quarter."

New Hampshire Spy, August 6, 1791

"Mrs. Spillard Is induced to open a school for Females, whom she instructs in reading, and the various useful and ornamental branches of needle-work, etc., etc. A music, drawing and writing master, will also attend at proper hours if wished."

New Hampshire Gazette, November 3, 1791

"Mr. Bennett, Will open his Singing-School on Monday evening next, at the house of Mrs. Gregory, opposite the dwelling house of Dr. John Jackson.—Those who have made any proficiency in Singing, will be taught two evenings, each week, by themselves, at 6s. per Quarter; those who have not received any instruction before, will be taught likewise by themselves, two evenings, each week at 7s. per Quarter, exclusive of any further expense—the one half of a Quarter to be paid at entrance, the remainder at the expiration of a Quarter.—School hours from 6 to 9 o'clock; the division of the classes to be agreed on at the time of opening—a full meeting is requested.   Portsmouth, Nov. 3, 1791."

New Hampshire Spy, November 12, 1791

"Dancing-School. Mr. Civil's Dancing School is now opened at the Hall of the late Portsmouth Academy, from two to five o'clock P.M.—An Evening School for young Gentlemen will be opened as soon as a sufficient number applies.

"Miniature Painting—Done in the most elegant manner at Seven Dollars each—and if the likeness is not approved of, no money required.—Also, Devices in hair for Lockets, Rings or Bravelets.—Profiles taken and reduced to any size required, at a moderate price.   Portsmouth, November 11, 1791."

New Hampshire Spy, January 11, 1792

"The Subscribers for the Support of a Singing School in the first parish in this town, are hereby notified that said school will probably be opened on Monday next and it is desired they would, as soon as possible, hand to the wardens, the names of those of their respective families they wish should attend. Any other of the parishioners who are not subscribers, by applying to the wardens may know the terms on which they may be admitted.   Portsmouth, January 10, 1792."

New Hampshire Spy, May 30, 1792

"Mr. Civil Presents his respects to the Ladies and Gentlemen of this town, and informs them that his Dancing School will commense on Thursday afternoon next, the 31st inst. in the Assembly Room, twice a Week, viz. Thursday and Saturday, terms of Tuition 4 Dollars per quarter, one to be paid at entrance.—The French Language and Drawing will be attended to at the Theatre—French four times a Week, Monday, Wednesday, Thursday and Friday, from 6 to 8 o'clock in the Morning, Drawing every Day in the Week, from 12 to 1 o'clock, the same terms as dancing.

"Should any Ladies and Gentlemen wish to be instructed at their own Houses, Mr. Civil will wait upon them at 5 dollars per quarter.   Portsmouth, May 26, 1792."

New Hampshire Spy, December 22, 1792

"The subscriber takes this method to return his sincere thanks to those who have heretofore given him encouragement & informs them that he has again opened a singing-school in the house lately occupied by Capt. S. Nichols, near the fourth Meeting-house,—those who are desirous of being instructed in the rules of singing and will honor him with their tuition, may rely on his using his utmost endeavors to teach them. His terms are low, and may be known by applying to the house above mentioned.   John Reed, Portsmouth, December 15, 1792."

The Oracle of the Day, June 11, 1793

"Mr. Allen, Respectfully informs the young Ladies and Gentlemen of this Town, that he has opened a Dancing-School at Capt. Whidden's Assembly-Room, and will continue it every Thursday and Saturday, at 3 o'clock in the afternoon.

"Those Gentlemen who can not conveniently attend in the day time, will be waited upon at 7 o'clock, on the evenings of Thursday and Friday.   Portsmouth, June 11, 1793."

New Hampshire Gazette, August 27, 1793

"John Reed respectfully informs the public, that he purposes to open a Singing-School the second day of September next, at the house of Capt. Samuel Storer, opposite Mr. Samuel Hill's store, north end; where the scholars may depend on having every pain taken to instruct them in Singing. Terms may be known by applying to said Reed.   Portsmouth, August 13, 1793."

The Oracle of the Day, November 27, 1793

"Mr. Bennet, respectfully informs the young Ladies and Gentlemen of this town, that he intends opening a Singing-School, soon—his terms will be moderate—Those who wish to attend, may know them by applying to him.   Portsmouth, November 27, 1793."

The Oracle of the Day, November 23, 1793

"John Latham Berkenhead, Lately From Europe, Having from a very early period received his tuition under the most accomplished masters and performers of Music in Great-Britain, particularly the great Doctor Wainwright, and the celebrated Bomgarton, of London; respectfully informs the public, that on the most reasonable terms, he gives lessons on the Organ, Harpsichord, Piano-Forte, and other keyed instruments—Tunes and Repairs them—and punctually attends the commands of all those who are pleased to honour him with any.

"He takes this opportunity most gratefully to acknowledge the many favours he has already received from some of the most respectable characters in this town, in his professional line, which he begs leave to assure them, he shall, by the most strenuous exertions, endeavour to deserve.

"His terms may be known by applying to him at his lodgings, at Mr. John Davenport's near Mr. William Sheafe's store. Portsmouth, November 22, 1793."

The Oracle of the Day, December 11, 1793

"Mr. Bennet, respectfully informs the young Ladies and Gentlemen of this town, that his Evening Singing School will be opened on Monday Evening next, at Captain Smith's House, in Washington-Street, opposite Dr. Hall Jackson's—where he shall teach on moderate terms, those who may please to honour him with their company.   Portsmouth, December 11, 1793."

New Hampshire Gazette, March 8, 1794

"Mr. Duport, Dancing-Master from Paris Presents his respects to the ladies and gentlemen of this Town. He proposes giving Private Tuition in the polite accomplishment of Dancing—And he engages in three months to perfect those Ladies and Gentlemen, who shall please to honor him with their attendance. Several of the first Families at the Southward, he has perfected in this accomplishment, in that short period, from whom he has letters of Recommendation.

"A Subscription Paper is lodged at Capt. Whidden's Assembly Room; where the terms will be made known.—Provided suitable encouragement is given a school will be opened the first of April next in said room.   Portsmouth, March 8, 1794."

New Hampshire Gazette, September 9, 1794

"Dancing School. Mr. St. Amand has the honor to inform the Ladies and Gentlemen of Portsmouth, that he shall open his Dancing-School to-morrow, being Wednesday the 10th of September, at 10 o'clock, A.M. and from thence 'till 1 o'clock, P.M. on Thursdays and Fridays, the hours of attendance are from 2 to 5, P.M. He will pay the most unlimited attention to his scholars and flatters himself with obtaining the esteem of all those who favor him with their confidence. When his Scholars have arrived to a sufficient degree of perfection, a public ball will be given once a fortnight. Parents admitted at any hour. His terms are six dollars pr. quarter, two of which are to be paid at entrance.

"On Wednesday and Thursday evenings at 6 o'clock, his school will be open for the admission of young gentlemen, upon the same terms as above. If 12 subscribers should present, his evening school will be opened next week, at the Assembly-House. Portsmouth, September 8."

New Hampshire Gazette, September 23, 1794

"Dancing-School opened. Mr. St. Amand Most respectfully informs the Ladies and Gentlemen of the town of Portsmouth, that he has opened his Dancing-School at the Assembly-House, where he will receive their children for tuition, and use utmost endeavor to instruct them the very polite accomplishment of dancing.

"Days and hours of attendance for young ladies,

Tuesdays from 10 to 1 o'clock

Thursday & Saturday } from 2 to 5 o'clock, P.M.

For young gentlemen,

Tuesday, Thursday & Friday } from 6 to 9 o'clock, P.M."

The Oracle of the Day, October 11, 1794

"Alexander Outin, Educated in France, Proposes teaching the French Language if Encouragement is offered—Likewise, will give lessons on the Violin.—Inquire of the Printer, or of Anthony Chapouil. Portsmouth, October 10, 1794."

The Oracle of the Day, May 9, 1795

"Thomas Burkenhead[3] Returns his sincere thanks to his friends, and the inhabitants of Portsmouth in general, for the liberal encouragement he has experienced from them; he at the same time begs leave to solicit a continuance of their patronage and favour, and likewise to inform them that he teaches the Organ, Harpsichord, and Piano Forte, in their various stiles, etc.—Also, that he Tunes and Repairs Instruments in the best manner in town and country.

"Mr. Berkenhead flatters himself that he posseses Abilities, Politeness and Patience, which are so very necessary for a good Teacher.

"His Terms may be known by application to him, who will wait on either Ladies or Gentlemen at their houses.   Portsmouth, May 9, 1795."

The Oracle of the Day, September 1, 1795

"Francis Maurice, Master of the French Language, Dancing and Music at Medford Academy, and Harvard University, Having been solicited by several respectable Gentlemen in this town, to teach the polite accomplishment of Dancing & French Language, Those Ladies and Gentlemen who will honour him with their attendance, are desired to leave their names at Mr. Peirce's bookstore in Court-street.

Conditions

"The Dancing School will be attended every Tuesday and Friday afternoons, at Eight Dollars per Quarter, four on entrance, and the remainder at the end of the Quarter.

"The French Language will be taught every Wednesday and Saturday evening, at six dollars per Quarter.   Portsmouth, Sept. 1, 1795."

New Hampshire Gazette, September 22, 1795

"Music School. The subscriber proposes to open a School for Sacred Vocal Music in this town, to be kept 12 weeks; every other evening, from half past five, to eight o'clock. His design is to teach such Music as it is sung in congregations: and to fit those who may attend, either to join the choirs in public worship, or for their own private amusement. Those persons who may be kind enough to favor him with the attendance of their children, and those under their care, may depend that every suitable attention will be paid them by their humble servant.   Isaac Lane.

"The School will be opened to-morrow evening at half past 5

o'clock in Mr. Whidden's large hall, where there may be accommodations for two hundred scholars. It is desired that as many as conveniently can, would attend on the first evening (if not, on either of the two succeeding evenings) as Mr. Lane wishes to ascertain whether there be a prospect of having a school, so as to make it an object for him to tarry: (the terms are 6 shillings a scholar) otherwise he must be under the painful necessity of leaving this town immediately.

"Mr. Lane is willing, besides producing credentials, both as to moral character, and with regard to his abilities as a Musician, to submit to a strict examination as to his theoretical knowledge, from any person in this town: as to his skill as a performer, or his abilities as a teacher, time will determine, should he be so fortunate as to meet with the confidence of the people of this place.   Portsmouth, September 21, 1795."

The Oracle of the Day, September 26, 1795

"Music School. Mr. Lane, having obtained a number of Subscribers, will proceed in his School on Monday evening next, at six o'Clock, in Mr. Whidden's Hall, where he will pay every suitable attention to those whom he may have the pleasure to instruct.

"Mr. Lane is willing, besides producing credentials, both as to his moral character, and with regard to his musical abilities, to submit to a strict examination as to his theoretical knowledge from any person in this town: as to his skill as a performer, or his abilities as a teacher, time will determine, should be be so fortunate as to meet with the confidence of the people of this place.

"Any singing-books will answer the purpose the first evening. Portsmouth, September 26, 1795."

The Oracle of the Day, November 18, 1795

"Singing-School. The Subscribers inform their Friends, that their Singing-School will be opened this evening at Mr. Diman's Hall: Those who have subscribed are desired to attend. Any who have not given their names, and wish to be instructed in the sacred employment, will have an opportunity this Evening—Those Gentlemen who please to send their Children, may depend on having every attention paid to them.   Joseph Akerman, Jr.   Job Harris.   Portsmouth, November 18."

The Oracle of the Day, November 25, 1795

"Singing-School, At Mr. Diman's Hall. Those persons who wish to be instructed in the sacred employment, are requested to attend immediately—as none will be admitted (except those who have made some proficiency), after this week.   Portsmouth, November 24, 1795."

New Hampshire Gazette, March 12, 1796

"Francis Maurice Respectfully informs the Ladies & Gentlemen of the town, that he proposes to teach the most beautiful accomplishment of Dancing in this town, and will open his school the 1st of April, if a sufficient number of subscribers should offer:— The terms of admittance are 5 dollars for each scholar pr. quarter, 2 at entrance and the remainder at the end of the quarter, the subscription paper is lodged at Mr. Melcher's Printing-Office, where subscribers will please to leave their names.   Portsmouth, March 11, 1796."

New Hampshire Gazette, April 2, 1796

"Dancing School. Mr. Maurice presents his compliments to the Ladies and Gentlemen of the town of Portsmouth, respectfully informs them that he shall open his Dancing School at the Assembly-Room on Wednesday next, and will be very much oblige to those Ladies and Gentlemen who wish him to instruct their Children in the most beautiful accomplishment to send them by 3 o'clock in the afternoon. The School will be kept two afternoons in each week, and the strictest attention will be paid to the pupils.   Portsmouth, April 2, 1796."

The Oracle of the Day, May 12, 1796

"Mr. Johnson having already opened a school at Mr. Davenport's for the instruction of gentlemen in the science and practice of Instrumental Music, begs leave to solicit further patronage of the good people of Portsmouth—and also respectfully to inform them, that he proposes opening a school for the initiation of the youth of both sexes in the still more useful accomplishment of vocal harmony—His ability and long experience as a teacher will be sufficiently vouched by persons fully acquainted with both. His terms may be known by applying to him at his lodgings at the Ark."

New Hampshire Gazette, August 20, 1796

"Music. Mr. Johnson proposes opening a School for the instruction of Sacred Vocal Music, and should encouragement offer, will devote three nights in each week to that purpose, at the rate of two dollars per quarter, one half to be paid at entrance.—All the respectable musical characters in town will attest to his abilities in that science, and he hopes to merit the patronage of the public by his assiduity.   Portsmouth August 19, 1796."

New Hampshire Gazette, March 18, 1797

"Dancing-School. Mr. Maurice, After returning his most sincere thanks to the Ladies and Gentlemen of the town of Portsmouth, for the encouragement given him the last summer, begs leave again to tender his services, and assures them he will use his utmost abilities to instruct their children in the very polite accomplishment of dancing, and will pay every attention to their manners and behavior while under his tuition, on the terms following, viz.

"1st. For the first quarter six dollars, and for the second, and of those that have before attended his school one guinea each per quarter.

"2d. Two dollars of which to be paid at entrance.

"3d. The school to commence on the first Saturday of April next, at the Assembly-Room, at three o'clock in the afternoon, and to be continued Thursdays and Saturdays, from three o'clock to sunset.

"Mr. Maurice informs the Ladies that he intends if encouragement offers, to open a Music-School, will teach them the Fortepienno at their houses, or at his Music-School, where he will furnish those who wish with a Fortepienno to learn on; the school will be kept from six to twelve o'clock in the morning, two days in each week. Likewise

"Informs those young gentlemen who wish to be instructed the Violin, that he will if encouragement offers, teach them two evenings in each week at his Music-School, which will be opened as soon as twelve scholars apply. Further particulars may be known by applying to Mr. Maurice, at Mr. Jotham Rindge's foot of Daniel Street, Portsmouth. March 18, 1797."

New Hampshire Gazette, April 15, 1797

"Dancing-School Mr. Maurice Begs leave to inform the ladies and gentlemen of the town of Portsmouth, that he opened his Dancing School, agreeable to his former advertizement, on the 1st day of April, but being unavoidably called out of town, is under the necessity of postponing the same until Thursday the 27th day of April inst. at which time the quarter will commence at the Assembly-Room at 3 o'clock, and the school be continued on Thursdays and Saturdays in the afternoon from 3 o'clock to sunset. Mr. Maurice assures the parents that he will pay every attention in his power to the manners and behavior of his pupils, while under his tuition, and will take the greatest pains to teach them the polite accomplishment of dancing genteely . . . .

"Subscription paper still open for admission of scholars, one lodged at the Assembly-Room, and one at Mr. Melchor's Printing-Office and Book-Store where gentlemen will please to leave the names of the children they intend to send. Mr. Maurice would just observe, that it is by far the best way for the whole to begin on the first afternoon.   April 7, 1797."

New Hampshire Gazette, November 22, 1797

"Dancing School.—Messrs. Renard & Barbot Respectfully inform the public that they intend opening a Dancing School, in which they will teach Country-Dances, Cotillons, Minuet, Allemand, and Horn-Pipe. They will neglect nothing to deserve the approbation of those who will trust them with their tuition.

"The school will be open as soon as a sufficient number of subscribers are obtained. For terms apply to the printer hereof, who has lodged with him a subscription paper.   Nov. 21, 1797."

The Oracle of the Day, December 16, 1797

"Singing School. The subscribers inform their friends and the public that they intend opening a Singing school, should a sufficient number offer.—Terms may be known by applying to them or the clergymen in town, who hold subscription papers for the purpose.   Job Harris.   Jos. Akerman, Jun.   December 15, 1797."

New Hampshire Gazette, January 17, 1798

"Messrs. Renard and Barbot's. Dancing-School will be opened

this evening, at the Assembly-House; all those who wish for instruction, will find it to their advantage to attend on the first evening. Privae lessons will be given to those who make applications at their houses, on moderate terms.   Wednesday, January 17, 1798."

The Mirror, April 24, 1798

"Free School. Those persons who wish to improve the advantages of a Free School, of Vocal and Instrumental Music, are desired to attend at the Court-House, in this town, where they may receive the tuition of an ingenious and experienced Preceptor, gratis. The Amateurs of the divine Art, and those who have made considerable proficiency in it, may there indulge themselves, at times, and not only find an agreeable relaxation from business, but have the satisfaction of promoting and encouraging an important part of public worship; and those who have yet to learn its rudiments, may gain the laudable knowledge free of expense, by devoting a few of those hours every week which may be easily spared, are generally idled away, and which will not infringe in the least on their common avocations.   Concord, April 20, 1798."

New Hampshire Gazette, November 21, 1798

"Piano Forte—J. H. Smith, Organist and Professor of Music, Respectfully informs the Ladies and Gentlemen of Portsmouth and its vicinity, that he teaches the Piano Forte, Harpsichord, Spinnet, Singing, the Violin, Tenor, Bass Violin, and Flute.

"Mr. Smith has taught in the first families and young ladies boarding schools, in the United States and Europe. He begs leave to observe, that when parents send their daughters to boarding schools, either in Boston or New-York, they pay 4 dollars entrance, and 4 shillings a lesson.

"His terms will be two dollars entrance, and 2 s 6 a lesson.— He tunes instruments for 2 dollars. Mr. Smith hopes for some encouragement, and will punctually attend to any line or message left at Mr. Melchers printing office or at Capt. Smith's, Water Street near the Hotel."

New Hampshire Gazette, June 18, 1799

"Francis Maurice Professor of the French Language, Music, Dancing and Fencing. Proposes to teach those beautiful and useful arts in this town, if there appears sufficient encouragement; His Dancing-School is kept at the Assembly-Room, every Thursday and Saturday in the afternoon—Terms may be known by applying to him at the Hotel.   Portsmouth, June 14, 1799."

The Mirror, June 24, 1799

"Mr. W. Blodget, Proposes, if suitable encouragement is given to teach the Organ, Harpsichord, Piano Forte, and Violin. He will commence as soon as a sufficient number appears to make it worth his attention.

"He may be spoken with at his room, at Lieut. Wilkins;—where Drawing will be taught, and Limning done on reasonable terms.

"Blank Music Books, and Paper, as cheap as can be had in Boston. Music copied.   Concord, June 22, 1799."

APPENDIX B. Selected Opera Programs

New Hampshire Gazette, November 3, 1769

"By Authority This Evening, at Mr. Stavers Long Room, will be read an Opera, call'd Love in a Village. The Songs will be Sung by a Person who has Read and Sung in most of the great Towns of America. He personates all the Characters, and enters into the different Humours or Passions, as they change from one to another throughout the opera. The Songs in this Opera (of which there are Sixty-Nine) are set to Musick by the Greatest Masters. Tickets for Admission to be had at Mr. Stavers, and at the Printing-Office. Price Half a Dollar each."

New Hampshire Spy, April 21, 1792

"Theatre. On Monday evening, April 23d. will be performed a Comic Opera called The Reform'd Wife or Virtue Rewarded.

Lord Townly,	Mr. Watts.
John Moody,	Mr. Solomon.
James,	Mr. Redfield.
and Manley,	Mr. Murry.
Lady Grace,	Mrs. Murry.
and Lady Townly	Mrs. Solomon.

"Preceeding the Opera, a Prologue—in character of a drunken Sailor, by Mr. Watts.

"The favourite Song of heaving the anchor short-called 'Heo! Hoe!'—in the character of a sailor, by Mr. Solomon.

"The favourite hunting Song of the twins of Latona, by Mr. Murry.

"The Greenwich Pensioner, by Mr. Solomon.

"The picture of a Play House or Bucks have at ye all, by Mr. Watts.

"To which will be added the Comic Opera called The Poor Soldier.

Patrick (the poor Soldier)	Mr. Murry
Captain Fitzroy	Mr. Redfield
Father Luke	Mr. Watts
Dermot	Mr. Hicks
and Darby	Mr. Solomon
Nora	Mrs. Murry
and Kathleen	Mrs. Solomon

"The dissertation on Jealousy, to be delivered by Mrs. Solomon.

"The whole to conclude with the comic song call'd the Four and Twenty Fiddlers, by Mrs. Solomon.

"Tickets at 3s. each, to be had of Mr. Stavers—and at either of the Printing Offices. Doors to be opened at half past five—the curtain rise precisely at seven o'clock."

New Hampshire Gazette, May 24, 1792

"Theatre To-morrow Evening Will be presented an Opera, called The Beggar's Opera.

"To which will be added Garricks satyrical Farce called Lethe, or Aesop in the Shades, with many other entertainments, as will be expressed in the Bill of the day, which may be had gratis at this Office where Tickets at 2 shillings each are for sale."

New Hampshire Gazette, May 31, 1792

"Theatre To-morrow Evening will be presented the Opera-called The Elopement or Cunning Little Isaac Outwitted.

"The Picture of a Play-House, By Mr. Watts.

"A favourite Scotch Song, (To the Green Woods gang with me), by Mrs. Solomon.

"To which will be added a Comic Opera, called the Romp.

"The whole to be concluded with a farewell address to the ladies and gentlemen of Portsmouth—By Mrs. Solomon."

New Hampshire Gazette, September 17, 1796

"Theatre Assembly-Room, Next Monday Evening, (September 19th) Will be Presented the Devil to Pay or the Wives Metamorphos'd.

Jobson (a Cobler)
Conjurer
Butler   By gentlemen of
Cook   Portsmouth
Coachman
Sir John Loverule
Lady Loverule   By a Lady
Lucy   Miss Arnold
Nell (Cobler's wife)   Mrs. Arnold

"Epilogue to the Tragedy to be Spoken by a gentleman.
"Pit Half a dollar, Gallery quarter ditto. Doors to be open precisely at 6. Performance begin precisely at 7. Tickets to be had of Mrs. Arnold at the Assembly-Room."

New Hampshire Gazette, September 24, 1796

"Theatre Assembly-Room Next Monday Evening (September 26th) Will be performed The much admired comic opera of Rosina Or the Reapers.

Belville
William   By gentlemen of
Rustic   Portsmouth
Capt. **Belville**
Rosina   Mrs. Arnold
Dorcas   By a Lady
Phebe   Miss Arnold

"After which will be presented the admired popular Farce of the Apprentice . . . ."

The Oracle of the Day, February 15, 1797

"Theatre Assembly-Room This Evening Will be presented the celebrated Comic Opera of the Mountaineers.

Ectavian   Mr. Harper
Buchasin   Mr. King
Virulet   Mr. Peters
Killmallock   Mr. Clapham
Sadi   Mr. Tubbs
Floranthe   Mrs. Harper
Zorayda   Miss Arnold
Agnes   Mrs. Tubbs

"After which will be presented the much admired Farce of the Spoil'd Child.

Little Pickle (Spoil'd Child)	Miss Arnold
Old Pickle	Mr. Clapham
John	Mr. King
Tag	Mr. Tubbs
Miss Pickle (an old maid)	Mrs. Tubbs
Susan	Mr. Peters
Maria	Mrs. Harper

"Doors to be opened at 6, and Curtain drawn up precisely at 7 o'clock. Tichets of admission half a dollar each, to be had at the Assembly-Room, and at Mr. Peirce's Bookstore."

APPENDIX C. John Hancock and the Massachusetts Antitheatre Law of 1750

IT IS a well known historical fact that Governor John Hancock of Massachusetts was stoutly opposed to the repeal of the anti-theater blue law of 1750 and in December, 1792, went so far as to instruct the Attorney-General to begin legal proceedings against a group of players who were presenting theatrical entertainments to an eager Boston citizenry in the guise of "Lectures, Moral and Entertaining." [1]

John Hancock's objection to the theater in Massachusetts is curiously paradoxical and arouses a certain amount of warranted suspicion. For instance, a letter written while in London on business manifests a deeply rooted fondness for the theater. The letter, dated October 29, 1760, comments on the sudden death of King George the Second: "Every thing here is dull. All plays are stopt and no Diversions are going forward, that I am at loss how to dispose of myself. On Sunday last the Prince of Wales was proclaim'd King thro the City with great Pomp and Joy. His Coronation I am told will not be till April, that I can't yet determine whether I shall stay to see it but the rather think I shall, as it is the grandest thing I shall ever meet with." [2]

Samuel Adams, who attempted to speak in favor of the act in 1791,[3] in many letters had denounced the "pomp and parade" of Hancock's first administration. James Warren, writing to John Adams, deplored the fact that "our new Government has been ushered in with great splendor, balls, assemblies, entertainments, and feats equal to any thing you can tell of in Europe . . . the whirl of pleasures and amusements has taken into its vortex Deacons and the other good people who seldom used to be seen in public but at their devotions." [4]

At the unveiling of Hancock's monument in 1896, Governor Roger Wolcott alluded to him as "a man of dignity of presence, fond of elaborate ceremonial, elegant in his attire, courtly in his manner, a man of education and great wealth for that time." [5] Certainly this description does not befit one who stood out unalterably against histrionic indulgences.

One time when Governor John Hancock and "his Lady," a distant relative of Benning Wentworth and immediate relative of the Sheafes, were spending a week in Portsmouth, a "grand entertainment was prepared at Col. Wentworth's to his Excellency." According to Brewster, "At this entertainment all the elite of the town were present, and a son of Gov. Hancock, of five or six years richly attired, gave an attractive feature, by dancing a minuet." [6]

When the Bow Street Theatre, under the management of Mr. Civil and Horatio Garnet, brought its season to a close on July 31, 1792, the audience that evening included the family of the Massachusetts Governor. The *New Hampshire Spy* for August 1, 1792, however, reported that "Governor Hancock (the Patriot) being afraid of the evening air did not attend, but his family did; and we believe it is not stretching the truth too far when we affirm that they were highly pleased."

Perhaps it was political expediency which influenced John Hancock's[7] opposition to the repeal of the antitheater law.

Notes

CHAPTER I. THE SETTING

1. Melcalf, *New Hampshire in History*, p. 11.
2. *Ibid.*, p. 13.   3. *Ibid.*, p. 14.
4. McClintock, *History of New Hampshire*, p. 45.
5. Stackpole, *History of New Hampshire*, I, 56.
6. *Ibid.*, p. 57   7. *Ibid.*, p. 103.   8. *Ibid.*, p. 167.
9. Metcalf, *New Hampshire in History*, p. 24.
10. Mayo, *John Wentworth, Governor of New Hampshire, 1767-1775*, p. 32.
11. *Ibid.*, p. 32.
12. *New Hampshire*, American Guide Series, p. 57.
13. *Ibid.*, p. 58.
14. Sanborn, *New Hampshire*, p. 125.
15. Metcalf, *New Hampshire in History*, p. 13.
16. Mayo, *John Wentworth*, p. 33.
17. Sanborn, *New Hampshire*, p. 192.
18. Metcalf, *New Hampshire in History*, p. 19.
19. Sanborn, *New Hampshire*, p. 291.
20. Sonneck, *Early Opera in America*, p. 150.
21. Bell, *Memoir of John Wheelwright*, p. 2.
22. Lawrence, *The New Hampshire Churches*, p. 15.
23. "Inventory of the Church Archives of New Hampshire, prepared by the New Hampshire Historical Records Survey Service Division Works Project Administration," p. 10.
24. Lawrence, *The New Hampshire Churches*, p. 15.
25. Stackpole, *History of New Hampshire*, II, 304.
26. *Ibid.*, p. 309.
27. Lee, *Memoirs of Rev. Joseph Buckminster, D.D., and His Son Rev. Joseph Stearns Buchminster*, p. 39.

28. Rogers, *Glimpses of an Old Social Capital*, p. 12.
29. Mayo, *John Wentworth*, p. 62.
30. *Proceedings of the American Antiquarian Society*, XXXII, 270.
31. Lee, *Early American Portrait Painters*, p. 68.
32. Mayo, *John Wentworth*, p. 35.
33. Sanborn, *New Hampshire*, p. 121.
34. *Ibid.*, p. 120.
35. *Colonial Laws of Massachusetts*, p. 153.
36. See Bibliography.
37. See Bibliography.

CHAPTER II. INSTRUMENTS IN NEW HAMPSHIRE

1. Scholes, *The Puritans and Music in England and New England*, pp. 7-11.

2. *Ibid.*, p. 33. As quoted by Scholes.

3. *Ibid.*, p. 12.

4. *Ibid.*, p. 33. Here Scholes erroneously reports: "In the *Records and Files of the Quarterly Court of Essex County, Massachusetts* (vol. iii, p. 231) is to be found the will of Mr. Nathaniell Rogers of Rowley, 1664. It includes: 'A treble viall, 10s.'" Scholes seems to be confused between Ezekiel and Nathaniell Rogers. The same volume of the *Records,* page 229, lists Ezekiel Rogers of Rowley and Nathaniell Rogers of Ipswich. There is a discrepancy in the date as quoted—1655 instead of 1664.

The entire entry reads: "Inventory of the estate of Mr. Nathaniell Rogers of Ipswich taken Aug. 16, 1655, by Robert Lord and Moses Pengry and allowed 25:7:1655, in Ipswich." It includes "a treble viall, 10s."

It is relevant to note that "Nathaniell Rogers was pastor of the Church of Christ at Ipswich." This bit of information would have provided Scholes with some evidence in defence of the Puritan minister who has been too severely accused of discountenancing music outside the worship service.

From *Collections, Historical and Miscellaneous*, edited by J. Farmer and J. B. Moore (vol. II, Concord, published by J. B. Moore, 1823, p. 267), we glean some further information on the owner of the "treble viall." Rev. Nathaniell Rogers came to this country in 1636 and settled in the ministry at Ipswich. He was the father of John Rogers, President of Harvard College. His grandson, and son of John, was the Rev. Nathaniel Rogers who was ordained minister in Portsmouth, New Hampshire, May 3, 1699.

5. Scholes, *The Puritans and Music*, p. 33.

6. New Hampshire Historical Society, "Council Book, New Hampshire Province Papers, 1631-1684," MSS, I, 21.

7. *Ibid.*, p. 22.

8. New Hampshire Legislature, *Provincial and State Papers*, 1623-1686, I, 115.

9. Hurd, *History of Rockingham and Strafford Counties*, p. 68.

10. Scholes, *The Puritans and Music*, p. 389.

11. *Ibid.*, p. 390.

12. *Ibid.*, p. 293. As quoted by Scholes.

13. Brewster, *Rambles about Portsmouth*, I, 19. From the quotation it is assumed that Brewster was not familiar with the other "hautboy and recorder" entries.

14. Scholes, *The Puritans and Music*, p. 124.

15. There is a possibility that some overlapping might have occurred in the inventories; nevertheless, the number is impressive.

16. Chamberlain, *Lithobolia*, p. 16.

17. Sanborn, *New Hampshire*, p. 133.

18. The virginal is a little instrument also, and "to touch" is very applicable to it. However, if the instrument were a virginal he would go to it, not take it to play.

19. Naylor, *Shakespeare and Music*, p. 118.

20. Scholes, *The Puritans and Music*, p. 118.

21. *Ibid.*, p. 41.

22. *Ibid.*, as quoted by Scholes.

23. Sanborn, *New Hampshire*, p. 133. Unfortunately Sanborn does not quote his source.

24. *Massachusetts Historical Society Collections*, Fifth Series: "Sewall Papers, Vol. 1, 1674-1700," V, 506.

25. New Hampshire Historical Society, "Probate Records of Rockingham County" MSS, Book B, p. 277.

26. New Hampshire Legislature, *Provincial and State Papers*, I, p. 494.

27. *Massachusetts Historical Society Collection*, "Sewall Papers," V, 444.

28. *New Hampshire Historical Society*, "Probate Records," p. 350.

29. *Ibid.*, p. 113.

30. Foote, *Three Centuries of American Hymnody*, p. 78.

31. A kit was a small violin, about sixteen inches long with three strings.

32. Josselyn, *Two Voyages to New England*, p. 103. Josselyn makes another allusion to music, p. 149: "The Tenth day [September, 1667] we came from Salem about twelve of the clock back to Marble-head: here we went ashore and recreated ourselves with Musick and a cup of Sack and saw the Town, about ten at night we returned to our Bark and lay abourd." In this connection Scholes, *The Puritans and Music*, p. 42, draws a sharp line between vocal and instrumental music. By musick "is meant instrumental performance, singing being the term otherwise employed; this is the general usage of the period." He concludes: "Some British music teachers still observe the distinction, announcing themselves as Teachers of Singing and Music."

33. *New Hampshire Gazette*, November 18, 1757.

34. The term 'silver bases' (probably silver basses) undoubtedly refers to bass-viol (cello) strings.

35. *New Hampshire Gazette*, July 18, 1766.

36. *Ibid.*, December 18, 1767.   37. *Ibid.*, February 7, 1772.

38. *Ibid.*, July 10, 1772.   39. *Ibid.*, August 20, 1773.

40. *New Hampshire Spy*, March 20, 1789.

41. *Oracle of the Day*, November 23, 1793.

42. Sonneck, *Suum Cuique: Essays in Music*, p. 73.

43. Curtis, *A Topographical and Historical Sketch of Epsom, New Hampshire*, p. 10.

44. New Hampshire Historical Society, "Pedigree of John Tucke of Gosport" MS.

45. *New Hampshire Gazette*, February 22, 1765.

46. Brewster, *Rambles about Portsmouth*, p. 47.

47. *Ibid.*

48. Foote, *Three Centuries at American Hymnody*, p. 83.

49. *Ibid.*

50. Brewster erroneously refers to it as the 'ancient spinnet,' *Rambles about Portsmouth*, p. 102.

51. Sanborn, *New Hampshire*, p. 200.

52. "Longman & Broderip," *Grove's Dictionary of Music and Musicians*, Vol. V, 5th ed., 1954.

53. A recent account of the famous harpsichord appearing in

the July 29, 1954, *Portsmouth Herald* still holds to the two-centuries-old romance.

54. Adams, *Annals of Portsmouth*, p. 313.

55. *Brewster, Rambles about Portsmouth*, I, 177.

56. *Oracle of the Day*, October 10, 1795.

57. This description is based on my own inspection of the instrument.

CHAPTER III. RELIGIOUS MUSIC

1. New Hampshire Legislature, *Provincial and State Papers*, I, p. 78.

2. Hood, *History of Music in New England*, p. 21.

3. *The Bay Psalm Book*. Being a Facsimile Reprint of the First Edition Printed by Stephen Daye at Cambridge, in New England in 1640.

4. *Ibid.*, Preface.

5. "Records of the First Church Portsmouth from 1671 to 1718" (Typescript, no date), p. 4. A copy is in the New Hampshire Historical Society.

6. Scholes, *The Puritans and Music*, p. 260.

7. Foote, *Three Centuries of American Hymnody*, p. 60.

8. Scholes, *The Puritans and Music*, p. 265.

9. Bouton, *History of Concord*, p. 531.

10. Coffin, *History of Boscawen and Webster*, p. 295.

11. Cutter, *History of the Town of Jaffrey*, p. 154.

12. *Ibid.*, p. 154.

13. This is the title of the third edition. Neither the title nor date of the original edition is known. From the fifth edition on it was known as *An Introduction to the Singing of Psalm Tunes in a plain and Easy Method with a Collection of Tunes in Three Parts.*

14. Foote, *Three Centuries of American Hymnody*, p. 99. For additional information on John Tufts's singing book, see Irving Lowens, "John Tufts's Introduction to the Singing of Psalm-Tunes (1721-1744): The First American Textbook," *Journal of Research in Music Education*, II (Fall, 1954), 89-102.

15. Foote, *Three Centuries of American Hymnody*, p. 99.

16. *Ibid.*   17. *Ibid.*, p. 103.   18. *Ibid.*, p. 104.

19. Coffin, *History of Boscawen and Webster*, p. 294.

20. *Ibid.*, p. 15.

21. Walker was pastor of the church from 1730 to 1782.

22. Bouton, *History of Concord*, p. 531. Bouton was pastor of this church from 1825 to 1867.

23. Lyford, *History of Concord, New Hampshire*, II, 708.

24. Cutter, *History of the Town of Jaffrey*, p. 154.

25. *Ibid.*   26. *Ibid.*

27. The manuscript is in the Portsmouth, New Hampshire, Historical Society.

28. Lawrence, *The New Hampshire Churches*, p. 141.

29. Belknap, *Sacred Poetry consisting of Psalms and Hymns*, 3rd. ed. (Boston, 1801); 1st edition dated 1795.

30. Quint, *The First Parish in Dover*, p. 68.

31. *Ibid.*, p. 68.   32. *Ibid.*   33. *Ibid.*

34. Coffin, *History of Boscawen and Webster*, p. 296.

35. Bouton, *History of Concord*, p. 531.

36. Lyford, *History of Concord*, II, 696.

37. *Ibid.*, p. 531.

38. Lawrence, *The New Hampshire Churches*, p. 141.

39. Cutter, *History of the Town of Jaffrey*, p. 155.

40. The national god of the Philistines.

41. Cutter *History of the Town of Jaffrey*, p. 153.

42. Lord, *Life and Times of Hopkinton, N.H.*, p. 297.

43. Urania; or, A Choice Collection of Psalm-Tunes, Anthems, and Hymns. From the most approved Authors, with some Entirely New; in Two, Three, and Four Parts. The whole Peculiarly adapted to the Use of Churches and Private Families: To which are pre-fix'd The Plainest, & most Necessary Rules of Psalmody. By James Lyon, A. B. Philadelphia, Price 15s. Hen. Dawkins Fecit 1761. Facsimile of the title page is taken from Brigham, *Paul Revere's Engravings*, p. 14. Hood, Foote, and Grove give 1762 for date of publication. Sonneck gives "1761 or 1762."

44. A Collection of The best Psalm Hunes, in two three and four Parts; from the most approved Authors, fitted to all Measures, and approv'd of by the best Masters in Boston, New England; to which are added some Hymns and Anthems; the greater part of them never before Printed in America. By Josiah Flagg. Engrav'd by Paul Revere: Printed and sold by him and Josiah Flagg, Boston, 1764."

45. Hood, *History of Music in New England.* p. 164.

46. Fielding, *Dictionary of American Painters, Sculptors and Engravers*, p. 138. Fielding assumes that Exeter is in Massachusetts.

However, a check reveals no Exeter in Massachusetts, and a study of the Gilman Genealogy leads the writer to assume that this is John W. Gilman of Exeter, New Hampshire.

47. For a history of the much misunderstood fuging tune, see Irving Lowens, "The Origins of the American Fuging Tune," *Journal of the American Musicological Society*, VI (Spring, 1953), 43-52.

48. Ellinwood, *The History of American Church Music*.

49. The only other mention of this work is found in Evans's *American Bibliography*, II, 239 (32468). Evans gives title page in part but quotes no source.

50. There appears to be no trace of the promised work ever having been published.

51. In the preface Merrill gives Exeter as his address.

52. We have not been able to establish any relationship between David Merrill and Richard Merrill.

53. Foote, *Three Centuries of American Hymnody*, p. 147.

54. *The Christian History*, "Rev. Mr. Shurtleff's Account of the Revival of Religion at Portsmouth, N.H." pp. 383-394.

55. *Ibid.*, p. 390.

56. Stackpole and Thompson, *History of the Town of Durham*, I, 192.

CHAPTER IV. SECULAR MUSIC

1. Scholes, *The Puritans and Music*, p. 117.

2. Jenness, *The Isles of Shoals*, p. 140. This is the most authoritative work on the subject by a historian who did much of his research in England.

3. *Ibid.*, p. 172.   4. *Ibid.*

5. Lord, "Manners and Customs in Hopkinton," *Granite Monthly*, II (March, 1879), 188.

6. *Ibid.*, p. 189.

7. Aldrich, *Walpole as It Was and as It Is*, p. 188.

8. Bouton, *History of Concord*, p. 252.

9. New Hampshire Historical Society, John Wentworth Letter Book MSS, 3v. in 1, John Wentworth to William Bayard, July 3, 1767, I, 6.

10. Mayo, *John Wentworth*, p. 90.

11. *Ibid.*, p. 92.   12. *Ibid.*   13. *Ibid.*, p. 85.

14. New Hampshire Historical Society, John Wentworth Letter Book MSS, 3v. in 1, John Wentworth to Paul Wentworth, September 17, 1769, III, 276.

15. Ford, *Thomas Jefferson*, p. 209.

16. *New Hampshire Gazette*, November 23, 1759.

17. *Ibid.*, October 9, 1788.

18. Evans, *American Bibliography*, VII, 334 (No. 21955).

19. Hans Gram was organist of the Brattle Square Church in Boston and was one of the compilers, with Oliver Holden and Samuel Holyoke, of the *Massachusetts Compiler*.

20. Shipton, *Isaiah Thomas, Printer, Patriot and Philanthropist 1749-1831*, p. 48.

21. *New Hampshire Gazette*, August 23, 1792.

22. *Ibid.*, July 30, 1793.   23. *Ibid.*, April 4, 1798.

24. *Oracle of the Day*, June 7, 1800. Customarily, sale advertisements appeared from five to ten times over a period of several weeks.

25. *Ibid.*, June 11, 1793.   26. *Ibid.*, April 2, 1794.

27. *Ibid.*, March 19, 1799.

28. Sonneck, *A Bibliography of Early Secular American Music*, p. 386.

29. *Ibid.*, p. 195.

30. Names of composers and dates of publication are taken from Sonneck's *A Bibliography of Early Secular American Music*, passim.

31. *Ibid.*

32. *Farmers Weekly Museum*, March 11, 1795.

33. Marquis de Chastellux, *Travels in North America in the Years 1780-81-82*, translated from the French, by an English Gentleman, p. 312.

34. *Ibid.*

35. Fitzpatrick, "The Bands of the Continental Army," *Daughters of the American Revolution Magazine*, LVII (April, 1923), 194.

36. *Ibid.*, p. 188.

37. Sonneck, *Early Concert-Life in America*, p. 262.

38. *Ibid.*, p. 263.

CHAPTER V. MUSIC FOR PUBLIC OCCASIONS

1. *Courier of New Hampshire*, February 29, 1797. The year 1797 was not a leap year; the date of the newspaper should read February 28, 1797.

2. *Ibid.*, July 11, 1797.

3. *New Hampshire Gazette*, May 30, 1766.

4. *Ibid.*, January 24, 1772.

5. *Ibid.*, September 25, 1772.

6. *Ibid.*, August 26, 1774.

7. *Concord Herald*, August 31, 1791.

8. Gould, *History of Church Music in America*, p. 65.

9. *Concord Herald*, August 31, 1791.

10. Gould, *History of Church Music in America*, p. 62, conjectures that this is Holyoke's first book, *Harmonia Americana*, published the same year and entirely of his own composition.

11. *Concord Herald*, August 31, 1791.

12. In the village of Canterbury, Independence Day (July 4, 1797) was celebrated in grand style and with great patriotic ardor. As the joyful festivities drew to a close, the inhabitants listened to "martial music on a neighboring hill" which, affirms *The New Star* (July 18, 1797), "added to the romantic pleasantness of the evening."

13. New Hampshire.

14. *New Hampshire Gazette*, June 26, 1788.

15. Complete texts to these setting may be found in the June 26, 1788, *New Hampshire Gazette*.

16. The following account is summarized from the *New Hampshire Gazette* of November 5, 1789.

17. Probably Jonathan Mitchell Sewall. In comparing the three odes to several similar works in his volume of *Miscellaneous Poems* (Portsmouth, 1801), the literary style which emerges suggests the ever-present J. M. Sewall, Portsmouth's favorite patriotic versifier.

18. *New Hampshire Gazette*, November 5, 1789.

19. Horatio Garnet (see Chapter VII) was probably the director.

20. *Oracle of the Day*, March 2, 1799.

21. An oratorio by Handel.

22. *New Hampshire Gazette*, January 8, 1800.

23. No first name given.

24. Sonneck, *A Bibliography of Early Secular American Music*, p. 257, reveals that Isaac Stanwood was the Portsmouth agent for "von Hagen's piano forte warehouse," of Boston. The firm, established late in 1797 (or early in 1798) dealt chiefly in publications.

25. *Oracle of the Day*, January 4, 1800.

26. Sonneck, *A Bibliography of Early Secular American Music*, p. 197, lists "Hymns By George Richards composed on the death

of Gen. Washington; and sung, at the Universal meeting-house Portsmouth, N. H., January 1800."

27. *New Hampshire Gazette,* January 8, 1800.

28. *Ibid.,* January 30, 1793.   29. *Ibid.,* April 7, 1795.

30. Sonneck, *A Bibliography of Early Secular American Music,* p. 524. Sonneck lists Sewall as composer on the basis of this song, although there appears to be no trace of the music. From the other references to Sewall encountered in this study we can not support the opinion that he did actually compose music.

31. *New Hampshire Gazette,* January 30, 1793.

32. Bouton, *History of Concord,* p. 321.

33. *Courier of New Hampshire,* March 13, 1798.

34. Bouton, *History of Concord,* p. 321.

35. *New Hampshire Gazette,* July 9, 1789.

CHAPTER VI. OPERA BEFORE THE REVOLUTION

1. Sonneck, *Early Opera in America,* p. 80.

2. Sonneck, *Suum Cuique: Essays in Music,* p. 41.

3. The Massachusetts legislature actually voted the repeal in in 1794 against Governor John Hancock's opposition. On February 4 of the same year the authorities, ignoring the ban, allowed the opening of the Federal Street Theatre.

4. New Hampshire Legislature, *Provincial and State Papers,* IV, 832.

5. *Ibid.,* p. 833.   6. *Ibid.,* pp. 833-834.   7. *Ibid.,* pp. 831-832.

8. *New Hampshire Gazette,* September 8, 1769.

9. *Ibid.,* November 3, 1769.

10. See Sonneck, *Early Opera in America,* pp. 133-134, for an advertisement (quoted from without source) of a reading of the *Beggar's Opera* on March 23, 1770, in Boston. The terms of the advertisement are remarkable in that they are so nearly the ones which occur in the *New Hampshire Gazette* advertisement of *Love in a Village.* The *Gazette* advertisement is in the November 3, 1769, issue, and interestingly enough the same type of reading performance of the play was given in Boston in July and in October of the same year. This strongly suggests that Mr. Joan, whom Sonneck identifies "with the would be American Stradivari James Juhan" (Sonneck, *Early Opera,* p. 134), repeated his Boston reading in Portsmouth. John Rowe's diary is Sonneck's source for the note that Mr. Joan "read but indifferently but sung in taste." These

1769 performances of *Love in a Village* marked the introduction of this famous work into America.

11. Sonneck, *Early Concert-Life in America*, p. 265.

12. *New Hampshire Gazette*, July 10, 1772.

13. Sonneck, *Early Concert-Life*, p. 11.

14. *New Hampshire Gazette*, October 23, 1772.

15. *Ibid.*, November 13, 1772.

16. Sonneck in *Early Opera in America*, p. 35, asserts that such plays as *Lethe, Theodosius, Romeo and Juliet*, and *Macbeth* were "interspersed with dirges, marches, songs, etc." In 1787 this work became known as *Aesop in the Shade*, a farce turned into an entertainment of music. (*Ibid.*, Table A).

17. *New Hampshire Gazette*, November 27, 1772.

18. *Ibid.*, December 4, 1772.

19. Sonneck, *Early Opera in America*, p. 198.

20. *Ibid.*, p. 258.   21. *Ibid.*, p. 262.   22. *Ibid.*

23. *Ibid.*, p. 268.

24. New Hampshire Legislature, *Provincial and State Papers*, XIII, p. 276.

25. *Ibid.*, p. 277.

26. Sonneck, *Early Concert-Life in America*, p. 266.

27. *Ibid.*

28. New Hampshire Historical Society, "Journal of the House 1770-1775," MS, VIII, 136.

29. Sonneck, *Early Concert-Life in America*, p. 266.

30. *Ibid.*, p. 267.   31. *Ibid.*, p. 263.   32. *Ibid.*, p. 269.

CHAPTER VII.   OPERA AFTER THE REVOLUTION

1. *New Hampshire Spy*, July 11, 1789.

2. Seilhamer, *History of the American Theatre*, II, 242-243. McPherson gave his "Lecture on Heads" at Philadelphia on June 19, 1788, and according to Seilhamer "was never heard of afterwards!"

3. *New Hampshire Spy*, August 29, 1789.

4. *Ibid.*, September 5, 1789.

5. *Ibid.*, August 1, 1789.

6. No first name given.

7. *New Hampshire Spy*, November 30, 1791.

8. See Appendix B.

9. *New Hampshire Spy*, August 1, 1792.

10. *Ibid.*, December 14, 1791.

11. *Ibid.*, August 1, 1792.   12. Mr. Civil.

13. *New Hampshire Spy*, August 1, 1792.

14. Hornblow, *A History of the Theatre in America*, p. 116. "Although most of the theatre advertisements of the time contained the notice: No persons admitted behind the scenes, the pernicious practice of allowing male spectators to mingle with the actors and actresses—a custom dating from Shakespeare's time and which led to many abuses and immoralities—was still common and occasioned many scandals."

15. *New Hampshire Spy*, August 1, 1792.

16. *Ibid.*,   17. *Ibid.*, December 17, 1791.

18. *Ibid.*,   19. December 21, 1791.

20. *Ibid.*, April 28, 1792.

21. *Ibid.*, December 14, 1791.   22. *Ibid.*

23. *Ibid.* "Fisher's Minuet" (Joh. Christian Fischer) was a set of variations for keyboard instrument by Mozart on a theme by Fischer. According to Sonneck's *A Bibliography of Early Secular American Music*, p. 142. it was "printed and sold at Carr's Music Store, Baltimore ca. 1800." If this is the first American publication, then it is possible that Garnet used, or was familiar with, a European printing.

24. *New Hampshire Spy*, December 31, 1792.

25. *Ibid.*, March 10, 1792.   26. *Ibid.*, April 18, 1792.

27. *Ibid.*, April 28, 1792.   28. *Ibid.*, May 19, 1792.

29. *Ibid.*, August 1, 1792.   30. *Ibid.*, April 18, 1792.

31. No first name given.

32. Sonneck, *Early Opera in America*, p. 158.

33. *New Hampshire Spy*, April 21, 1792.

34. *Ibid.*

35. This opera is not listed in Sonneck's *A Bibliography of Early Secular American Music*.

36. *New Hampshire Gazette*, May 10, 1792.

37. *Ibid.*, May 24, 1792.   38. *Ibid.*, May 31, 1792.

39. Sonneck, *A Bibliography of Early Secular American Music*, p. 358, erroneously notes "the first American performance of the *Romp* at Philadelphia, October 22, 1792."

40. *New Hampshire Spy*, April 21, 1792.

41. *Ibid.*

42. An idea of Watts' company can be gained from quoting the cast of this opera:

Patrick (the Poor Soldier)	Mr. Murry
Captain Fitzroy	Mr. Redfield
Father Luke	Mr. Watts
Dermot	Mr. Hicks
Dalby	Mrs. Solomon
Nora	Mrs. Murry
Kathleen	Mrs. Solomon

43. *New Hampshire Gazette*, May 10, 1792.

44. *New Hampshire Spy*, May 19, 1792.

45. *New Hampshire Gazette*, May 31, 1792.

46. *Oracle of the Day*, April 19, 1794.

47. Sonneck, *Early Opera in America*, p. 158.

48. *Ibid.*, p. 127. See also Sonneck, *Suum Cuique: Essays in Music*, p. 45. wherein the author notes that during the Federal Convention at Philadelphia in July, 1787 George Washington, who was known to have "opposed the narrow-minded restrictions" against the theater, attended a performance of the *Tempest*, which had been previously advertised as "an opera called the Tempest, or the Enchanted Island (altered from Shakespeare by Dryden). To conclude with a Grand Masque of Neptune and Amphitrite: With entire new Scenery, Machinery, etc. The music composed by Dr. Purcell."

49. *Ibid.*, p. 159.

50. Fitzpatrick, *The Diaries of George Washington 1748-1799*, IV, 45.

51. *New Hampshire Gazette*, January 24, 1772.

52. *The Portsmouth Book*, p. 48.

53. *Ibid.*   54. *Ibid.*

55. *Oracle of the Day*, September 2, 1794.

56. *Ibid.*, September 6, 1794.   57. *Ibid.*, August 26, 1794.

58. *Ibid.*, August 30, 1794.

59. *New Hampshire Gazette*, September 3, 1796.

60. *Ibid.*, October 22, 1796.

61. Moreland, "The Early Theatre in Portland," *The New England Quarterly*, XI (June, 1938), 335.

62. *New Hampshire Gazette*, October 22, 1796.

63. *Ibid.*, September 3, 1796.   64. *Ibid.*, September 10, 1796.

65. *Ibid.*, September 17, 1796.   66. *Ibid.*, Stepember 24, 1796.

67. *Ibid.*, October 15, 1796.   68. *Ibid.*, October 22, 1796.

69. *Ibid.*, October 29, 1796.   70. *Ibid.*, September 10, 1796.

71. *Ibid.*, October 15, 1796.   72. *Ibid.*, September 3, 1796.

73. *Ibid.*, September 10, 1796.   74. *Ibid.*, October 22, 1796.

75. Also in *Oracle of the Day*, November 2, 1796.

76. *Oracle of the Day*, November 9, 1796.

77. Sonneck, *Early Opera in America*, p. 151.

78. See Moreland, "The Early Theatre in Portland," pp. 334-347 for a complete account of this episode.

79. *Ibid.*, p. 335.

80. Sonneck, *Early Opera in America*, p. 151.

81. *Ibid.*

82. Morenland, "The Early Theatre in Portland," p. 335.

83. *Ibid.*

84. *New Hampshire Gazette*, February 4, 1797.

85. *Oracle of the Day*, February 15, 1797.

85. *Oracle of the Day*, February 15, 1797.

86. *New Hampshire Gazette*, February 25, 1797.

87. *Oracle of the Day*, March 1, 1797.

88. Moreland, "The Early Theatre in Portland," p. 337. As quoted by Moreland from the *Eastern Herald & Gazette of Maine*, Thursday, December 22, 1796.

89. *New Hampshire Gazette*, March 14, 1798.

90. *Ibid.*, March 21, 1798.   91. *Ibid.*, March 28, 1798.

92. *Ibid.*, March 14, 1798.   93. *Ibid.*

94. *Oracle of the Day*, May 10, 1800.

95. Sonneck, *Early Opera in America*, p. 137.

96. *Ibid.*, p. 146.   97. *Ibid.*, p. 152.

98. Sonneck, *A Bibliography of Early Secular American Music*, p. 57, states that "whether Michael Kelly's music for *The Castle Spectre* was used at all in these American performances we do not know."

99. Sonneck, *Early Opera in America*, p. 127. It is conceivable that the entire drama was interspersed with the appropriate music of Thomas Arne.

100. Moreland, "The Early Theater in Portland," p. 339.

101. *Oracle of the Day*, May 17, 1800.

102. *Ibid.*, June 21, 1800.   103. *Ibid.*, June 14, 1800.

104. *New Hampshire Gazette*, June 10, 1800.

105. *Oracle of the Day*, June 21, 1800.

106. *Ibid.*   107. *Ibid.*

108. The glee is a piece of vocal music in at least three parts

and for solo voices, usually those of men. It is generally performed without accompaniment. During the period under investigation, the glees were characteristically popular songs of the day whose authors were still living. They were sung during intermissions of operas, concerts and plays.

109. Moreland, "The Early Theatre in Portland," p. 339. "Mr. Jones announced that he would sing 'Information, Suffocation, Botheration, Mortification, and Population.'"

110. Wadleigh, *Notable Events in the History of Dover, New Hampshire,* p. 181.

111. Moreland, "The Early Theatre in Portland," p. 335.

112. Sonneck, *Early Opera in America,* p. 151.

113. Seilhamer, *History of the American Theatre,* III, 261.

114. For a further discussion of John Hubbard, see Chapter X.

115. *Farmers Weekly Museum,* August 27, 1798.

CHAPTER VIII. CONCERT LIFE

1. Sonneck, *Early Concert-Life in America,* p. 312.

2. *Ibid.* 3. *Ibid.,* p. 319.

4. *New Hampshire Spy,* July 22, 1788.

5. *Ibid.,* June 23, 1789. 6. *Ibid.,* July 7, 1789.

7. Sonneck, *A Bibliography of Early Secular American Music,* p. 309.

8. *New Hampshire Gazette,* September 24, 1789.

9. *New Hampshire Spy,* June 23, 1792.

10. Sonneck, *Early Concert-Life in America,* p. 284.

11. Sonneck, *A Bibliography of Early Secular American Music,* p. 524. William Selby (1738-1798), "Organist, harpsichordist and composer. First mentioned in 1771 on a Boston concert program as organist. Resided at Boston until his death. During the Revolution, when the musical life of Boston came to a standstill, Selby made his living as a liquor dealer and grocer. With the year 1782 he started anew on his career as organist, teacher, musical editor, composer and arranger of excellent concerts. The rapid progress of music at Boston was largely prepared by him, and it is unfair not to mention William Selby among the musical pioneers of Boston. He was organist at the Stone Chapel until his death, when he was succeeded by P. A. von Hagen." Sonneck (*Early Concert-Life in America* p. 282) conjectures that William Selby conducted the above performance.

12. Sonneck (*Early Concert-Life in America,* p. 283) says "This

was not correct as 'Jonah, an oratorio, composed by S. Felsted' was performed at New York on June 11, 1788."

13. For a complete account of this performance see Sonneck, *Early Concert-Life in America*, pp. 282-285.

14. *New Hampshire Spy*, December 21, 1791.

15. *Ibid.*, December 24, 1791.

16. Lee, *Memoirs of Rev. Joseph Buckminster, D.D. and of His Son, Rev. Joseph Stevens Buckminster*, p. 29.

17. *Ibid.* 18. *Ibid.*, p. 214.

19. Sonneck, *Early Concert-Life in America*, p. 297.

20. Brooks, *Olden-Time Music*, p. 56.

21. Gould, *History of Church Music in America*, p. 67.

22. Robert Wainwright (1748-1782), English organist and composer, was granted a Bachelor and a Doctor of Music degrees on April 29, 1774. In 1768 he succeeded his father as organist of the Collegiate Church at Manchester, and in 1775 he became organist of St. Peter's Church in Liverpool. He composed services and anthems as well as an oratorio, "The Fall of Egypt." (See *Grove's Dictionary of Music and Musicians*, 5th. ed. revised, IX, 126).

23. Karl Friedrich Baumgarten, Lubeck 1740—London 1824, German organist, violinist and composer. He settled in London about 1758. Directed operas at Haymarket Theatre and at Covent Garden. As an organist he possessed "great skill in modulation" and a "thorough knowledge" of his instrument, but as a violinist, both in concerted music and as a leader, he was "wanting in energy." Haydn wrote in his diary, "a sleepy orchestra, was led by him." Baumgarten was a man of considerable ability and accomplishments; his pupils were numerous and eminent; he composed quartets, violin sonates, piano-forte pieces, several operas as well as a quantity of other incidental works for the stage. (See *Grove's Dictionary of Music*, I, 507).

24. *Portsmouth Oracle of the Day*, November 23, 1793.

25. *Ibid.*, May 10, 1794.

26. Sonneck, *Early Concert-Life in America*, p. 298.

27. Ibid., p. 301.   28. *Ibid.*, p. 298.   29. *Ibid.*, p. 314

30. *Ibid.*, p. 297.

31. *Oracle of the Day*, October 13, 1795.

32. *New Hampshire Spy*, December 4, 1789.

33. *New Hampshire Gazette*, July 23, 1796.

34. *Ibid.*, August 13, 1796.   35. *Ibid.*, June 27, 1797.

36. Sonneck, *Early Opera in America,* p. 146, records that J. B. Williamson and G. L. Barrett were vocalists from Covent Garden who were brought to America by Charles Stuart Powell in 1796.

37. Sonneck, *Early Concert-Life in America,* p. 43.

38. *Ibid.,* p. 54. 39. *Ibid.,* p. 305.

40. *Ibid.,* p. 306. Graupner settled in Boston early in 1798. He came there as oboist in the Federal Street Theatre orchestra and advertised in March his services as teacher of the oboe, German Flute, violin, etc. He was born about 1740, became oboist in a Hanoverian regiment, and went to London in 1788, where he played under Haydn. For detailed information about Gottlieb Graupner, the attention of the reader is directed to the unpublished typescript copies of a biography of Graupner by his granddaughter, Catherine Graupner Stone, now in the Library of Congress and the New York Public Library, as well as to the extensive treatment of Mr. and Mrs. Graupner in H. Earle Johnson's *Musical Interludes in Boston, 1795-1830,* pp. 165-200, with portraits (p. 184), Graupner's activities as a publisher (pp. 230, 243-247), and a very full list of his publications (pp. 305-332).

41. Johnson, *Musical Interludes in Boston, 1795-1830* p. 159. The change in spelling of the name occurred when the Van Hagens came to Boston; no reason is given.

42. *New Hampshire Gazette,* June 3, 1800.

43. *Ibid.*

44. *Oracle of the Day,* June 7, 1800.

45. Sonneck, *Earley Concert-Life in America,* p. 320.

46. *Concord Town Records,* 1732-1820, p. 273.

47. Bouton, *History of Concord,* pp. 582-583. Asa McFarland. D.D. (1769-1827), was a native of Worcester, Massachusetts. He was graduated from Dartmouth College in 1793. Five years later (1798) he was ordained the third pastor of the First Congregational Church in Concord and continued in this trust until 1824. During his college years, in order to defray part of his educational expenses, he taught music. Dr. McFarland was a leader in vocal music and did much to promote good singing in the divine worship. He possessed a fine bass voice and sang with great power—as tradition holds, "Making the house tremble."

48. Israel Evans.

49. *Concord Town Records,* p. 297.

50. *Courier of New Hampshire,* January 3, 1797.

51. Choir director.

52. New Hampshire Historical Society, "Records of the Concord Musical Society 1799-1865" MS, pp. 1-7.

53. *Ibid.*   54. *Ibid.*, p. 13.

55. Bouton, *History of Concord*, p. 532.

56. Today the annual interest derived from the Hall fund benefits the First Congregational Church Chancel Choir of Concord. The writer was the musical director of this organization from April of 1950 to June, 1955.

57. *The New Star*, September 19, 1797; Part 1, p. 192.

58. *Farmers Weekly Museum*, August 27, 1798.

59. *Ibid.*, July 10, 1798. "The Power of Music," an editorial written by Joseph Dennie.

60. Pope, *The Cheney Genealogy*, p. 87. Abner Cheney was born November 10, 1765. He "graduated from Dartmouth College in 1796; taught, the following year, the Academy at Charlestown, N.H., where he won great respect, and gave much promise of usefulness. But he died at the close of the year. An inspection of the inventory of his effects shows us his Greek Testament and other tokens of Theological study, and books of literary cast; along with a bass viol and books of vocal and instrumental music. Evidently he had a versatile, talented nature, and was one who might have been widely beloved and greatly useful. Great was the mourning, we learn, over his early death. But surely one so in harmony with the True, the Beautiful, and the Good, must find place and field in His loved Father's higher realm!"

61. *Ibid.*, October 18, 1796.

CHAPTER IX. THE TEACHERS

1. Chase, *History of Old Chester*, p. 323.

2. Bush, *History of Education in New Hampshire*, p. 55.

3. Hood, *History of Music in New England*, p. 51. The theses to which this quotation refers were lost in a conflagration which destroyed the college library in 1764.

4. *Ibid.*   5. *Ibid.*, p. 140.

6. Sonneck, *Early Concert-Life in America*, p. 251.

7. It would be impractical to footnote the large number of isolated references in this directory.

9. Reverend James Lyon of Philadelphia.

8. John Bull (circa 1562-1728). *Grove's Dictionary of Music* does not list an oratorio.

10. Chapter XII is devoted entirely to Benjamin Dearborn.

11. Barriskill, "The Newburyport Theatre in the 18th Century," *Essex Institute Historical Collection*, XCI (July, 1955), 217, notes that "Mr. Samuel H. Flagg from Portsmouth, N.H., announced his 'Concert of vocal and instrumental Music' for the fifth of August in the Town House" in the July 29, 1789, Newburyport *Essex Journal*.

12. Sonneck, *A Bibliography of Early Secular American Music*, p. 504, records: Louis Landrin Duport "(ca. 1755-ca. 1840) Dancing master and composer of dances. Emigrated to the United States in 1790." He composed "Cotillions, Dance tunes, etc, No. 1 of a new sett of cotilions [sic], Two new favorite cotillions, United States country dances."

13. Bentley, *The Diary of William Bentley, D.D.* II, 268, notes that "Mr. Turner, the English Master, & Mr. Outein [sic], have their Dancing School" in Salem.

14. *Ibid.*, p. 357. "The Music was good . . . & was assisted by Monsieur Maurice, Teacher of Music and Dancing in Salem. This French gentleman was excellent upon the violin."

15. *Ibid.*, p. 191. "A curious Mr. Lane from Bedford in Town to sell Anthems."

16. Gould, *History of Church Music in America*, p. 73.

17. *History of New Ipswich*, p. 263.

18. *Ibid.*, p. 264.

19. *Biographical Catalogue of the Trustees, Teachers and Students of Phillips Academy Andover 1778-1830*, p. 13.

20. For background the reader is referred to Weeden, *Economic and Social History of New England, 1620-1789*, and *Laws of New Hampshire*, Volumes III-VI.

21. The pistole was valued at about four dollars.

22. Johnson, *Musical Interludes in Boston 1795-1830*, p. 283.

23. About twenty-eight shillings.

24. *New Hampshire Gazette*, March 19, 1773.

25. Sonneck, *Early Councert-Life in America*, p. 156.

CHAPTER X. MUSIC IN THE ACADEMIES

1. Bush, *History of Education in New Hampshire*, p. 49.

2. *Ibid.*, p. 103.

3. Bentley, *The Diary of William Bentley*, II, 392.

4. Bush, *History of Education in New Hampshire*, p. 51.

5. Marr, *Atkinson Academy, The Early Years*, p. 36.

6. *Ibid.*, p. 65.   7. *Ibid.*, p. 67.   8. *Ibid.*, p. 66.
9. *Ibid.*, p. 67. As quoted by Marr.
10. *Ibid.*, p. 32.   11. *Ibid.*, p. 40.   12. *Ibid.*, p. 80.
13. *Ibid.*, p. 16.   14. *Ibid.*, p. 17.   15. *Ibid.*, p. 14.
16. Gilman, *Contributions to Literature*, pp. 199-201.

CHAPTER XI. JOHN HUBBARD

1. Hubbard, *An Essay on Music.*
2. Gould, *History of Church Music in America*, p. 65.
3. Lord, *A History of Dartmouth College, 1815-1909*, p. 559.
4. Parish, *An Eulogy on John Hubbard . . . September, 1810*, p. 7.
5. *History of New Ipswich*, p. 262.
6. *Ibid.*, p. 263.   7. *Ibid.*, p. 264.
8. *Farmer's Museum*, June 10, 1799.
9. *Ibid.*, June 24, 1799.   10. *Ibid.*, July 8, 1799.
11. *Proceedings of the Massachusetts Historical Society, 1860-1862*, V, 255.
12. Parish, *An Eulogy on John Hubbard*, p. 8.
13. Hubbard, *The American Reader*, p. 8.
14. Parish, *An Eulogy on John Hubbard*, p. 9.
15. Hubbard, *An Essay on Music*, p. 16.
16. *Ibid.*   17. *Ibid.*, p. 17   18. *Ibid.*   19. *Ibid.*
20. Lord, *A History of Dartmouth College*, p. 552.
21. *Ibid.*
22. *Dwight, Travels; in New England and New York*, II, 117
23. Lord, *A History of Dartmouth College*, p. 553.
24. *Ibid.*, p. 554.
25. Ritter, *Music in America*, pp. 105-106.
26. Lord, *A History of Dartmouth College*, p. 559.
27. New Hampshire Historical Society, "Orford and Piermont Hubbard Musical Society, Constitution and Records, 1816-1832" MS (unpaged).
28. The term "musician" as used here may be taken to imply instrumental performer. Perhaps, because of the scarcity, they were accorded preferential treatment.
29. "Orford and Piermont Hubbard Musical Society, Constitution and Records" MS.
30. This may be the first instance of Handel's name being used to identify a musical society in our country.
31. Rev. Samuel Worcester, D.D. (Hollis, N.H. 1770-Brainerd, Tenn. 1821) attended New Ipswich Academy where he came under

the direct influence of Hubbard. As a student at Dartmouth, he "cherished and improved his taste for music." Taught several singing schools in an effort to improve sacred music. In this respect he fostered Hubbard's ideals. He published a collection of Psalms and hymns known as the *Christian Psalmody* in 1815.

32. Worcester, *An Address on Sacred Music ... Sept. 19, 1810*, p. 22.

33. *New Hampshire Patriot*, August 28, 1810.

34. Worcester, *An Address on Sacred Music*, p. 21.

35. Name of paper not given.

36. *New Hampshire Patriot*, September 18, 1810.

37. Gould, *History of Church Music in America*, p. 66.

38. Evans, *American Bibliography*, VII, 326, lists a work by Hubbard entitled "Harmonia Selecta printed at Worcester by Isaiah Thomas, 1779." This is a most curious entry. Evans gives no source. Gould, who knew Hubbard, does not mention the work, and assiduous investigation has revealed no hint of its existence.

39. Gould, *History of Church in America*, p. 66.

40. Richardson, *History of Dartmouth College*, I, 256.

CHAPTER XII. BENJAMIN DEARBORN

1. Lippencott, "Dearborn's Musical Scheme," *The New-York Historical Society Quarterly Bulletin*, XXV (October 1941), 134-142.

2. *Ibid.*, p. 134. Lippencott erroneously quotes the date as "March 29, 1782," and also erroneously notes that this is the "earliest ... advertisement" of Dearborn's singing school.

3. *New Hampshire Gazette*, October 6, 1778.

4. Lippencott, "Dearborn's Musical Scheme," p. 134.

5. *New Hampshire Gazette*, April 1, 1785.

6. Lippencott, "Dearborn's Musical Scheme," p. 135.

7. The writer has in his possession a microfilm reproduction of the original.

8. *Ibid.* Lippencott erroneously gives April 24, 1754, as Dearborn's baptismal date.

9. "Records of the First Church Portsmouth," p. 191.

10. *New Hampshire Gazette*, February 4, 1777.

11. *Ibid.*, April 20, 1779.   12. *Ibid.*, June 15, 1779.

13. *Ibid.*, September 29, 1791.

14. Evans, American Bibliography, VI, 163 (17510).

15. *Ibid.*, VIII, 276 (24250).

16. *Ibid.*, X, 58 (28543).

17. *New Hampshire Gazette*, Januari 22, 1791.

18. *Ibid.*, April 30, 1791.

19. *New Hampshire Spy*, March 19, 1791.

20. Ogden, *An Address Delivered at the Opening of Portsmouth Academy On Easter Monday A.D. 1791*, p. 20.

21. *Ibid.*

22. Lippencott, "Dearborn's Musical Scheme," *passim.*

23. Evans, *American Bibliography*, XI, 176 (32031). Unfortunately a copy of this work has been thus far unlocatable.

24. Gould, *History of Church Music in New England*, p. 52.

CHAPTER XIII. SAMUEL HOLYOKE

1. *Biographical Catalogue of Phillips Academy, Andover, Mass. 1778-1830*, p. 30.

2. *Concord Herald*, August 31, 1791.

3. Bentley, *Diary of William Bentley*, Vols. II, III, IV, *passim.*

4. Gould, *History of Church Music in New England*, p. 63.

5. This is an error; the date should read October 15.

6. *Biographical Catalogue of Phillips Academy*, p. 15.

7. Elson, *History of American Music*, p. 13.

8. Moore, *Complete Encyclopaedia of Music*, p. 435.

9. This is an error; Holyoke was from Boxford.

10. Pratt and Boyd, eds. *Grove's Dictionary of Music and Musicians; American Supplement* (4th ed., rev.), p. 387. Pratt's difficulty in dating this work (he gives "1800 or '02") would seem to us solved by this editorial reference to it.

11. The writer of this editorial was probably George Hough, the first printer in Concord and publisher of the *Courier*. Hough was appointed chorister of the Concord Musical Society in 1801 and again in 1810, according to Bouton in his *History of Concord* (p. 533). He was also leader of the choir in the "old North meeting-house" (First Congregational Church). His interest in music caused him to devise an "entire new plan" for rendering "the art of singing less difficult for young beginners." His idea involved doing away with the current systeem of expressing the seven degrees of the scale with four names, "which tends to perplexity," and replacing it by using the first seven letters of the alphabet. The whole book, like Benjamin Dearborn's *Scheme*, makes no use of traditional musical characters; it is printed with regular type. The book includes sixty-four pages: title page, copyright page, eight music

instruction, fifty-three music, one for index. The title page reads: "Modern Harmony or The Scholar's Task Made Easy. Being An Original Composition, in Three and Four Parts. Written on an Entire New Plan. Particularly to Lessen the Labor of Beginners. Containing, An Introduction The Grounds of Music, With A Number Of Tunes And Anthems, Suitable For Divine Worship, And For The Use Of Musical Societies. Concord: Printed by George Hough—1808. Sold at his Book-Store, wholesale and retail." A copy of Hough's book is in the New Hampshire Historical Society.

12. Metcalf, *American Writers and Compilers of Sacred Music*, p. 116. Metcalf, who is in possession of the original contract of Holyoke and Ranlet, erroneously assumes that the *Instrumental Assistant* appeared in 1807 because the date in the manuscript is slightly obscured.

13. A copy is in the New Hampshire Historical Society.

14. Sonneck, *A Bibliography of Early Secular American Music*, p. 209.

CHAPTER XIV. THE VILLAGE HARMONY

1. Pratt, *Grove's Dictionary of Music and Musicians, American Supplement*, pp. 385-386.

2. *Ibid.*, p. 387, erroneously gives 1797 as the year of the first edition.

3. Copies of editions 5, 6, 7, 10, 11, 13, 16, and 17 are in the New Hampshire Historical Society. The writer has been unable to locate copies of the first four editions.

4. Evans, *American Bibliography*, X, 237 (29793).

5. *Ibid.*, XI, 96 (31494).   6. *Ibid.*, XI, 330 (33123).

7. *Ibid.*, XII, 228 (34930).

8. James Avison Baker, grandson of James Baker, donated this book to the New Hampshire Historical Society on October 3, 1911. He recorded on the inside of the cover that "the calf was raised, leather tanned, goose raised, quills made and ink made by him and the work done by the light of a candle."

9. In all probability, the publication data quoted here are similar to those of the first printing of the fifth edition.

10. Bell, *History of the Town of Exeter, New Hampshire*, p. 304.

11. Bentley, *Diary of William Bentley*, II, 393.

12. *Biographical Catalogue of Phillips Academy*, p. 14, records that Amos Blanchard was a "Teacher of Writing and Music" there

in 1803-1805 and 1811-1812. He was born in Wilton, New Hampshire, January 14, 1773, and died in Andover, Massachusetts, August 17, 1847.

13. Daniel Read.

CHAPTER XV. MUSIC THEORY

1. Sonneck, *Francis Hopkinson and James Lyon*, p. 166.
2. *Ibid.*
3. *New Hampshire Gazette*, May 26, 1769.
4. In 1688 Salmon wrote a book on temperament, *A proposal to perform Music in Perfect and Mathematical Proportions;* in 1672 he published "An Essay to the Advancement of Musick, by casting away the perplexity of different Cliffs and uniting all sorts of Musick in one universal character." (See *Grove's Dictionary of Music*, 5th ed., VII, 381).
5. *The Village Harmony*, 5th ed., p. i.
6. *Ibid.*
7. Holyoke, *The Instrumental Assistant*, I, 17-19.
8. *The Village Harmony*, 5th ed., p. iii.
9. *Ibid.*, p. ii.   10. *Ibid.*, pp. iv-v.   11. *Ibid.*, p. iv.
12. Gould, *History of Church Music in New England*, p. 94.
13. Earle, *The Sabbath in Puritan New England*, p. 222.
14. Gould, *History of Church Music in New England*, p. 94.
15. *Ibid.*, p. 122.   16. *Ibid.*

APPENDIX A. TEACHERS' ADVERTISEMENTS

1. This date, not part of the advertisement, indicates the issue in which the notice was found. These announcements customarily appeared in the press several times.
2. This date, when included in the advertisement, usually indicates the day on which the notice was purchased.
3. John Lathan Berkenhead.

APPENDIX C. JOHN HANCOCK AND THE MASSACHUSETTS ANTITHEATER LAW OF 1750

1. Sonneck, *Early Concert-Life in America*, p. 135.
2. *Proceedings of the Massachusetts Historical Society*, "Letter to Rev. Daniel Perkins, Bridgewater," p. 193.
3. Sonneck, *Early Opera in America*, p. 134.
4. *Proceedings of the Massachusetts Historical Society*, Vol. LX, "S. Adams and the Sans Souci Club in 1785," p. 339.
5. Hoar, *John Hancock, His Book*, p. 246.

6. Brewster, *Rambles about Portsmouth*, I, 115.

7. Seilhamer, *History of the American Theatre*, III, 14, writes with reference to this incident: "It was said that the Governor of the State, who was at Portsmouth at the time, was only prevented by illness from attending the performance, but his wife gave it the sanction of her presence." In the first instance, Seilhamer confuses historical fact by assuming that Hancock is the Governor of New Hampshire; and in the second instance, Seilhamer's allusion to "sanction of her presence" presupposes an existing opposition to the theater, and hence the need for the official sanction of a governor's wife. Neither Portsmouth nor the remainder of New Hampshire needed any one's "sanction"; there were no laws against theatrical exhibitions.

Bibliography

PUBLISHED MATERIAL

Adams, Nathaniel. Annals of Portsmouth. Exeter: C. Norris, 1825.

Aldrich, George. Walpole as it Was and as It is. Claremont: Claremont Manufacturing Company, 1880.

Barriskill, James M. "The Newburyport Theatre in the 18th Century," *Essex Institute Historical Collections,* XCI (July, 1955), 211-295.

Bay Psalm Book, being a facsimile reprint of the first edition, printed by Stephen Day at Cambridge, in New England in 1640. New York: Dodd Mead and Co., 1903.

Belknap, Jeremy. The History of New Hampshire. 3 vols. Dover, N.H.: O. Crosby and J. Varney, 1812.

——— Sacred Poetry Consisting of Psalms and Hymns. 3d ed. Boston: Thomas and Andrews, 1801.

Bell, Charles H. History of the Town of Exeter, New Hampshire. Boston: Farewell & Co., 1888.

——— Memoir of John Wheelwright. Cambridge, Massachusetts: John Wilson and Son, 1876.

Bentley, William. The Diary of William Bentley, D.D., 1874-1819. 4 vols. Salem, Mass.: The Essex Institute, 1905-1914.

Bio-bibliographical Index of Musicians in the United States of America from Colonial Times. Washington, D.C.: Music Division, Pan American Union, 1941.

Biographical Catalogue of the Trustees, Teachers, and Students of Phillips Academy, Andover, 1778-1830. Andover, Mass.: The Andover Press, 1903.

Birge, Edward B. History of Public School Music in the United States. Boston: Oliver Ditson Company, 1928.

Bouton, Nathaniel. History of Concord. Concord, N.H.: Benning W. Sanborn, 1856.

Bradford, Ephraim P. A Discourse [on music], delivered at New-Boston [N.H.] to the Handellian Society, February 22, 1807. Amherst, N.H.: Joseph Cushing, 1807.

Brewster, Charles W. Rambles about Portsmouth. 2 vols. Portsmouth: L. W. Brewster, 1859-73.

Brigham, Clarence S., History and Bibliography of American Newspapers. 2 vols. Worcester: American Antiquarian Society, 1947.

——— Paul Revere's Engravings. Worcester: American Antiquarian Society, 1954.

Brooks, Henry M. Olden-Time Music. Boston: Ticknor and Company, 1888.

Brown, Francis. An Address on Music: Delivered before the Handel Society, Dartmouth College, August, 1809. Hanover, N.H.: Charles and William S. Spear, 1810.

Bush, George Cary. History of Education in New Hampshire. Washington: Government Printing Office, 1898.

Chamberlain, Richard. Lithabolia. Reprint. Tarrytown, N.Y.: William Abbatt, 1923. (Originally published: London, Whitlock, 1698).

Chase, Benjamin. History of Old Chester. Auburn, N.H.: Published by the author, 1864.

Chase, Gilbert. America's Music. New York: McGraw-Hill Book Company, Inc., 1955.

Chastellux, Marquis de. Travels in North America in the Years 1780-81-82. Translated from the French, by an English Gentleman. New York: no publisher given, 1828.

Coffin, Charles C. History of Boscawen and Webster. Concord, N.H.: Republican Press Association, 1878.

Colonial Laws of Massachusetts; reprinted from the edition of 1660. Boston: Rockwell and Churchill, 1889.

Concord Herald. Concord: George Hough, Jan. 6, 1790, to Jan. 30, 1794.

Concord Town Records, 1732-1820. Concord, N.H.: The Republican Press Association, 1894.

Courier of New Hampshire. Concord: George Hough, Feb. 13, 1794, to 1805.

Curtis, Jonathan. A Topographical and Historical Sketch of Epsom, New Hampshire. Concord: J. B. Moore, 1823.

Cutter, Daniel B. History of the Town of Jaffrey. Concord, N.H.: Republican Press Association, 1878.

Dwight, Timothy. Travels: in New England and New York. Vol. II. New Haven: S. Converse, 1821.

Earle, Alice Morse. The Sabbath in Puritan New England. New York: Charles Scribner's Sons, 1891.

Edwards, George Thornton. Music and Musicians of Maine. Portland: The Southworth Press, 1928.

Ellinwood, Leonard. The History of American Church Music. New York: Morehouse-Gorham Company, 1953.

Ellis, Harold Milton. Joseph Dennie and His Circle. Austin: University of Texas 1955.

Elson, Louis C. The History of American Music. New York: The Macmillan Company, 1904.

Emerson, Caleb. A Discourse on Music, pronounced at Amherst, N.H., before the Handellian Musical Society, September 13, 1808. Amherst, N.H.; Joseph Cushing, 1808.

Emerson, Reuben. An Oration on Music, pronounced before the Handel Society, Dartmouth University, August 23, 1814. Andover, Mass.: Flagg and Could, 1814.

Engel, Carl, comp. Music from the Days of George Washington. Washington, D.C.: United States George Washington Bicentennial Commission, 1931.

Essex County, Massachusetts: Quarterly Courts. Records and Files 1662-1667. Vol. III. Salem: Essex Institute, 1913.

Evans, Charles. American Bibliography. 13 vols. Chicago: Blakely Press, 1903-1955.

Farmer, John and Jacob B. Moore, eds. Collections, Historical and Miscellaneous. 3 vols. Concord, N.H.: J. B. Moore, 1822-1831.

Farmer's Weekly Museum: New Hampshire and Vermont Journal. Walpole: Isaiah Thomas and David Carlisle, April 11, 1793. With the April 1, 1794, issue the title was changed to the Farmer's Museum or Lay Preacher's Gazette, and with the Feb. 17, 1800, issue, to Farmer's Museum or Literary Gazette.

Fielding, Mantle. Dictionary of American Painters, Sculptors, and Engravers. Philadelphia: Lancaster Press, Inc., n.d.

Fisher, William Arms. One Hundred and Fifty Years of Music Publishing in the United States. Boston: Oliver Ditson Company, 1933.

Fiske, Abel. A Discourse Delivered in Lyndeborough, (N.H.) February 26, 1801, at a Singing Lecture. Amherst, N.H.: Samuel Preston, 1801.

Fitzpatrick, John C. "The Bands of the Continental Army," *Daughters of the American Revolution Magazine*, LVII (April, 1923), 187-199.

———— Ed. The Diaries of George Washington, 1748-1799. Vol IV. Boston: Houghton Mifflin Company, 1925.

Flexner, James T. First Flowers of Our Wilderness. Boston: Houghton Mifflin Company, 1947.

Foote, Henry W. Three Centuries of American Hymnody. Cambridge, Massachusetts: Harvard University Press, 1940.

Frost, Maurice. English & Scottish Psalm & Hymn Tunes c. 1543-1677. London: Oxford University Press, 1953.

Gilman, Samuel. Contributions to Literature. (Includes "Memoirs of a New England Village [Atkinson, N.H.] Choir."). Boston: Crosbey, Nichols and Company, 1856.

Gould, Nathaniel D. An Address Delivered at New-Ipswich, N.H., May 16, 1818, at the Request of Bethel Lodge, and the Hubbard Musical Society. Amherst: R. Roylston, 1818.

———— History of Church Music in America. Boston: Gould and Lincoln, 1853.

Grove's Dictionary of Music and Musicians. 9 vols. 5th ed., revised. Ed. by Eric Blom. London: Macmillan & Co. Ltd., 1954.

History of New Ipswich. Boston: Gould and Lincoln, 1852.

Hoar, John F. John Hancock, His Book. Boston: Lee and Shepard, 1898.

Hood, George. History of Music in New England. Boston: Wilkins, Carter and Co., 1846.

Hornblow, Arthur. A History of the Theatre in America. 2 vols. Philadelphia: J. B. Lippincott Company, 1919.

Howard, John T. Our American Music. 3d ed. New York: Thomas Y. Crowell Co., 1951.

———— The Music of George Washington's Time. Washington, D.C.: United States George Washington Bicentennial Commission, 1931.

Howe, Granville L. A Hundred Years of Music in America. Chicago: G. L. Howe, Publisher, 1889.

Hubbard, John. An Essay on Music, pronounced before the Middlesex Musical Society, Sept. 9, A.D. 1807, at Dunstable, Mass. Boston: Manning & Loring, 1808.

—— The American Reader. 4th ed. Walpole: Thomas & Thomas, 1808.

Hubbard, W. L., ed. History and Encyclopedia of Music. History of American Music, Vol. VIII. New York: Irving Squire, 1910.

Hurd, D. Hamilton. History of Rockingham and Strafford Counties. Philadelphia: J. W. Lewis and Co., 1882.

Jackson, George Pullen. White and Negro Spirituals. New York: J. J. Augustin Publisher, 1943.

Jenness, John S. The Isles of Shoals. New York: Hurd and Houghton, 1873.

Johnson, Earle H. Musical Interludes in Boston, 1795-1830. New York: Columbia University Press, 1943.

—— "The Musical Von Hagens," The New England Quarterly, XVI (March, 1943), 110-117.

Josselyn, John. Two Voyages to New England. Boston: William Veazie, 1865.

Kouwenhoven, John Atlee. "Some Unfamiliar Aspects of Singing in New England," The New England Quarterly, VI (September, 1933), 567-588.

Lang, Paul Henry. Music in Western Civilization. New York: W. W. Norton & Company, Inc., 1941.

Lawrence, Robert F. The New Hampshire Churches. Claremont, N.H.: Claremont Manufacturing Co., 1856.

Lee, Cuthbert. Early American Portrait Painters. New Haven: Yale University Press, 1929.

Lee, Eliza Buckminster. Memoirs of Rev. Joseph Buckminster, D.D., and his son Rev. Joseph Stevens Buckminster. 2d ed. Boston: Ticknor, Reed, and Fields, 1851.

Lippencott, Margaret E. "Dearborn's Musical Scheme," New-York Historical Society Quarterly Bulletin, XXV (October, 1941), 134-142.

Lord, Charles C. Life and Times of Hopkinton, N.H. Concord, N.H.: Republican Press Association, 1890.

—— "Manners and Customs in Hopkinton," Granite Monthly, II (March, 1879), 186-191.

Lord, John King. A History of Dartmouth College, 1815-1909. Concord, N.H.: The Rumford Press, 1913.

Lowens, Irving. "John Tufts' Introduction to the Singing of Psalm-Tunes (1721-1744): The First American Textbook, "*Journal of Research in Music Education,* II (Fall, 1954), 89-102.

―――― "The Origins of the American Fuging Tune," *Journal of the American Musicological Society,* VI (Spring, 1953), 43-52.

―――― and Britton, Allen P. "The Easy Instructor (1798-1831)," *Journal of Research in Music Education,* I (Spring, 1953), 30-55.

Lyford, James O. History of Concord, New Hampshire. Vol. II. Concord, N.H.: Rumford Press, 1903.

McClintock, John N. History of New Hampshire. Boston: B. B. Russell, 1888.

Marr, Harriet Webster. Atkinson Academy, The Early Years. No place given: John E. Stewart Company, 1940.

Mayo, Lawrence Shaw. John Wentworth, Governor of New Hampshire, 1767-1775. Cambridge, Massachusetts: Harvard University Press, 1921.

Metcalf, Frank J. American Writers and Compilers of Sacred Music. New York: The Abingdon Press, 1925.

Metcalf, Henry M. New Hampshire in History. Concord, N.H.: W. B. Ranney Co., 1922.

Miller, Perry. The New England Mind: From Colony to Province. Cambridge, Massachusetts: Harvard University Press, 1953.

Mirrour. Concord: Elijah Russell, Sept. 6, 1792, to Nov. 15, 1796; Nov. 7, 1797, to Sept. 2, 1799.

Moore, John W. Complete Encyclopedia of Music. Boston: John P. Jewett and Company, 1854.

Moreland, James, "The Early Theatre in Portland," *The New England Quarterly,* XI (June, 1938), 331-342.

Morin, Raymond. "William Billings, Pioneer in American Music," *The New England Quarterly,* XV (March, 1941), 25-33.

Naylor, Edward W. Shakespeare and Music. London: J. M. Dent and Co., 1896.

New Hampshire Gazette, with the Freshest Advices Foreign and Domestick. Portsmouth: Daniel Fowle, Oct. 6, 1756. Continued with some alterations in title until after 1820.

New Hampshire: a Guide to the Granite State. American Guide Series. Boston: Houghton Mifflin Co., 1938.

New Hampshire: Legislature. Provincial and State Papers. Vol. I (1623-1686), Concord: George E. Jenks, 1867; Vol. IV (1722-1737), Manchester: John B. Clark, 1870; Vol. XIII (1790-1800), Concord: Parsons B. Cogswell, 1884.

New Hampshire Mercury and the General Advertiser. Portsmouth: Robert Gerrish, 1784 to 1788.

New Hampshire Patriot. Concord: Isaac Hill, Apr. 18, 1809, to Feb. 2, 1819.

New Hampshire Spy. Portsmouth: George Jerry Osborne, Oct. 26, 1786, with alterations in title to 1793.

New Star. Concord: Russel & Davis, Apr. 11, 1797, to Oct. 3, 1797. Ogden, John Cosens. An Address Delivered at the Opening of Portsmouth Academy on Easter Monday, A.D. 1791. Portsmouth: George Jerry Osborne, 1791.

Ninde, Edwards S. The Story of the American Hymn. New York: The Abingdon Press, 1921.

Oracle of the Day. Portsmouth: Charles Peirce, June 4, 1793. After 28, 1799, the title was altered to *The United States Oracle of the Day.*

Park, Lawrence. "Joseph Blackburn-portrait painter," Proceedings of the American Antiquarian Society, XXXII (1923), 270-329.

Parker, John R. A Musical Biography, or, Sketches of the Lives and Writings of Eminent Musical Characters. Boston: Published by Stone & Farwell, 1825.

Parish, Elijah. An Eulogy on John Hubbard, Professor of Mathematics and Natural Philosophy in Dartmouth College: Who Died August 14, 1810. Pronounced at the College, September, 1810. Hanover, N.H.: C. W. S. & H. Spear, 1810.

Pope, Charles H. The Cheney Genealogy. Boston: Published by Charles H. Pope, 1897.

The Portsmouth Book. Boston: Geo. H. Ellis, n.d.

Pratt, Waldo Selden. The Music of the Pilgrims. Boston: Oliver Ditson Company, 1921.

——— ed. Grove's Dictionary of Music and Musicians. American Supplement, Vol. VI. New York: The Macmillan Company, 1934.

Proceedings of the Massachusetts Historical Society. Vol. V (1862); Vol. XLIII (1910); Vol. LX (1927). Boston: The Society.

Quint, Alonzo H. The First Parish in Dover. Boston: Alfred Mudge and Son, 1884.

Richardson, Leon Burr. History of Dartmouth College. Vol. I. Hanover: Dartmouth College Publications, 1932.

Ritter, Frederic Louis. Music in America. New York: Charles Scribner's Sons, 1884.

Rogers, Mary C. Glimpses of an Old Social Capital. Boston: Merrymount Press, 1923.

Sabin, Joseph. A Dictionary of Books relating to America, from Its Discovery to the Present Time. 29 vols. New York: 476 Fifth Avenue, 1868-1936.

Sanborn, Frank B. New Hampshire. Boston: Houghton Mifflin and Co., 1904.

Scholes, Percy A. The Puritans and Music in England and New England. London: Oxford University Press, 1934.

Seilhamer, George O. History of the American Theatre. 3 vols. Philadelphia: Glober Printing House, 1888-1891.

Sewall, Jonathan Mitchell. Miscellaneous Poems. Portsmouth: William Threadwell, & Co., 1801.

Sewall, Samuel (1652-1730). Diary. 3 vols. Boston: Massachusetts Historical Society, 1878-1882.

Shipton, Clifford K. Isaiah Thomas, Printer and Philanthropist 1749-1831. Rochester: The Printing House of Leo Hart, 1948.

Shurtleff, William. "Rev. Mr. Shurtleff's Account of the Revival of Religion at Portsmouth, N.H.," Christian History, No. 48-49 (Jan.-Feb., 1743), pp. 383-394. Boston: S. Kneeland and T. Green, 1744.

Smyth, Mary W. "Contemporary Songs and Verses about Washington," The New England Quarterly, V (April, 1932), 281-292.

Sonneck, Oscar G. A Bibliography of Early Secular American Music. Revised and enlarged by William T. Upton. Washington: Library of Congress, 1945.

—— Early Concert-Life in America. Leipzig: Breitkopf and Haertel, 1907.

—— Early Opera in America. New York: G. Schirmer, 1915.

—— Francis Hopkinson and James Lyon. Washington, D.C.: H. L. McQueen, 1905.

—— Miscellaneous Studies in the History of Music. New York: Macmillan Company, 1921.

—— Suum Cuique: Essays in Music. Boston: G. Schirmer, 1916.

Stackpole, Everett S. History of New Hampshire. Vol. I, II. New York: American Historical Society, 1916.

—— and Lucien Thompson. History of the Town of Durham. Vol. I. Concord, N.H.: Rumford Press, 1913.

Upton, William Treat. Art-Song in America. Boston: Oliver Ditson Company, 1930.

Wadleigh, George. Notable Events in the History of Dover, New Hampshire. Dover: Tufts College Press, 1913.

Weeden, William Babcock. Economic and Social History of New
England, 1620-1789. Vol. I. Boston: Houghton Mifflin Co., 1890.

Wheelock, John. An Essay on the Beauties and Excellencies of
Painting, Music, and Poetry, pronounced at the Anniversary
Commencement at Dartmouth College, A.D. 1774. Hartford:
Printed by Even. Watson, n.d. Reprinted by C. Spear, Hanover,
n.d.

Worcester, Samuel. An Address on Sacred Music, Delivered before
the Middlesex Musical Society and the Handel Society of Dartmouth College at a joint meeting held at Concord, N.H., Sept. 19,
1810. Boston: Manning and Loring, 1811.

UNPUBLISHED MATERIAL

"Council Book, 1631-1684." Vol. I Manuscript, 302 pp. New Hampshire Historical Society.

"Orford and Piermont Hubbard Musical Society Constitution and
Records, 1816-1832." Manuscript (unpaged), New Hampshire
Historical Society.

"Pedigree of John Tucke of Gosport." Manuscript, 13 pp. New
Hampshire Historical Society.

"Probate Records of Rockingham County, Book B." Manuscript,
390 pp. New Hampshire Historical Society.

"Records of the Concord Musical Society 1799-1865." Manuscript
(unpaged), New Hampshire Historical Society.

TUNE BOOKS

Unless otherwise noted, copies of the following tune books are
in the new Hampshire Historical Society.

Belcher, Supply. The Harmony of Maine. Boston: Isaiah Thomas
and Ebenezer T. Andrews, 1794.

Billings, William. New England Psalm-Singer. Boston: Edes and
Gill, 1770. Boston Public Library.

—— Psalm Singer's Amusement. Boston: Printed and sold by
the author, 1781. Boston Public Library.

—— Singing Master's Assistant. Boston: Draper and Folsom,
1778. Boston Public Library.

Blanchard, Amos. The Newburyport Collection of Sacred, European Music. Exeter: Ranlet & Norris, 1807.

—— The American Musical Primer. Exeter: Norris and Sawyer,
1808.

Dearborn, Benjamin. A Scheme for Reducing the Science of Music to a More Simple State and to Bring All Its Characters within the Compass of a Common Fount of Printing-Types. Portsmouth, New Hampshire: 1785. New York Historical Society.

Flagg, Josiah. A Collection of the Best Psalm Tunes in Two, Three and Four Parts. Boston: Paul Revere and Josiah Flagg, 1764. Boston Public Library.

Holyoke, Samuel. A Dedication Service containing An Introductory Ode, Three Hymns, A Doxology, and A Concluding Anthem. Exeter, New Hampshire: Henry Ranlet, 1801.

⸺ Exeter: For Thanksgiving. (An Anthem.) Exeter: Printed by Henry Ranlet, 1798.

⸺ The Columbian Repository of Sacred Music. Exeter, New Hampshire: Henry Ranlet, n.d. (ca. 1800).

⸺ The Instrumental Assistant, Vol. I. Exeter, New Hampshire: H. Ranlet, n.d. (This edition ca. 1806), Vol. II. Exeter, New Hampshire: Ranlet and Norris, 1807.

⸺ The Vocal Companion. Exeter, N.H.: Norris & Sawyer, 1807.

Hough, George. Modern Harmony; or, The Scholar's Task Made Easy. Concord, N.H.: Printed by George Hough, 1808.

Hubbard, John. A Volume of Sacred Musick. Newburyport, Mass.: Published by E. Little & Co., C. Norris & Co., Printers [Exeter, N.H.], 1814.

Ingalls, Jeremiah. The Christian Harmony; or, Songster's Companion. Exeter, New Hampshire: Henry Ranlet, 1805.

Kimball, Jacob. The Essex Harmony. Exeter, New Hampshire: Henry Ranlet, 1800.

Knapp, William. New Church Melody. 5th ed. London: Printed for R. Baldwin and S. Crowder, 1764.

Larkin, Samuel. The Nightingale: A Collection of the Most Popular Ancient and Modern Songs. Portsmouth: Printed for William and Daniel Treadwell, 1804.

Law, Andrew. A Collection of Hymn Tunes from the Most Modern and Approv'd Authors. Cheshire, Conn.: Printed by Wm. Law, n.d. (ca. 1782 to 1792).

⸺ Select Harmony. n.d. (ca. 1778 to 1792).

Lyon, James. Urania. Philadelphia: 1761. (Probably the 2d or a later impression of the 1st ed.). Boston Public Library.

Merrill, David. The Psalmodist's Best Companion. Exeter, New Hampshire: Henry Ranlet, 1799.

Merrill, Richard. The Musical Practitioner; or, American Psalmody. Newburyport, Mass.: William Barrett, 1797.

Read, Daniel. The American Singing Book. New Haven: Printed for and sold by the Author, 1787.

Robbin, Charles. The Drum and Fife Instructor. Exeter, N.H.: C. Norris & Co., 1812.

Swan, Timothy. The Federal Harmony. n.d. (ca. 1785 to 1792).

Tans'ur, William. Elements of Music Display'd; or, Its Grammar or Ground-Work Made Easy. London: Printed for Stanley Crowder, M.DCC.LX.II (1762). Boston Public Library.

—— Royal Melody Compleat; or, New Harmony of Zion. London: M.DCC.LX (1760). Boston Public Library.

Village Harmony. 5th ed., 1st printing. Manuscript copy "by James Baker New-Holderness N.H. February 1799." New Hampshire Historical Society.

—— 5th ed., 2nd printing. Exeter: Henry Ranlet, 1800.

—— 6th ed. Exeter: Henry Ranlet, 1803.

—— 7th ed. Exeter: Ranlet & Norris, 1806.

—— 8th ed. Exeter: Charles Norris & John Sawyer, 1807. Boston Public Library.

—— 10th ed. Exeter: C. Norris & Co., n.d. (ca. 1811).

—— 11th ed. Exeter: C. Norris & Co., 1813.

—— 12th ed. Exeter: C. Norris & Co., 1815. Boston Public Library.

—— 13th ed. Exeter: C. Norris & Co., 1816.

—— 14th ed. Exeter: C. Norris, 1817. Boston Public Library.

—— 16th ed. Exeter: J. J. Williams, 1819.

—— 17th ed., 1st printing. Exeter: J. J. Williams, 1820.

—— 17th ed., 2nd printing, Exeter: J. J. Williams, 1821.

Williams, Aaron. The American Harmony; or, Universal Psalmodist. Newburyport, Mass.: Daniel Bayley, 1769. Boston Public Library.

Wood, William. Harmonia Evangelica: A Collection of Sacred Music. Exeter, N.H.: C. Norris & Co., 1810.

Index